# The church under siege

The quarrelsome rings

**M. A. SMITH**

# The church under siege

**Inter-Varsity Press**

© INTER-VARSITY PRESS, LEICESTER, ENGLAND
*Universities and Colleges Christian Fellowship,*
*38 De Montfort Street, Leicester LE1 7GP*

INTER-VARSITY PRESS
*Box F, Downers Grove,*
*Illinois 60515*

*First published September 1976*

INTERNATIONAL STANDARD BOOK NUMBERS:
UK 0 85110 578 5
USA 0 87784 855 6
*Library of Congress catalog card*
*number: 76-12304*

# 3018031

*Printed in Great Britain by*
*Billing & Sons Limited,*
*Guildford, London and Worcester*

# Contents

# Acknowledgments

I should like to express my thanks to my wife, Diana, who read through the draft copies of this book and its forerunner, *From Christ to Constantine*. Her suggestions and criticisms have made these books far more readable and comprehensible than they would have been without her help.

My thanks are also due to the staff of the Inter-Varsity Press for their assistance in producing both volumes.

**Photographs:** pp. 18, 23, 35, 52, 60, 75, 89, 102, 131, 155, 157, 194, 210, 211, 213, 228, 229, 235, 240 British Museum, London, reproduced by courtesy of the Trustees; pp. 24, 30, 100, 119, 146, 150, 151, 153, 158, 159, 166, 173, 175, 181, 200, 203, 208, 224 The Mansell Collection, London; p. 40 Turkish Tourism Information Office, London; p. 47 Rheinisches Landesmuseum, Trier; p. 80 National Museum of Naples; p. 113 French Government Tourist Office, London; pp. 205, 206 Camera Press, London; p. 217 St Martin's Church, Canterbury; cover, pp. 117, 246, 247 The Manx Museum, Isle of Man.

# Illustrations

# Time chart

| Secular | Eastern | Western |
|---|---|---|
| | | 311 Caecilian bishop of Carthage<br>Donatism begins |
| 312 Battle of Milvian Bridge<br>313 Licinius defeats Maximin | 313 Alexander bishop of Alexandria | 313 Synod at Rome on Donatism<br>314 Synod at Arles |
| | 318/9 Beginnings of Arianism | 320 Persecution of Donatists followed by toleration |
| 324 Defeat of Licinius by Constantine<br>325 Deaths of Crispus and Fausta | 324 Council at Antioch<br>325 Council of Nicaea<br>330 Athanasius persecutes Melitians<br>Eustathius deposed<br>335 Council of Tyre<br>336 Exile 1 of Athanasius | |
| **337 Baptism and death of Constantine the Great**<br>**Constantine II, Constans and Constantius emperors** | 339 Death of Eusebius of Caesarea<br>Exile 2 of Athanasius | |
| **340 Death of Constantine II** | 340 Athanasius and Marcellus at Rome<br>Persecution in Persia<br>341 Death of Eusebius of Nicomedia<br>Dedication council at Antioch | 340 Firmicius Maternus |
| | 343 Council of Sardica | |
| | 346 Return of Athanasius<br>Death of Pachomius | |
| | | 347 'Times of Macarius' at Carthage |
| **350 Death of Constans**<br>**Constantius sole emperor**<br>351 Battle of Mursa | | 355 Synod of Milan<br>Death of Donatus<br>Conversion of Marius Victorinus |
| | 356 Exile 3 of Athanasius | |
| | 357 'Blasphemy of Sirmium' | |
| | 359 The 'Dated Creed' | |
| | 361 Return of exiled bishops | |
| **361 Death of Constantius**<br>**Julian emperor**<br>**Pagan reaction**<br>**363 Death of Julian**<br>**364 Jovian emperor**<br>**365 Valentinian I and Valens emperors** | Apollinaris of Laodicaea<br>Exile 4 of Athanasius<br>363 Schism at Antioch<br>365 Exile 5 of Athanasius<br>370 Basil the Great *fl.*<br>373 Death of Athanasius | 366 Damasus/Ursinus riots at Rome<br>374 Ambrose bishop of Milan |
| **375 Death of Valentinian I**<br>**378 Death of Valens**<br>**Theodosius I, Gratian and Valentinian emperors** | 378 Gregory of Nazianzus at Constantinople<br>381 Council of Constantinople | |
| **383 Death of Gratian**<br>**Magnus Maximus usurper** | c. 383 Death of Ulfilas | 384 Dispute of altar of victory |

|  |  | 385 Execution of Priscillian<br>Jerome goes to Palestine<br>386 Conversion of Augustine |
|---|---|---|
| **388 Death of Magnus Maximus** | 388 Affair at Callinicum<br>390 Massacre at Thessalonica |  |
| 391 State ban on paganism<br>392 Revolt of Arbogast<br>394 Defeat of Arbogast at river Frigidus |  |  |
| **395 Death of Theodosius I** |  |  |
|  |  | 397 Deaths of Martin of Tours and Ambrose of Milan<br>c. 400 Ninian *fl.* |
|  | 398 John Chrysostom bishop of Constantinople<br>404 Exile of John Chrysostom |  |
| 406 Barbarians cross Rhine<br>408 Execution of Stilicho | 407 Death of John Chrysostom |  |
| **408 Theodosius II eastern emperor**<br>410 Alaric captures Rome |  |  |
|  |  | 411 Start of Pelagian controversy<br>418 Final condemnation of Pelagianism |
| 415 Death of Athaulf, king of the Goths | 415 Murder of Hypatia |  |
| 421 Constantius marries Galla Placidia | 420 Death of Jerome |  |
| **425 Death of Constantius<br>Valentinian III emperor of West**<br>429 Vandal invasion of North Africa |  |  |
|  |  | 430 Death of Augustine<br>Palladius to Ireland<br>?c. 431 Patrick to Ireland |
|  | 431 Council of Ephesus (Nestorius condemned)<br>433 Cyril of Alexandria and John of Antioch reach agreement |  |
| 438 *Codex Theodosianus* |  | 440 Leo bishop of Rome |
|  | 444 Death of Cyril of Alexandria |  |
|  | 449 'Robber Synod' at Ephesus | 448 Death of Germanus of Auxerre<br>450 Salvian *fl.* |
| **450 Death of Theodosius II**<br>451 Aetius defeats Attila<br>Death of Galla Placidia | 451 Council of Chalcedon<br>Condemnation of Dioscorus<br>Death of Nestorius |  |
| 452 Death of Attila<br>453 Murder of Aetius<br>**454 Death of Valentinian III**<br>455 Vandals capture Rome |  | 452 Leo the Great and Attila |

**Eastern**
457 Murder of Proterius of Alexandria
Narsai flees to Nisibis

**474 Zeno eastern emperor**

**Western**
457 Death of Deogratius at Carthage

461 Death of Leo the Great
? Death of Patrick
469 Sidonius bishop of Clermont
474 Euric captures Clermont

|  |  |
|---|---|
|  | 476 **Deposition of Romulus Augustulus** (**last western emperor**) |
|  | 477 Death of Gaiseric the Vandal |
| 481 Zeno's *Henoticon* | *c.* 485 Death of Sidonius |
|  | 486 Clovis destroys kingdom of Soissons |
| **491 Anastasius emperor** | 493 Death of Odoacer |
|  | Theodoric king of Italy |
|  | 496 Baptism of Clovis |
|  | 502 Caesarius bishop of Arles |
| 503 Death of Narsai | 511 Battle of Vouillé |
|  | 517 Death of Clovis, king of the Franks |
| **518 Justin I emperor** | 520 Gildas *fl.* |
|  | 524 Death of Boethius |
|  | 526 Death of Theodoric the Great |
| **527 Justinian emperor** |  |
| 533 *Codex Justinianus* |  |
| 534 'Nika' riot | 534 Bellisarius conquers North Africa |
|  | 540 Cassiodorus retires |
|  | 542 Death of Caesarius of Arles |
| 543 Death of Leontius of Byzantium |  |
| 544 'Three Chapters' controversy | 547 Death of Benedict of Nursia |
| 548 Death of empress Theodora |  |
| 553 Second Council of Constantinople (fifth ecumenical council) | 553 Narses defeats Goths at Battle of Busta Gallorum |
|  | 554 Pragmatic Sanction |
| 559 Repulse of Kutrigur Huns | 565 Lombards invade Italy |
| **565 Death of Justinian** |  |
| **Justin II emperor** |  |
| Death of Procopius |  |
| **578 Tiberius II emperor** | 573 Gregory bishop of Tours |
| *c.* 578 Death of Joseph Baradaeus |  |
| **582 Maurice emperor** |  |
|  | 589 Council of Toledo |
|  | End of Visigothic Arianism |
|  | 590 Gregory the Great bishop of Rome |
|  | 594 Death of Gregory of Tours |
|  | 597 Augustine lands in Kent |
|  | Deaths of Fredegund, queen of the Franks, and Columba |
|  | 600 Isidore bishop of Seville |
|  | *c.* 600 Death of Venantius Fortunatus |
| **602 Murder of Maurice** |  |
| **Phocas emperor** | 603 Conference of Augustine and Celtic bishops |
|  | 604 Deaths of Gregory the Great and Augustine of Canterbury |
| 610 Heraclius emperor |  |
| 612 Muhammad flees to Medina | 613 Death of Brunhild, queen of the Franks |
|  | 615 Death of Columbanus |
| 616 Siege of Constantinople by Persians and Avars | 619 Death of Laurence of Canterbury |
| 626 Final defeat of Persians by Heraclius | 627 Paulinus goes to Northumbria |
|  | 629 Dagobert king of the Franks |
| 632 Death of Muhammad | 632 Oswald king of Northumbria |
|  | Aidan in Northumbria |
| 636 Battle of Yarmuk | 636 Death of Isidore of Seville |
| Arabs take Palestine |  |

11

641 Death of Heraclius
642 Arab conquest of North Africa and
    Egypt

642 Oswald killed by Penda
    Death of Martin of Rome
655 Death of Penda of Mercia
664 Synod of Whitby
669 Theodore the Greek archbishop of
    Canterbury
670 Death of Oswy of Northumbria
c. 675 Muirchu fl.
680 Death of Hilda of Whitby
685 Cuthbert bishop of Lindisfarne
687 Battle of Tertry, Pepin of Heristal
    supreme among Franks
    Death of Cuthbert
690 Death of Theodore the Greek
700 End of 'Three Chapters' schism
709 Death of Wilfred at Oundle
    Arabs conquer Spain
714 Charles Martel mayor of palace of Franks

680 Third Council of Constantinople
    condemns Monothelitism

**717 Leo the Isaurian emperor**
718 Arabs besiege Constantinople
720-30 Leo repulses Arabs from Asia
      Minor

732 Battle of Poitiers
    Defeat of Arabs by Charles Martel
735 Death of Bede
739 Death of Willibrord

**740 Constantine V emperor**
741 Persecution of icon-worshippers

741 Death of Charles Martel
    Pepin the Short mayor
751 Pepin anointed king of the Franks
754 Martyrdom of Boniface
    Pepin campaigns in Italy
756 Death of Aistulf, king of the Lombards
767 Death of Pepin the Short
    Charlemagne and Carloman kings
771 Death of Carloman
774 Charlemagne conquers Lombards
775 Charlemagne's wars against the Saxons

**775 Death of Constantine V**
    End of iconoclasm

778 Incident at Ronscevalles
781 Alcuin comes to Aachen
787 Charlemagne's ecclesiastical reforms
794 Synod of Frankfurt (condemnation of
    Felix of Urgel)
795 Death of Paul the Deacon

787 Second Council of Nicaea (seventh
    ecumenical council)

**800 Charlemagne crowned emperor**

**797 Irene murders son and becomes
empress**

804 Death of Alcuin
    Norse raids on Britain

**802 Death of Irene**

**814 Death of Charlemagne**
Einhard retires to Seligenstadt

**Louis the Pious emperor**
821 Death of Theodulf of Orleans
833 Louis the Pious deposed and reinstated

**840 Death of Louis the Pious**
Division of Charlemagne's empire
844 Death of Einhard

# Introduction

The period of church history from Constantine the Great to Charlemagne is of great interest for several reasons.

First, it holds a story worth telling for its own sake. It is an inspiration to see Christians of other ages facing the task of living the Christian life and spreading the gospel of Christ.

Second, an understanding of Christian history can help us to understand present-day theological issues. While we cannot take over patristic solutions wholesale, the theological ground-work of past ages is extremely valuable. It can show us where the heart of a problem lies. It can save us from wasting time investigating solutions which have already been found unsatisfactory. Doctrines of God, the Person of Christ, grace, salvation, liturgy and worship are relevant study today. But it essential to know that they have also been relevant study for centuries.

Third, Christian history can speak to our own day and situation. Like the people of the period under study, we live in times of totalitarian régimes, cultural debasement and collapse, and sometimes military and civil turmoil. We can be encouraged when we see that other Christians have had to face these troubles and have successfully survived them. And we can learn from the past, if only to avoid making the same mistakes twice.

Fourth, significant change is gradual. By studying a long period of history we can see the long-term movement of events. This will put us in a better position to pick out the important straws in the wind of change in our own day.

The ultimate aim in studying Christian history is to make us better fitted to serve Christ in our generation. Few Christians, and even fewer evangelical Christians, give much thought to the period from Constantine to Charlemagne. It is my conviction that a thoughtful look at this neglected part of Christian history will make us more capable of serving Christ today.

# 1

# Life in the fourth century

The reign of Constantine is 300 years away from the climax of classical Roman civilization under Augustus. And the lapse of time had done the Empire no good, although the worst damage had been done during the years of chaos of the third century. The middle and latter part of the third century had been notable for the frequent civil wars and changes of emperor, as well as various external invasions which were only just beaten off. The anarchy had been temporarily stopped when Diocletian became emperor in 284, and his scheme of four emperors to rule the unwieldly empire promised well. But the early years of the fourth century saw fresh civil wars, from which Constantine and Licinius emerged as the supreme rulers of the West and East respectively.

But such a history had left its mark. The fairly benevolent despotism of Augustus had been replaced by military autocracy. The emperor was fast becoming an eastern despot, with all the trappings of absolute power. The splendid robes, the imperial diadem and the elaborate court ceremonial made him very much more than merely the 'first citizen'.[1] Successive purges had rendered the Senate largely impotent, but under Diocletian's reforms at the end of the third century it was robbed even of the vestiges of power. The Senate remained mainly as a rich man's club which provided the various entertainments of the city of Rome. The executive power of the Empire was in the hands of a bureaucracy which, though technically under the surveillance of the emperor, nevertheless had a certain autonomy. Although most of these

[1] Augustus took as his title 'Princeps', which I have rendered as 'first citizen', but later on the technical term for emperor became 'Imperator', a word originally meaning 'commander-in-chief of the armed forces'.

officials had the courtesy rank of Senator, they seldom if ever attended the Senate. They were elaborately stratified according to their posts, and only members of the highest echelons had access to the emperor's presence. Many were scattered far and wide because of their posts as government officials in various provinces. Even after Constantine had given his official blessing to Christianity, the great majority of the government officials were not Christians, and the last stronghold of the old paganism was to be found in the Senate.

## The decay of the cities

Below the rich, ruling classes came the smaller landholders and the local worthies who formed the town councils of the cities. And it was here that a disastrous rot had set in. Under the early Empire the Roman world had been town-centred. Paul described himself as a citizen of Tarsus.[2] The old Greek city-state had survived as the Roman city with its civic pride and its own carefully regulated hierarchy. The economy on which the city depended was largely agricultural, supported by a certain amount of commerce and manufacture. And it was in this area that the ravages of the third century were never repaired. Galloping inflation and poor harvests had driven many small farmers to bankruptcy. The central government bureaucracy and the hard-pressed army made increasing demands for support on the cities. The large landowners could afford to buy out the smaller farmers, and in the end set up estates that were virtually self-supporting.[3] Commerce suffered badly during the wars of the third century. Manufacturing industries such as the potteries of Gaul, which produced the *terra sigillata* or Samian ware,[4] came to an abrupt halt during the troubles; and although resuscitated under the dynasty of Constantine they never attained their former prosperity. Under such pressures the towns withered. Townsmen fled to avoid debt or the tax-collector. Some even sold themselves as slaves to some rich man rather than face starvation. But the government and the army still demanded

[2] Acts 21:39.
[3] Many economic historians point to this as the start of the mediaeval feudal system.
[4] The red-glazed, patterned pottery which was the first-grade table-ware in the Western Roman Empire.

money. Once, it had been an honour to be a 'decurion',[5] and so by family birthright to be eligible to hold office in the town council. Then the emperor decreed that the members of the council should be personally liable for collection of taxes. If the required sum was not forthcoming, the wretched councillors were expected to make up what was lacking. Needless to say, people soon became unwilling to undertake public office. They looked for ways of avoiding it, whether by flight to the desert, enrolling in the army or being ordained. Eventually laws were passed making service on town councils compulsory, and exemption from such duties was granted only to a favoured few.

But it was not only the decurions who were forced to remain in the role they inherited. Because of economic circumstances, many trades showed little profit; but the tradesmen were compelled by law to make their children follow in the father's profession. This artificial caste system was made applicable to such diverse trades as pig-breeding and the merchant-shipping service. In some areas it was difficult to find taxpayers at all, especially as the lords of the large estates did not welcome tax-collectors and even had private armies to keep them at bay.

Below the hard-pressed middle ranks of society were the crowds of the poor. In the country many were in a position analogous to that of the mediaeval villein. They were tenants tied to the soil, without freedom to move away, and owing allegiance to the rich landowner. In the towns they formed mobs which were often merely sources of trouble. The unemployable mobs at Rome (and later at Constantinople) were fed by state subsidy,[6] and entertained by the rich. Elsewhere the cities tended to contract in size. Venerable monuments of the past were broken up to help build walls to protect the towns from the possible depredations of invading barbarians or wandering brigands.[7] Such culture as there was looked back to the golden age of the past, and found its last bastion in the pagan majority on the Senate at Rome. A brooding air of pessimism was setting in over the Empire.

[5] See, for example, Cicero's speech *Pro Archia* (delivered in the mid-first century BC), where being a decurion could entitle a man to Roman citizenship.

[6] Called the *annona*; there were even shrines to the goddess Annona!

[7] *E.g.* the funeral monument of Julius Classicianus, procurator of Britain in the mid-first century, now restored from various broken fragments and on display in the British Museum.

**The funeral monument of Julius Classicianus.** It was broken up and used for wall-building in the fourth century.

## The churches in late Roman society

It was against this background that the Christian churches took their place as newly accepted components of society. It is a mistake to imagine them as suddenly emerging from the Catacombs, still bearing the scars of the final great persecution which had ended only in 313. Many congregations already had their own buildings.[8] In some outlying areas little congregations might still meet in homes, but this was becoming less usual. The organization of the churches was already quite complex. Each local church would be ruled by a bishop, who was elected from that congregation and who was expected to pastor the same flock until he died. He was assisted

---

[8] Like the impressive one at Nicomedia, which was destroyed as the first act of the last great persecution under Diocletian. Lactantius, *On the Deaths of the Persecutors* 11–13, cited in J. Stevenson (editor), *A New Eusebius* (SPCK, 1957; hereafter referred to as *NE*), p. 286.

by a group of elders (who would take charge of outlying groups of the congregation), and also a group of deacons who were his personal assistants and from whom his successor was often chosen. There was also a large number of minor officials, such as readers and doorkeepers. The bishop would preside at the communion service each Sunday (this was the main Sunday service). He would preach regularly to the congregation, prepare the people for baptism, visit the sick and be guide and disciplinarian to his flock. He would dress no differently from other people, and would perform the tasks which we should expect nowadays from the minister of any town church. The bishops of the churches in the big cities tended to gain a superior position;[9] and because of the rule which stopped bishops from transferring from one church to another[1] such positions were often fought for with considerable bitterness. An able bishop of a small church, however, could make his influence felt at councils of bishops (these met sporadically to decide on major problems), and a nonentity who was bishop in an important city would find that the size of his city or church counted for little.

The average church member was part of a society within a society. The corrupt Empire carried on its life around him, but he was a privileged member in the family of God. Each Sunday he would come to worship, to hear the bishop teach and to take part in the great mystery of the eucharist. The church was in effect a lifeboat in an otherwise very stormy sea of life. The churches were far from inward-looking, however. In times of plague or famine the bishop and his deacons were usually the only people who could or would organize relief. From the records of the searches of churches during the Diocletian persecution, it is obvious that even small congregations had stores of clothes and shoes,[2] and perhaps also food, with which they could help some of the casualties of society. On occasion bishops used church funds to ransom those captured by barbarians. Whatever the demands of the tax men, people were still able to give both in kind and in money to support the clergy and their charitable works. And while the church was in no position to change the system, it did do much to alleviate the hardships which the system caused.

[9] E.g. the primacy of the bishop of Alexandria over the Egyptian churches.

[1] E.g. canon 15 of the Council of Nicaea (325), cited in NE, p. 362.

[2] E.g. the search at Cirta, cited in NE, pp. 287-9.

## The 'barbarians'

One of the main reasons for hardship was that the Roman Empire of the fourth century was an embattled camp surrounded by pressing hordes of barbarians. Outside the frontiers, tribes were on the move. Those in contact with the frontiers were mainly Germanic, but they were being pushed by nomadic Asiatic tribes. The Roman army was an expensive means of defence for the beleaguered Empire. Already, differences were becoming apparent between the classic Roman legion and the army units of the fourth century. Instead of being a citizen army, it was fast becoming a mercenary one, and many barbarians were being enrolled in the ranks. Soon they rose by virtue of their ability to become officers, and by the end of the fourth century many generals were barbarians. Cavalry was becoming increasingly important, and barbarian weapons were being adopted (*e.g.* the broadsword in place of the short two-edged Roman sword). The problem of recruitment was caused mainly by depopulation within the Empire, where the peasant farmer, who had once been the strength of the legion's rank and file, was now becoming a rarity. With the decrease of farmers, many tracts of land had reverted to uncultivated scrub, and this in turn meant that there was less from tax revenue, and less actual food with which to provide for the army. Pay was often in arrears, and supplies were chaotic. Soldiers often had to resort to plunder just to live. In an attempt to remedy this situation, a considerable section of the army was settled in small-holdings along the frontiers, to act as a new peasant militia. The *élite* units formed a mobile reserve, which it was hoped could be brought up wherever there was serious trouble.

But it would be wrong to see the imperial frontiers as barriers against an unrelieved sea of barbarism. The term 'barbarian' included cultured Persians as well as wild Germanic tribes; in fact it could be applied to anyone who was not part of Graeco-Roman civilization. Yet many barbarians on the frontiers were half-Romanized. Some had spent long years at the imperial court. Traders moved beyond the imperial frontiers with considerable freedom, and some Romans even lived permanently among the barbarians in order to evade the tax men. Christian preachers, often working all their lives among barbarian tribes, not only laid the foundation of Christian groups beyond the frontiers but also ensured that when the great invasions of the early fifth century came, many of the invaders had a considerable respect both for Christians and for church property. While it is anachronistic to think of people like Ulfilas and Ninian[3] as modern-style missionaries, they and many like them did penetrate widely among the barbarian tribes. The fact that all the first wave of barbarian invaders except the Franks were to some extent Christianized proves that there had been some Christian preaching among them.

Within the Empire there was much regional diversity. The fourth century saw a resurgence of regional languages and culture. In North Africa (modern Tunisia and Algeria) the Punic language flourished among the lower classes. Those who spoke Punic formed an enveloping sea which backed on to the desert and surrounded the Graeco-Roman towns on the coast. And here the language barrier also tended to be the division between the rich and the poor. In Egypt, the Coptic dialects (Sahidic, Bohairic, *etc.*) produced a similar divide between the peasants and the Greek-speaking *élite*. But it was not such a deep cleavage; and thanks to the career of Athanasius[4] and his repeated terms of exile among the Coptic-speaking hermits of the desert, the pope (or patriarch) of Alexandria became the leader of Egyptian aspirations in rivalry with the power of the central government at Constantinople. Further east, the Syriac dialects were spoken on both sides of the eastern frontier. Christian churches in the Persian Empire kept friendly links with the churches of the western Orient, but could also be strongly independent. Here also, large segments eventually broke off to run their own separate organizations.

Christianity was still first and foremost an urban movement. It is true that in Egypt, North Africa and parts of Syria and Asia Minor it had penetrated quite deeply into the countryside, but there were many enclaves even here where paganism went on unabated. In the West the countrymen of many areas were still unevangelized. But paganism lacked any real vitality. When Julian the Apostate (emperor, 361–3)[5] tried to restore paganism at the expense of Christianity, he was struggling to revive a corpse. The pagan *literati* in the Roman Senate remained, but they were increasingly out of touch with contemporary life. In the remote valleys a few peasants would still continue old rites, but the main stream of

[3] See below, pp. 93ff. and 97 and also Glossary.
[4] See below, chapters 2 and 3.
[5] See below, pp. 50–68, and Glossary.

thought and culture had passed them by without their noticing.

Independent political thought and action under the later Empire was virtually impossible, and this contributed to the popularity of theology. For here was a subject where public debate was possible. Training in rhetoric was the staple diet of fourth-century Roman education. Therefore there were many people who could make persuasive use of the pulpit. There was ample opportunity for the ambitious to climb high. And compared with engaging in politics, theology was fairly safe. Although later in the fourth century, when emperors took sides in theological disputes, one might be exiled for holding a particular view, this was infinitely preferable to summary execution; a frequent penalty in the political arena. And the prizes for an able or unscrupulous prelate were many. He could become confidant of the emperor, and hold court in state surrounded by an admiring congregation of one of the large churches. Wealth and the friendly attentions of the rich could be his. Can it be wondered at if such prizes caused men to engage in street battles, as when in the latter part of the fourth century Damasus and Ursinus left piles of corpses in the streets of Rome as they fought to become bishop?[6]

It is also small wonder that, faced with an invasion of the churches by the unscrupulous social climbers, many of the more Christlike and dedicated Christians became sick of the whole affair and opted out. They left the corrupt church in the corrupt world and took refuge in the desert to contemplate. Others, slightly wiser, retreated to form communes where they could live out the Christian life undisturbed by the lure of fame and position. Such people could, in their turn, become introverted and self-seeking, but even the desert was not immune from life outside. Visitors would come for spiritual advice, and on several occasions a desperate congregation would come out and demand that some holy hermit or abbot should return to the world as bishop of a church in need.

Such was the background to life in the fourth century, the century which opened with the triumph of Constantine and the end of persecution of the Christians. We now turn to the events of the years after Constantine's victory in 312.

---

[6] See the account of Ammianus Marcellinus, cited in J. Stevenson (editor), *Creeds, Councils and Controversies* (SPCK, 1966; hereafter referred to as *CCC*), pp. 86–7.

# 2

# Constantine and the start of the 'Christian Empire'

When Constantine marched into Rome after winning the Battle of the Milvian Bridge (312), he probably felt as if he had just touched something very powerful which he did not fully comprehend. He had gone into action against Maxentius, trusting in the sign of the Christians' God; and rather unexpectedly he was entering Rome as victor. Here was a new and powerful God, who had favoured him. And at all costs Constantine must keep on the right side of Him. Anything which would upset the proper worship of this

**A page of Codex Sinaiticus** (4th century), one of the earliest complete manuscripts of the whole Bible. The 'codex' or notebook form, rather than the scroll, came into common use in the 2nd century, and was adopted from the start for New Testament writings. This page contains John 21 :1–25. British Museum, London.

ultra-powerful deity could not be tolerated. Such a God would make too powerful an enemy, were Constantine to risk His displeasure. And so, throughout the rest of his reign, one of Constantine's main aims was to see that the Empire and the imperial dynasty continued to receive God's blessing.

With the generosity of a recent victor, Constantine decided that it was only right and fitting to retain God's favour by making princely donations to the churches in his domains. Official letters went out to the various governors, instructing them to hand over the necessary payments to the accredited church officials. At the same time, Constantine put in orders for fine and accurate copies of the Christian Scriptures.[1]

**The Milvian Bridge, Rome,** scene of Constantine's vision and his victory over Maxentius. The bridge was originally built in 109 BC.

[1] The order for copies of the Scriptures is cited by B. J. Kidd (editor), *Documents Illustrative of the History of the Church,* vol. ii (OUP, 1922), pp. 2, 3. The *Codex Sinaiticus* in the British Museum and the *Codex Vaticanus* (description in B. M. Metzger, *The Text of the New Testament: its Transmission, Corruption and Restoration*[2] (OUP, 1669), pp. 47–8) are probably survivors of this or a subsequent order.

At first all went well. Constantine was wisely guided by Hosius, the bishop of the church of Cordoba in Spain. But just as everything seemed tranquil, there came a disturbing report from North Africa. The governor there reported trouble. He could not decide which of two rival groups was the accredited church of the one true God. On the surface, it would seem that a certain Caecilian was the bishop of the church at Carthage (and, by virtue of this post, leader of the North African Christians). But a deputation had presented itself to the governor, with a petition and a dossier of complaints. The governor felt quite out of his depth, and so he asked Constantine to intervene. And in intervening, Constantine was to have his first taste of church politics.[2]

## The beginnings of Donatism

North Africa had not been severely affected by Diocletian's persecution, which had just ended. Indeed, there had been little or no persecution in North Africa since 306. But even during that comparatively short period of persecution, many clergy had either committed, or were suspected of committing, acts which would normally exclude them from continuing in their positions. And, as had happened after a similar persecution fifty years before, Christians had become split into two camps. One group was in favour of being comparatively lenient with those who had weakened during the persecution, while others were against any concessions. While in the previous persecution the test had been whether or not people had actually taken part in pagan sacrifices and so denied Christ, now the point at issue was whether or not clergy had handed over copies of the Christian Scriptures to the Roman officials for destruction.[3] If they had, they were held to be barred from carrying out their official duties. And there were many involved.

An account of one screening of bishops survives (it was conducted by the leading bishop of Numidia, modern Algeria). Various bishops had to give account of their actions. One pleaded his innocence on the ground that he had hidden and had not been

[2] The main documents for the early stages of this dispute were gathered together in a dossier by Optatus, Catholic bishop of Milevis (*fl.* 365–85), and are available in *NE*, pp. 313–31.

[3] The offence was called *traditio*, and one guilty of it was called a *traditor*; hence our word 'traitor'.

found when the Roman officials came to search. Another had given the searchers only letters. Another had deceived the Roman officials by giving them books on medicine instead of his Bible: Another pleaded that he had handed over only damaged copies. Then one bold spirit, a certain Purpurius, bishop of the congregation at Limata, got up and challenged the inquisitor himself. 'How did you come to be set free unless you surrendered something?' he asked. Even though Purpurius was a violent man who had not scrupled to kill some of his family during the persecution (for what reasons we are not told), his question was so embarrassing that the primate agreed to leave the whole question to be solved by God on judgment day!

The question needed answering, however, because three blameless bishops were required to conduct the proper ordination of a new bishop. If even one of the consecrators had been guilty of a moral lapse, the ordination would be invalid. And it was this point which formed the substance of the charges which were brought in the dossier to the governor of North Africa, and which eventually came to Constantine himself. Constantine would most likely think that if there were irregularities concerning those appointed to lead the worship of the Almighty, then perhaps there would be dire consequences for the state.

In actual fact, there was a lot more behind the trouble at Carthage than this one issue. When the bishop of Carthage had died a few years previously, a good many people in Carthage wanted the chief deacon, Caecilian, to succeed him. But there was a custom that the primate of Numidia (in this case Secundus of Tigisis, who had conducted the investigation into the conduct of bishops mentioned above[4]) should consecrate the new bishop of Carthage. And there were fears that he would not approve of Caecilian. So the ceremony took place before Secundus and the Numidian contingent arrived; and one of the bishops who took part was a certain Felix, bishop of Aptungi.

But Caecilian had enemies in Carthage. There was a rich lady called Lucilla whom he had rebuked for excessive superstition (she had habitually kissed the bone of an alleged martyr before receiving communion). There were also two church elders who had misappropriated some church property which had been entrusted to them for safe-keeping during the troubles, and who

[4] See above, p. 25.

# Map 1

## Spain and North Africa

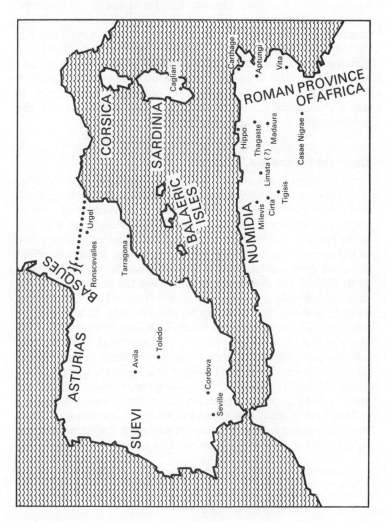

had subsequently been publicly shown up by Caecilian. These were joined by the Numidian contingent, arriving hot and dusty and furious that the old traditions had been slighted. Caecilian suggested that if they objected to his ordination they could perform the ceremony again. But Purpurius of Limata probably spoke for them all when he said that if Caecilian came to him for laying on of hands he would get beaten over the head. But the Numidians and the disaffected Carthaginians could not get their own way. They left the church building where Caecilian was with most of the congregation, and held a meeting elsewhere at which they consecrated a certain Majorinus (said to be a member of Lucilla's household) as bishop of Carthage in opposition to Caecilian. It was a deputation from this dissident group which came to the governor with their petition and dossier.[5]

## Constantine and the Donatists

In fact, the petition was not as extreme as one might have thought. The petitioners asked Constantine to appoint judges from Gaul (who presumably would be impartial) to investigate the whole affair. In particular, they alleged that Felix of Aptungi, who had taken part in Caecilian's consecration, had previously been guilty of handing over the Scriptures to the persecutors, and was therefore debarred from conducting a valid ordination. In hindsight, many have blamed the dissidents for involving the state in a church dispute. But really they only wanted unbiased judges. Constantine, though, seems to have made up his mind already. In his letters he refers to 'the Catholic church over which Caecilian presides'.[6] He thought that he could get peace by backing the majority party in the dispute. What Constantine did not realize was that he was dealing with something much deeper than merely a quarrel over a disputed election. Some of the underlying issues in this quarrel were basic to the whole understanding of the Christian message.

Many half-hidden reasons added venom to the dispute. There was the regional rivalry between the advanced Roman province of Africa, with its opulent civilization, and the more backward areas

[5] Constantine was already aware of trouble in the North African churches (see *NE*, p. 316), but had left the affair in the hands of the local governor until this point.

[6] Eusebius, *Church History* x. 7.2, cited in *NE*, p. 304.

of Numidia. There was the hatred of the down-trodden peasants for the landowners, made more noticeable by the fact that the peasants spoke Punic while the landed gentry spoke Latin. On top of these was the clash of personalities and theologies. But at the root of the dispute were two mutually exclusive ideas of what constituted the 'church'.

For Caecilian and his friends, the church was a universal society, taking its place in the civic life of the towns and now at last receiving even imperial patronage. It was a widely-based society where room could be found for most people, and where mercy could be shown to those who fell short of the highest standards. The church could co-operate with the state (now ruled by a pro-Christian emperor) in upholding and bettering the established order. But to Caecilian's opponents, the church was an embattled minority group, engaged in a truceless war with the agents of the devil. The state, in spite of its pro-Christian guise, was still the agent of persecution. Since the church was on a war footing, there was no room for the cowards or deserters. God's people were to be an *élite* body, presided over spiritually by the martyrs who had made the supreme sacrifice in defence of the faith. In slightly muted form, these are still the two theories of the church, and they are mutually incompatible.

Since he only dimly understood the problem, Constantine probably acted wisely when he turned over the documents and the conduct of the investigation to Miltiades, the bishop of Rome. Here was a man who was leader of the most important church in Constantine's domains, and who seemed to Constantine eminently suitable to chair the meetings which would have to be held. Perhaps Constantine would have liked to hear other opinions, but he was in no position to consult the bishops of the important churches in the eastern provinces because they were in the territory of his rival, the eastern emperor Licinius. At that very moment Constantine was in the process of relieving Licinius of the Balkan provinces. Although they were officially colleagues, Constantine was sure that eventually Licinius would have to suffer the fate of the usurper Maxentius (whom Constantine had defeated at the Battle of the Milvian Bridge). But he would bide his time for the moment. And in the mean time Constantine had to take care that he did not lose the favour of the God whose help he would assuredly need when the final battle came.

Meanwhile, Miltiades held a small council of Italian bishops, along with three bishops from Gaul, and they came up with the decision that Constantine wanted. The appeal by the anti-Caecilian party was dismissed, and Caecilian was solemnly declared to the legal bishop of Carthage. But this was not good enough for Caecilian's opponents. They asked Constantine to convene a Gallic council to settle the argument. And Constantine, presumably anxious that justice should be seen to be done, duly convened a council of bishops at Arles in the following year (314). To prevent the two factions coming to blows, he laid elaborate plans for them to travel to Arles by separate routes!

Having seen the various clergy assembled at Arles,[7] Constantine left them to settle their differences. They did not spend all their time dealing with the North African situation. The bishops reached

**The Roman amphitheatre, Arles.** The church at Arles was the leading church in the south of France.

[7] There were thirty-three bishops there, including three from Britain; the bishop of the church at Arles presided.

an agreement over the dating of Easter; they left it to the bishop of Rome to circularize the others each year informing them of the correct date. They came to a compromise over the problem of what to do about converted heretics who sought admission to orthodox churches.[8] The bishops also legislated on various points of church discipline. But, most important from Constantine's point of view, they again dismissed the appeal of Caecilian's opponents. They did so on the grounds that the charges against Felix of Aptungi could not be substantiated from written records made by public officials during the persecutions.[9] Meanwhile, Majorinus, the schismatic bishop of Carthage, had died. His place was taken by Donatus, who was to give his name to the whole dispute. From then on it is strictly accurate to call the anti-Caecilian party 'Donatists'.

## The rift in the North African churches

Who was this man Donatus, who came from an obscure little village on the edge of the desert salt flats? Why was it that this man from Casae Nigrae (Black Cottages) was to exert a lasting influence in this bitter conflict? Donatus is a shadowy figure, but he is representative of the people of rural North Africa.

In the past fifty years paganism had dramatically collapsed in Donatus' country. The hallowed stones of pagan temples, even plaques commemorating votive offerings, were being used to pave streets or mend walls.[1] Every little village had its own church presided over by its own bishop. And already they were becoming known as 'the churches of the martyrs'. The local village feast days were now held on the anniversaries of the deaths of local martyrs, and were often accompanied by night-long feasts held at the martyr's grave in the cemeteries (a practice which the more spiritual Christians frowned upon). Sometimes the martyr's tomb containing

[8] If they had already received a Trinitarian baptism, they were to be received into communion by the laying on of hands; if they had not received a Trinitarian baptism, they were to be baptized properly.

[9] There is also mention in this particular canon of the validity or otherwise of ordinations by morally unworthy clergy, but the exact sense is not clear. See *NE*, p. 324.

[1] W. H. C. Frend, *The Early Church* (Hodder & Stoughton, 1952), p. 121.

his relics served as the altar table of the local church.[2] At times the cult of the martyrs almost exceeded the reverence given to God Himself. To speak ill of the revered martyr was a blasphemy not to be forgiven. It was significant that a most damaging charge levelled at Caecilian was that he had been lukewarm in helping the 'confessors'[3] in prison during the last persecution. To the Punic-speaking inhabitants of the little villages, all their aspirations and grievances were taken up into their devotion to the 'churches of the martyrs' and their opposition to the 'Catholic church' of the Latin-speaking city-dwellers. And the prophet of this rural resistance church was Donatus.

Although Donatus was the able leader of a schismatic church which his 'Catholic'[4] opponents hated, they could never charge him with any evil deeds[5]. From 314 until his death in exile in 355 he was the inspiration of the North African Christians, and even after his death his influence lingered on. People swore by him, in the same way as they would invoke God. In people who often seemed capable only of bitter hatred, Donatus inspired affection and devotion. He took the anti-Caecilian movement and gave it a positive theology and aim. He planned to set up a universal 'church of the martyrs' in opposition to the 'collaborating churches' of which Caecilian was the head in North Africa. With this end in view, he appointed a 'true bishop' at Rome. and a continuing Donatist congregation there dates from Miltiades' time (Miltiades had held the council which had first rejected the appeals against

[2] This is the origin of the Roman Catholic custom, now insisted upon under canon law, of having relics of the saints under the altar.

[3] Though originally almost synonymous with 'martyr', the term 'confessor' was normally used of those who suffered in the cause of Christ but did not die for the faith.

[4] The term 'Catholic' means 'universal', and was taken by the opponents of Donatus because they claimed to be the representatives of the 'universal church' throughout the world as opposed to the Donatist church which was limited to the geographical region of North Africa. But during the fourth century the word 'Catholic' began to be used in the sense of 'doctrinally orthodox', to distinguish mainstream churches from heretical sects. Because of the misconceptions caused by the present-day meaning of the word 'Catholic', I have generally preferred to use terms like 'official', 'orthodox' or 'mainstream' even in contexts where the original writers use the term 'Catholic'.

[5] Nearly all our information about the Donatist dispute comes from anti-Donatist writers.

Caecilian). Donatus wrote many letters and received many visitors from abroad. His zeal and organizing ability were enormous. While Caecilian and his successors remained as ciphers with the legal rank of bishop of Carthage, the common people openly spoke of 'Donatus of Carthage' as if he were the real bishop. Against such a man, Constantine's alternate acts of conciliation and repression were futile.

After the Council of Arles, Donatist attempts to discredit Caecilian continued. But they misfired. Constantine, notwithstanding the decisions of two councils, decided to see that everyone's scruples were respected. So he instituted an enquiry to see if Felix of Aptungi really had been guilty of handing over the Scriptures. It must have seemed strange to some elderly Roman civil servants when they were ordered by one emperor to search out and destroy all copies of the Christian Scriptures, and then were ordered by the next emperor to find out which Christian bishops had actually assisted them in their former task!

At the enquiry, a Donatist called Ingentius came forward with written evidence from the town magistrate of Aptungi. It was a document giving details of the government search, with an appendix incriminating Felix. But only the first part of the document (the innocuous part) was genuine. The damning appendix was the work of Ingentius himself. He was arrested and presumably produced as the conclusive piece of evidence which would silence Donatist complaints. Unfortunately, silence was not forthcoming. When Constantine came back from his first struggle with Licinius, he found peace in the North African churches nowhere nearer. So he resorted to force.

Years later the Donatists remembered the 'persecution of Caecilian'. In the name of unity Constantine ordered that the Donatists be forced to give up their separatist stance. When they refused, strong measures were taken, and some Donatists were killed by government troops. Caecilian's supporters were utterly fed up with the Donatists, and were not at all sorry to see them outwardly crushed. With the 'Catholics' rejoicing at the government action, the Donatists blamed Caecilian for their sufferings. The bitterness grew deeper; and even when a leading Donatist bishop (Silvanus of Cirta) was publicly discredited and shown to have been guilty himself of handing over copies of the Scriptures to the persecutors, the movement was not halted.

Constantine could not keep troops in North Africa when they were badly needed elsewhere. Barbarian tribes were causing trouble on the Rhine–Danube frontier, and Constantine had no choice but to let the repression of the Donatists lapse while he dealt with a serious threat to the safety of the Western Empire. Immediately he was gone, Donatus organized his people, and they openly took over churches once owned by 'Catholic' congregations. Perhaps Constantine began to have second thoughts about the rights of the struggle, for when the 'Catholics' complained to him, he merely advised them to be patient and tolerant. On at least one occasion Constantine actually gave orders for a new church building to be erected for a group of 'Catholics' who had been evicted by Donatists.

## Constantine becomes sole emperor

Constantine was now busy planning his master stroke against his erstwhile colleague and co-emperor, Licinius. There was no love lost between them, and the only basis for their friendship had been the fact that at one time both Constantine and Licinius had the same enemies. Although they both had declared themselves in favour of the Christians, Licinius was beginning to show signs of regretting this. To be sure, Eusebius of Caesarea, the church historian, had ended his first edition of his church history with laudatory sections on both Constantine and Licinius;[6] but Licinius knew full well that Constantine could get great support in the East through posing as a 'Christian emperor'. Licinius started a niggling campaign of harassment against Christians, and waited for an opportunity to move against Constantine. Constantine moved large forces into the Balkan provinces, ostensibly to repel raids of Sarmatian barbarians from across the Danube. In an action against these barbarians, Constantine happened to cross the demarcation line and enter Licinius' territories. And immediately Licinius retaliated.

The war was of relatively short duration. Constantine defeated Licinius on land, and forced him back to Byzantium. But Licinius had a large fleet, and looked like being able to block the crossing of the Bosphorus. Constantine's eldest son, Crispus, was in charge of a much smaller fleet, but he had already shown himself to be a

[6] The first edition consisted only of books 1 to 9. Book 10 was added after the defeat of Licinius, and various emendations were made in earlier books, to water down Licinius' support for Christianity.

**Constantine the Great, emperor 307–337.** A coin in the British Museum, London.

**The emperor Licinius (emperor 308–324).** A portrait on a coin in the British Museum, London.

very capable general in the campaigns on the Rhine–Danube frontier. And it was Crispus' master stroke which won the day. He took his small fleet swiftly through the narrows of the Hellespont and destroyed Licinius' fleet by a surprise attack. Although Licinius retreated across the Bosphorus, he was soon surrounded and forced to capitulate. Constantine bided his time, perhaps unwilling to kill his old colleague out of hand. But soon he was told of plots against him, organized by Licinius; and Constantine ordered that Licinius be executed. Constantine was then sole emperor, but in his very hour of triumph he was presented with his second church dispute. And this one was to prove almost as intractable as Donatism.

### The beginning of the Arian controversy

Constantine found the whole of the East divided into two camps. Furious accusations and counter-accusations were being hurled around. Although the storm centred originally around an elder from Alexandria called Arius[7] and the disciplinary action taken against him by the bishop of Alexandria (called Alexander), bishops from many other parts had also become involved. The arguments were about various statements of belief. And theology was Constantine's weakest point. He had to be guided by others, and so he turned to Hosius of Cordoba, his trusted adviser. Hosius was sent east to investigate[8] and if possible to bring peace. It was only when the controversy showed no signs of abating that Constantine

[7] For the origins of Arianism, see documents in *NE*, pp. 340–51.
[8] *NE*, pp. 352–4.

himself took a hand in proceedings. But before coming to this, we must go back to the beginning of this set of troubles.

The beginnings of the Arian controversy (so called because it began with the dissension over the opinions of Arius) were somewhat similar to those of Donatism. The background was a dispute over who should be bishop of Alexandria. During Diocletian's persecution, bishop Peter of Alexandria was imprisoned. While he was in prison, a certain bishop called Melitius took it upon himself to take charge. This might have been forgiven if it had been only a temporary measure, but Melitius had ambitions to become the next bishop of Alexandria. In the event, he failed. Peter managed to discipline him, and the affair went underground when Peter was martyred during the last phase of the persecution. Melitius was not appointed as Peter's successor, but he had many supporters among the Coptic-speaking peasants, and he continued to bear a grudge against those who succeeded Peter as bishops of Alexandria. One of Melitius' former supporters was Arius.

Arius had been trained by Lucian of Antioch, the revered, scholarly presbyter who had been martyred during the persecution. Lucian had been the teacher of many men who were subsequently to rise to high office, and Arius therefore had many influential friends. Although once a supporter of Melitius, Arius had managed to get into favour with the successors of Peter of Alexandria, and at the present time was in charge of a nice suburban church at Baucalis. There the tall, slightly round-shouldered, learned cleric was a favourite especially with the religious ladies in the congregation. His piety was suitably noted, and he kept up his contacts, especially with his old student-friend Eusebius, bishop of Nicomedia.[9] And it was while at Baucalis that his heterodox views were first heard.

To modern readers, it often appears bizarre that so much fuss was made over points of doctrine in the early churches. When such concern is coupled with decidedly unchristian behaviour in the course of the dispute, many would be tempted to condemn all ancient theological disputes as not worth study. But the ancient theologians realized how much was at stake, and their concern is shown by the lengths to which they were prepared to go in defence

[9] Not to be confused with Eusebius of Caesarea, the church historian, whom Arius also knew quite well.

of what they believed to be the truth. For unless there was true belief, a person's very salvation was in doubt. If Constantine was worried about the safety of his Empire, the church leaders were worried about the eternal safety of their souls. And for both, being right with God was of supreme importance. Should we wonder, then, that they were prepared to fight tooth and nail against anyone who seemed to be endangering eternal salvation? Of course, there were other, more earthy, motives involved. The more important bishoprics and the confidence of the emperor were worth fighting for. But virulent theological disputes were fought so frantically because not only this world but also the world to come was thought to be at stake.

In the eastern churches at this time, the main scheme of theology saw the Trinity in terms of three Persons, very distinct and almost arranged in a graded hierarchy. This was due to the influence of the thought of Origen.[1] He saw God the Father as the fount of all deity, with God the Son as the mediator between God and man. If there were adequate safeguards, Origen had even been willing to speak of God the Son as a 'second God'. Most eastern theologians held views which were some sort of approximation to this, but often the subtle distinctions and safeguards which Origen had used were abandoned. So there was a distinct tendency to view Jesus as in some way not quite equal to God the Father, and this was to be found especially among the disciples of Lucian of Antioch. In spite of wide divergences, however, the various views had, till now, peaceably coexisted. Part of the reason for this was that there was another view of the Godhead against which virtually all eastern theologians reacted most violently.

In the East at this time, if you wanted to blacken the name of a theological opponent, the quick and easy way was to suggest that he was a Sabellian, or that he followed the views of Paul of Samosata. The main reason why this particular theological view was so abhorrent was because it started from premises diametrically opposed to the general eastern view. Sabellius[2] had stressed the unity of God, and had viewed the Persons of Father, Son and Spirit as three different ways of looking at the one true God.

[1] The learned theologian of the early third century. For his career see my book *From Christ to Constantine* (IVP, 1971), pp. 122–7.

[2] We know very little about Sabellius with certainty. See *From Christ to Constantine*, pp. 119–20.

Paul of Samosata's teaching[3] may have been on similar lines, but the fact that he was said to have held 'low and degrading views about Christ' may mean that he also placed stress on the humanity of Jesus. But he had been condemned as a heretic by bishops who were supporters of Origen's theology. Few people in the East had a view of the Trinity like this, where the stress was on the oneness of God, but it was a view which was very much more congenial to western minds. Till now it had been treated as the theological bogy of the East. But Arius added a new trouble to the situation.

Basically, Arius took the Origenist theology of the East to its logical conclusion. But applying human logic to the study of the divine nature generally misfires. Arius complained that many teachers, including his own bishop Alexander, were making insufficient differentiation between Father and Son. Arius contended that the Son was positively inferior to God the Father, that He had a beginning and that 'there was when He was not'. In fact, the Christ of Arius' theology was a created demigod.

## The first moves against Arius

Alexander summoned his clergy to debate these views. Already he was suspecting that Eusebius of Nicomedia was using Arius to propagate his own theology. This Eusebius of Nicomedia was an unsavoury cleric who had recently moved from the church at Berytus[4] and become bishop of Nicomedia (then the capital of the eastern part of the Empire ruled by Licinius). When he heard that Alexander had summoned a council of over a hundred bishops, and that they had condemned Arius' teaching on the ground that it was unscriptural and a novelty, he immediately started to rally support for Arius from among the former students of Lucian of Antioch. And with the whole of the East taking sides, this was where Constantine came in.

It might well be asked, however, why Arius' theology was so damaging to Christianity. Arius himself insisted that he was being biblical, but in fact he was also markedly influenced by the Neo-Platonic philosophy. In this philosophy the uncreated, ineffable, divine essence was thought to be imperfectly mediated to mankind

[3] There is some confusion over what exactly were the views of Paul of Samosata. Some of the evidence is collected in *NE*, pp. 277–80.
[4] Modern Beirut in the Lebanon.

by the visible world. All the things in the visible world were shadows of the one great reality. But this great reality, the divine essence, was one, indivisible and unknowable. For Arius, God the Son was the nearest approach to a perfect reflection of the divine essence; and although unlike the other members of the created order, Jesus was still separate and distinct from the divine essence which was God the Father. Thus Jesus, the Word of God, was in Arius' thinking effectively demoted to the status of a demigod. Yet, if Jesus were not fully God, the revelation which He claimed to make of God the Father was called in question. If He were only an imperfect reflection of God the Father, how could there be any certain knowledge of God? And, far more seriously, if God the Son was not fully God, how could we be sure that He was in a position to save mankind? These were the corollaries of Arius' theology. To Constantine, bewildered and lamentably ignorant of Christian doctrine, it might seem like the disputes of two different schools of philosophers. But to any Christian aware of the issues at stake, it was a battle over the most important articles of belief.

When Constantine's envoy Hosius arrived in Antioch, he summoned a council of bishops there.[5] The doctrines of Arius were condemned, especially the idea that there was some point even before time when God the Son did not exist, and the suggestion that the divine Word[6] was a created being. God the Son is described as being 'of the very substance of the Father', and all ideas of His having a changeable nature (in contrast to God the Father who is unchanging), or being begotten at a point in time, are anathematized. Three bishops, however, members of the Lucianist clique, dissented from the findings of the council. They were led by Eusebius of Caesarea. Because of their dissent, they were put under temporary excommunication until the meeting of a full synod at Ancyra.

On receipt of this news, Constantine acted quickly. One suspects that he did not want to see his flattering friend Eusebius of Caesarea punished. Also, it was well known that Marcellus, bishop of Ancyra, was a man with theological views which were at the opposite extreme to those held in most of the East.[7] If a synod were

[5] For this important new evidence, see *NE,* pp. 354–7.
[6] The term 'Logos', as used in the prologue to John's Gospel.
[7] Many eastern bishops considered his theology to be Sabellian, and he was officially disowned even by the orthodox later on.

held on Marcellus' home ground, there would be no reprieve for several highly influential churchmen. Constantine may possibly have been aware that Marcellus and Eusebius of Caesarea had already engaged in bitter theological controversy over the very matter now at issue. Accordingly Constantine sent a letter to the bishops of the East informing them of a change of venue for the synod. Various reasons were given for the change. In view of the fact that bishops from the West could more easily attend, Constantine suggested the pleasant climate of Nicaea would commend that town as a suitable meeting place. But it was also very close to the imperial capital of the East, and he himself would be present.

## The Council of Nicaea

In spite of the fact that the Council of Nicaea was one of the most important Christian gatherings ever held, and the creed which it issued has become one of the great treasures of Christendom, it is surprising how little we know of its proceedings.[8] We are not helped by the fact that Eusebius of Caesarea, our main informant,

[8] Most of the material is assembled in *NE*, pp. 358–72.

Nicaea, where the first Ecumenical Council was summoned by Constantine the Great in 325. The picture shows the city wall and an old gate.

was an interested party. But reading between the lines of the letter which he sent back to his church at Caesarea, we can gain some idea of what happened.

It is probable that about 300 bishops (traditionally reckoned as 318) assembled at Nicaea, nearly all of them from the eastern provinces. Constantine presided (even though, since he was unbaptized, he was not even a church member), and the first item was the rehabilitation of Eusebius of Caesarea. He was required to read out the text of the creed which he had learnt when he was baptized. This was adjudged by the emperor to be orthodox, and to be fair it must be said that it contained no statement that even a most acute theologian could object to. Its only defects were in what it did not say. Anyway, Constantine prevented any debate by declaring Eusebius orthodox immediately after that cleric had finished his speech.

With Eusebius of Caesarea rehabilitated, the council then got down to the business of formulating a creed which would rule out the teachings of Arius. Constantine, who wanted only peace and agreement, was in favour of having Eusebius' own creed with the addition of the word 'consubstantial' (Greek *homoousios*) to describe the relation of Christ to God the Father. But why this word? Some have thought that Hosius of Cordoba suggested it. Or was it suggested by Alexander, the bishop of Alexandria, because he knew that Arius did not like it? We cannot be certain, but it was a word with a troubled history before it was ever used at the council of Nicaea.

In view of its importance both now and in the ensuing debates, it is worth while to pause and consider the meaning and use of this word. It originally meant 'made of the same stuff'. But it had been used in two theological controversies which were remembered either now or later with interest by the theologians of the East. The notorious Paul of Samosata had used it, (we do not know in what context) and this was enough to make it suspect. It had also been used in the famous debate of the previous century when Dionysius of Rome and Dionysius of Alexandria had clashed over Trinitarian doctrine. In both cases it seems to have been used by people who stressed the unity of the Godhead in an attempt to guard against excessive stress on the threeness of the Persons in the Godhead. And as such it would be viewed with distaste by many eastern theologians. But more recently, when Arius had been writing to his bishop Alexander, he had mentioned the word 'consubstantial' as one to be avoided when describing the relation of Father to Son. So, if one wanted to exclude Arius, it was obviously a useful weapon to use.

Constantine, however, did not get his way when he proposed that this controversial word should be added as the sole addition to Eusebius of Caesarea's creed, and that this should be the test of orthodoxy. A committee was set up to compose a creed (Eusebius does not say who was on the committee), and they came out with a creed which is the basis of our present Nicene Creed.[9] The creed which the committee proposed was much clearer in its definitions than Eusebius' own creed. Eusebius could say that God the Son was 'God from God', but Arius and his followers could interpret this as 'secondary god from the one true God'. The committee's creed shut the loopholes. Christ is described as 'from the substance of the Father' and 'consubstantial with the Father', as well as 'true God from true God'. To make assurance doubly sure, certain statements were explicitly anathematized in an appendix. The statement 'There was when He was not', and the belief that Christ was 'of another substance' or 'created' or 'changeable', were all explicitly banned.

Eusebius did not like the new creed. His own theology was at least half Arian, for although stopping short of believing that Jesus was a creature without any special link with God the Father, Eusebius certainly believed that Christ had some point of beginning and was to be clearly differentiated from God the Father in status. But Eusebius also saw that Constantine wanted unity. Constantine wanted that unity on the basis of the creed which his Council of Nicaea had formulated. So, in the end, nearly everyone signed the creed. Arius did not, and he was supported by two unimportant Egyptian bishops. Otherwise even the Lucianist clique fell into line. Eusebius of Nicomedia liked the creed even less than his namesake from Caesarea, and pledged himself to get it altered. When Constantine heard about this mutinous attitude, he promptly sent the scheming cleric into exile for a short time. On the promise of good behaviour, however, Constantine soon allowed

[9] Creed in *NE*, p. 366. The popularly named 'Nicene creed' as used in churches today dates from 381, but apart from the addition of the article on the Holy Spirit and the deletion of the anathemas at the end, it is not substantially different.

him back. And Eusebius of Nicomedia bent all his energies to rallying the former students of Lucian and to destroying all who supported the creed of Nicaea.

## After Nicaea

But at this point in time Constantine was involved in a domestic upheaval which occupied all his attention. We do not know exactly what were the causes, but the pious front on display at Nicaea was quickly dropped. Constantine's eldest son, Crispus, was summarily executed by his father. Constantine had married twice, and his second wife, Fausta, had three sons. From this it would seem on the surface as if it was just a case of a jealous stepmother's intriguing in favour of her own children. But the plot thickens when we also hear that Fausta herself was executed shortly afterwards. The reasons for such summary and ruthless actions are not known. Clearly Constantine feared treachery, but it is not known who was plotting with whom. Rumours of treason and immorality were whispered widely, but the truth is lost for ever. The whole episode left a dark stain on the career of Constantine.

Three years after the Council of Nicaea, bishop Alexander of Alexandria died. To the exceeding annoyance of Eusebius of Nicomedia and his clique, a strong opponent of Arius was elected as successor. This man, who was to become the centre of the Trinitarian controversy, remained bishop of Alexandria, in spite of five periods of exile, until 373. His name was Athanasius. He soon came to Constantine's notice, because Constantine was still trying to obtain complete unity in the eastern churches. And so the emperor suggested to Athanasius that perhaps if Arius abjured his heresy he might be allowed back into fellowship again. But Athanasius, well aware of how slippery Arius could be, refused point blank. So Constantine marked him down as a potential trouble-maker.

Athanasius was not the only church leader who came into Constantine's disfavour. There was the elderly and outspoken bishop of Antioch, called Eustathius. When Constantine's mother, Helena, made a royal visit to the Holy Land to see all the biblical sites, Eustathius made some scathing remarks about all the ostentatious ceremony which accompanied the royal lady. Constantine's ecclesiastical advisers, led by Eusebius of Caesarea, were quick to suggest that such behaviour should be punished, and Constantine allowed them to convene a synod and depose Eustathius. What Constantine did not realize was that Eustathius was a strong supporter of orthodoxy, and that the main reason for animosity against him was that he held one of the main churches of the East. When Eustathius was deposed and a pro-Arian bishop appointed in his place, a minority in the church refused to accept the new man. They began to meet as a separate church under the leadership of a young presbyter called Paulinus, and the church at Antioch remained divided for most of the remainder of the century.

Eustathius was the first of the new martyrs by exile, the men who suffered because of the intrigues of fellow churchmen. The next victim was Marcellus, the bishop of Ancyra. We have already mentioned his unusual theological views, and he was an obvious target for Eusebius of Nicomedia to attack. His theological views were not nearly so abhorrent in the West, however, and although exiled he made common cause with Athanasius later on. With Eustathius and Marcellus out of the way, the time seemed ripe to attack the last outstanding opponent of Arius, Athanasius of Alexandria himself.

## The building of the 'Christian Empire'

Meanwhile, Constantine was becoming dissatisfied with Rome as the capital of his Empire. There was a discreet hostility among the Roman Senate towards the emperor's support for the Christians. The city itself was not well situated to deal with troubles on the frontiers. And Constantine wanted to make a fresh start. During his war against Licinius, he had already noticed the city of Byzantium, and he decided that this should become the new capital of the 'Christian Empire'. It was well sited on a peninsula jutting into the Sea of Marmara, and both the troublesome frontiers (the Rhine–Danube line and the Persian frontier) were easily accessible. But, above all, its paganism was easy to overshadow. By encouraging people to migrate there, and by establishing a nominally Christian Senate, along with large building programmes for churches, Constantine succeeded in making it a 'Christian' city from the start. At least, the ethos was to be officially Christian, even though in actual fact its city mob was just as ill behaved as that at Rome. When Constantinople was dedicated in 330, however, Constantine felt very pleased with his achievement.

# Map 2

## The Eastern Mediterranean Area

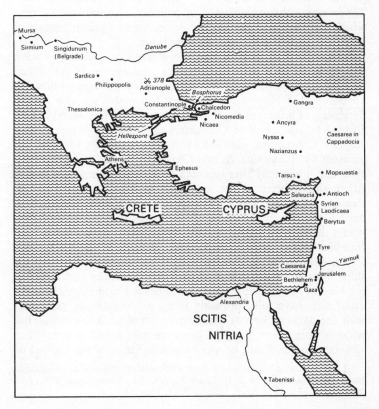

## Constantine and Athanasius

Constantine now set his mind to obtain peace in the churches. And seeing Athanasius as the main stumbling-block to this, he was quite ready to allow a synod to be convened to investigate charges against him. And there were some very damaging accusations raised against him. Athanasius had had considerable trouble with the Melitians. Although Melitius himself was now dead, a redoubtable Copt called John Arcaph had taken over the leadership. Athanasius had retaliated with strong-arm methods. He had imprisoned and beaten certain Melitian clerics, and had generally taken all steps possible to crush the movement. This much was true.[1] But when John Arcaph and his friends arrived at the council (it was convened at Tyre) they had other accusations as well. These were either exaggerated or patently false, but the support which the Melitians gave to the Arian moves against Athanasius made Athanasius' own position precarious.

Athanasius had made a bad move when he refused to allow Constantine's own agents to conduct enquiries in Egypt. When he came to Tyre he found all his enemies ranged against him, led by Eusebius of Nicomedia. But when Athanasius saw that he had no chance of a fair hearing, he did not wait for the council to end. Instead he rushed off to Constantinople with a few friends. The emperor Constantine was riding just outside the city when he was accosted by Athanasius. At first Constantine could not believe his eyes, and it was only after repeated pleas that he consented to give Athanasius a personal hearing. Back in Tyre, the council was already dispersing. Only a few of the court bishops remained, headed naturally by Eusebius of Nicomedia. Less capable plotters would have been dismayed at Athanasius' clever move. But Eusebius had an even more powerful weapon. He sent a message to Constantine saying that Athanasius had threatened to stop the ships from Egypt which carried corn supplies to the capital. It was the kind of foolish thing which a hot-headed man like Athanasius could well have said, probably more to demonstrate his power with the dock-workers at Alexandria than as an actual threat. But without corn from Egypt, Constantinople would starve. When Constantine heard this, he was furious. Athanasius was allowed no

[1] Letters written by Melitians among themselves tell of the persecution. Some are collected in H. I. Bell and W. E. Crum, *Three Coptic Texts with Jews and Christians in Egypt* (Kegan Paul, 1924).

**Porta Nigra, Trier, north Gaul.** Athanasius spent his first period of exile here.

opportunity even to reply, but was exiled to Trier, a town in Northern Gaul near the Rhine where he was cordially received by the bishop Paulinus. It was 336, and although Constantine did not know it, he had less than a year to live.

## Constantine, the first 'Christian' emperor

Although Constantine deferred his baptism until he was dying, his legislation shows marks of having been influenced by Christian humaneness.[2] He abolished crucifixion as a punishment, and prohibited branding of criminals on the face. He decreed that all prisoners should be allowed to come out of their cells and see the light of day at least once a day. But for offences such as kidnapping and rape he maintained the most savage penalties. He made

[2] Details in the *Codex Theodosianus*, a collection of laws made by Theodosius II (eastern emperor 408–50), edited by T. Mommsen (Berlin, 1905).

47

Sunday a public holiday, thus putting this day on a par with other festivals when markets and law courts were closed. His law concerning Sunday expressly permitted farmers to do necessary work on that day, however, and his support for Christians did not mean that he allowed town councillors to evade their tax-paying duties by becoming ordained.[3]

Although Constantine's usual method of bringing about theological peace was to repress all dissidents, he was wise enough to exercise tolerance where possible. For example, the small puritanical sect called Novatianists were generally hated and harassed by mainstream Christians because of their unyielding attitude towards those who had given way under persecution. When Constantine found that they were doctrinally orthodox, however, he enacted a law[4] expressly granting them protection from over-zealous, persecuting clerics. Even towards paganism Constantine showed remarkable leniency. Although he made no secret of his support for Christians, he refrained from making any legal enactments against non-Christians. He still nominally held the post of 'Pontifex Maximus' (chief priest of the imperial cult), and in general he left temples and ceremonies of the pagans undisturbed. Although describing himself as 'bishop of those outside the church' he limited his action to suppressing some immoral cults and to stealing a few fine works of art to embellish Constantinople, the city which was his pride and joy.

But Constantine left a legacy of problems. In North Africa the Donatist troubles continued unabated. In the East the ferment over Arianism was not settled, and Constantine understood so little of it that he allowed himself to be baptized by Eusebius of Nicomedia, the most redoubtable enemy of the creed which Constantine himself had supported at the Council of Nicaea. He delayed his baptism until he was dying, in case he should commit some great sin after baptism. There must have been something bizarre about preparing for an imperial baptism and an imperial funeral at the same time. But Constantine had decided that this was the way of pleasing the God of the Christians, and His favour must be kept at all costs.

To the last, Constantine never really made up his mind about

[3] This had apparently become a standard way for decurions to dodge holding public office in their towns and so becoming liable to see that taxes were paid. The edict is in *Codex Theodosianus* xvi.2.3.

[4] *Codex Theodosianus* xvi.5.2, cited in *NE*, pp. 335–6.

who was to succeed him. There were his three sons, but there were also brothers and nephews he had been busily promoting during his last years. In the end this was to be settled by a bloody purge as soon as the great man was dead. And so at last Constantine was baptized for the forgiveness of his sins at Easter 337. Five weeks later he was dying, dressed in the white robes traditionally worn by the newly baptized convert. With the best of intentions, and with an uncomprehending obtuseness, he had tried to please God whom he had only imperfectly known. In hindsight it is easy to condemn him for not having done any better, but many of his successors were to do considerably worse.

# 3

# Athanasius and the Trinitarian controversy

The fourth century saw what was probably the greatest doctrinal battle before the Reformation. And just as the Reformation is inexplicable without Luther, so the Trinitarian controversy of the fourth century can best be told as a story centred around Athanasius, the pope of Alexandria.

Fourth-century Alexandria was a cosmopolitan city, where many faiths and cultures alternately mingled with each other and fought against each other. There were many devotees of the old Egyptian gods, and there was a strong intellectual paganism against which Christian teachers had to argue. There was the Jewish quarter, consisting of a sizeable part of the city. Way-out sects of oriental origin canvassed their ideas and attempted to synthesize the traditions of Judaism and Christianity with the religions of the East. And there was the Christian church, ruled by a patriarch-bishop who had spiritual authority over the churches of Egypt. Egyptian Christianity had two distinct strains in itself. There was the intellectual, philosophical side, deriving its life from the great teachers of the third century, Clement of Alexandria and Origen. There was also the stream of popular Christianity, characterized by an indomitable and stubborn spirit which produced both mystical hermits and martyrs, but also intransigent political bishops and fanatical mobs. Athanasius was a typical Egyptian Christian in that he drew on both sides of the tradition. His greatness was that ultimately he turned both of these sides of his character to the exaltation of Christ.

We know virtually nothing of Athanasius' family or early years. From an early age he seems to have been under the special care of Alexander, the bishop of Alexandria. Athanasius received both secular and religious education, and was appointed deacon by Alexander. He went with his bishop to the Council of Nicaea in 325, but probably took little part in the debates there. His own theological position was naturally close to that of Alexander. He accepted the traditional orthodoxy of the East, but was gifted with a sharp insight which could spot loopholes and dangerous trends which went unnoticed by others. His ardent championship of the doctrine of the full deity of Christ, and his advocacy of the Nicene Creed as the only adequate safeguard were not so much fresh contributions to Christian theology, but rather were moves to buttress the doctrine already generally agreed. Some people think that Athanasius helped his bishop Alexander to draft some of his doctrinal letters issued early in the Arian controversy. Although this cannot be proved, Athanasius had certainly already proved his literary and doctrinal ability by writing two short works[1] to commend the Christian faith to pagans. When Alexander lay dying in 328, he indicated that he would like to see Athanasius succeed him, and when the church met after Alexander's death they voted for Athanasius. He was only about thirty when he became bishop, and was a zealous, impatient young man. And he inherited all the wars which his predecessor and father in God had been fighting.

We have already seen how his Egyptian stubbornness led to his first exile.[2] In trying to crush the former supporters of Melitius, he succeeded only in driving them into alliance with the Arians, and so when the emperor Constantine died we find Athanasius far away from Alexandria as an exile in Trier. But although in exile, Athanasius had many friends in Egypt. No doubt some supported him merely because they did not like to see outsiders, such as the slimy Eusebius of Nicomedia, interfering in the affairs of the Egyptian church. But there were many who had a strong personal attachment to Athanasius, and Athanasius' exile in the West had gained him friends there who were to be some of his most loyal supporters in the later struggles. Like most hot-blooded and

---

[1] There is some doubt as to when *Against the Nations* and *On the Incarnation* were written. Some scholars think it was later than this, but since there is no hint of the Arian controversy in either work they are probably to be dated early in Athanasius' life.

[2] See above, pp. 30, 31.

determined Christians, Athanasius inspired either love or hate. He was a man you could not be neutral about.

## Constantine's successors

The emperor Constantine had left in doubt the question of who should succeed him. His three sons settled the matter. With the help of the army they exterminated nearly all their other relatives. Almost the only survivor was a young nephew of Constantine called Julian, and this barbaric purge was one of the things which turned him permanently against Christianity.[3] In fairness it must be said, however, that any connection between New Testament Christianity and the doings of Constantine's sons was purely accidental.

The three sons divided the Empire between them. Constantine II took the western provinces. The second son, Constantius,[4] took the East, while the third son, Constans, was left with the Balkan provinces, Italy and North Africa. As far as theology was concerned, they probably understood little. But they took sides in church affairs with considerable enthusiasm. Constantine II and Constans tended to favour continuing their father's policy, and so favoured those who upheld the creed of Nicaea. Constantius gradually became more and more pro-Arian. The motives which the various brothers had for supporting theological parties, however, were mixed. With Constantius supporting those with Arian leanings, it was only natural that his rivals should support his theological opponents.

**Constans, emperor 337–350.** A coin in the British Museum, London.

[3] See below, pp. 74–9.
[4] In some text-books called Constantius II to distinguish him from the father of Constantine the Great, Constantius Chlorus (died 306).

After Constantine's death, his son Constantine II proclaimed a general amnesty to all those exiled during his father's reign. Therefore Athanasius was allowed to return to Alexandria.[5] In spite of the disgust felt by his enemies in the East, Athanasius returned to an enthusiastic welcome. Jubilant crowds received him back, and he must have been gratified to see the support he had. But one person in the crowd especially caught his attention. An aged, gaunt and unkempt Copt came forward. The crowds made way for the old man with awed reverence. For this was Antony, the famous hermit of the desert, now almost eighty. And he had actually deigned to come into the city from his desert cell to support the young pope of Alexandria and his stand for the truth. Athanasius received the old man warmly, and this was not merely a piece of astute public relations. Like many Egyptian Christians, Athanasius had a deep respect for those who had opted out of normal life and gone to seek God in the solitude of the desert. With the age of martyrs now a thing of the past (and there had been many martyrs in Egypt), popular imagination was caught by these shock-troops of the Christian army who were said to have fought the devil face to face on occasion. In the heart of many a church statesman there was a longing to leave the worldly battle-line and retire to fight the real spiritual battles in the desert.

## Athanasius under attack

Athanasius, however, was not left in peace at Alexandria for long. His enemies, led by Eusebius of Nicomedia, did not want a strong anti-Arian bishop in Alexandria. Although the out-and-out Arians were a comparatively small minority, they could enlist support from many eastern moderates, for two reasons. First, the creed of Nicaea was unpalatable to many easterners. This creed had been untouchable as long as Constantine was alive, but now there was a strong movement in the East to have it replaced. The moderates wanted a creed which would seem totally free from possible Sabellian overtones. The Arians, on their part, wanted a broader creed which would leave their theology tolerated. Both parties, therefore, could unite against the creed of Nicaea. Second, neither party liked Athanasius. Many eastern bishops, while by no means

[5] The main documents for this part of the Trinitarian controversy are assembled in *CCC*, pp. 1, 8–26, 31–56, 111–16, 143–50.

Arian, did not approve of the fact that Athanasius had been allowed back to his bishopric after having been deposed by a church council. The Arians, led by Eusebius of Nicomedia, wanted him out because he was becoming their most formidable opponent. The emperor Constantius was approached. He was informed that Athanasius was a threat to the peace, and was asked for help to depose him. But Athanasius was already gaining popular support in Egypt. It was no easy matter to remove him. The Alexandrian populace were furious when they heard that the emperor had decreed that Athanasius was to be deposed and exiled. Athanasius, not strong enough yet to defy the emperor, had to go. Even so, imperial troops were needed to enforce the decision of the emperor and the court bishops. Crowds who assembled to protest against the imperial action were savagely attacked by the troops, and many were killed or wounded. Complaining bitterly, Athanasius fled to his friends in the West. Eusebius of Nicomedia installed a pro-Arian bishop called Gregory, so as to prevent Athanasius returning.

Athanasius was accompanied by two friends of the hermit Antony when he fled to the West. Such was the spiritual stature of the exiled bishop that these two saintly men were willing to leave their life of contemplation to share the hardships of their friend in the worldly battles of church politics. Their sanctity and ascetic ways impressed many Christians in the West, since this was the first time that western Christians had even seen hermits. Athanasius went to Rome, and there met another notable refugee—Marcellus, the exiled bishop of Ancyra. Athanasius and Marcellus found common cause and asked for their case to be heard afresh before an unbiased assembly. With the support of Julius, the bishop of Rome, a council was convened. Athanasius and Marcellus were solemnly declared to be innocent of all charges against them, and to be rightful bishops of their respective churches. Western church leaders were now becoming worried about the strength of Arianism in the East, and they threw their weight into the struggle to uphold traditional Christian doctrine. But in spite of their efforts on Athanasius' behalf, a western council could not impose its will on the East.

Meanwhile, on the political front, Constantine II had decided to eliminate his brother Constans, his rival in the West. Unfortunately for him, his plans went wrong and he was defeated and killed. Constans now took charge of all the West (340). For

Athanasius this was a considerable help to his cause. Constans had met Athanasius, had been impressed by the determined bishop from Alexandria, and was ready to support him.

The prospects for peace in the churches were now much better because the controversial Arius was dead. There had been much talk of restoring Arius to communion, but he had died before this could happen. According to the friends of Athanasius, he had died in the public lavatory at Constantinople the night before he was to be received back into communion. With Arius gone, there was now some hope that an agreement on theology might result in harmony between East and West.

## The 'Dedication' council

In 341 nearly a hundred eastern bishops were present when Constantius, the eastern emperor, dedicated the 'Golden Church' at Antioch. It was a great occasion, and everyone felt that the time was highly suitable for holding a council to settle doctrinal difficulties. The eastern bishops, however, were still hag-ridden by their fears of Sabellianism. They still viewed the Nicene key word 'consubstantial' with suspicion, even though most of them had no desire to perpetuate the theology of Arius. The creeds issued by this council reflect their concerns.

At this juncture it is worth while to note that creeds were being used for an additional purpose to that for which they had originally been designed. Originally, the creed had been a summary of Christian doctrine learnt by heart by a candidate for baptism.[6] It was treated as a secret, and was not used regularly in public worship as happens nowadays in Anglican services. In cases of doctrinal problems, however, people whose doctrine was suspect were often asked what was the creed they had learnt when they were baptized (this was what had happened to Eusebius of Caesarea at the Council of Nicaea). Arising possibly from the practice at Nicaea, creeds were now being issued as tests of orthodoxy; hence the

[6] The creed began its life in the form of the three questions asked at baptism: 'Do you believe in God the Father?', 'Do you believe in God the Son?', 'Do you believe in God the Holy Spirit?' These had received doctrinal amplification, and later the questions were recast in a declaratory form. For a full discussion of this, see J. N. D. Kelly, *Early Christian Creeds* (Longmans, 1950), chapters 1 to 3.

proliferation of creeds in the fourth century and the detailed study of their wording.

Four creeds are associated with the council at Antioch in 341.[7] While they were quite orthodox in what they said, an acute theologian like Athanasius could see that they failed to be explicit enough to rule out Arianism entirely. Such has always been the defect of well-meaning clergy seeking for a peace formula which will meet with maximum support. The eastern bishops were not totally blind, however. They did condemn any suggestion that Christ was begotten at a point in time, and they were perfectly willing to call Him 'God from God'. But they jibbed at using the word 'consubstantial'.

Both the emperors, Constans and Constantius, wanted the church dispute over. They probably failed to realize how deeply both sides felt. And there was the added problem that even now East and West were linguistically drifting apart. The Latin-speaking West had genuine difficulty in communicating with the Greek-speaking East. For both parts of the Empire to meet and conduct technical theological discussions, there had to be men who were not only fluent in both languages but also conversant with the two different sets of thought forms which were developing. And such men were hard to find. Nevertheless, the two emperors arranged for an ecclesiastical summit meeting at Sardica, a town on the border between the two parts of the Empire.

## The Council of Sardica

The Council of Sardica was a fiasco. The eastern bishops arrived, but when they saw Athanasius and Marcellus of Ancyra there, they refused to take part. They said that these men had been legally deposed, and therefore had no right to be present. Even though the arch-plotter Eusebius of Nicomedia was now dead,[8] many eastern bishops did not like Athanasius after what they had heard about his heavy-handed treatment of the Melitian dissidents. But the westerners were adamant. Hosius of Cordoba (now in his late eighties) was presiding. He was supported by Julius, the bishop of

[7] Full details of their prominence in Kelly, *Early Christian Creeds*, pp. 263–74.
[8] He had become bishop of Constantinople in 338, and remained there till his death in 341/2.

Rome who had helped to exonerate the deposed bishops. They refused to convene the council unless Athanasius and his friends were allowed to take part. The situation was impossible, and the deadlock was broken only when the easterners walked out in a body, crossed back over the frontier and held a separate assembly at Philippopolis in Thrace. The only thing noteworthy about this council of the eastern bishops was the emergence of Valens, bishop of Mursa in the Balkans, as the new leader of the Arian party in succession to Eusebius of Nicomedia.

Meanwhile, the westerners, along with Athanasius and his friends, solemnly held council in Sardica. From opposite sides of the border, the two rival synods hurled anathemas at each other, but since neither side could implement them they were not worth the paper they were written on. The western council at Sardica also put out a doctrinal statement which could only be called provocative. Western Christians had always disliked the eastern method of viewing the Trinity as 'three substantial existences' (in Greek, three *hypostaseis*), and then trying to account for the unity of the Godhead. While in eastern ears this might seem perfectly orthodox, to westerners it sounded like a belief in three gods![9]

Because of this misunderstanding, the westerners at Sardica condemned as heretical the description of the Trinity as 'three substantial existences', demanding instead that the easterners should subscribe to a belief in 'one substantial existence'—a doctrine which the easterners would regard as rank Sabellianism and which would please no-one in the East except Marcellus of Ancyra. We do not know what Athanasius said on this occasion. No doubt he wanted true doctrine affirmed, but he dared not risk losing the support of the westerners by suggesting that they had got things wrong. At the time he kept a diplomatic silence, but later in his career he was heard to refer to 'that rubbish from Sardica'— his considered view on the doctrinal definition of that council.

The Council of Sardica had one strange result. Athanasius and his friends had appealed to Julius, the bishop of Rome, to reconsider

[9] The problem was caused by the fact that the Greek word *hypostasis*, which I have rendered as 'substantial existence', did not have the same meaning as the Latin *substantia*, its etymological equivalent. The Latin *substantia*, meaning substance or essence, was better translated by the Greek *ousia*, while the Greek *hypostasis* carried at least some of the meaning of the Latin *persona*.

the verdict of deposition passed against them by the Council of Tyre. There was no known precedent for this (although Julius believed one to exist) and so, to give the unusual step a semblance of legality, the Council of Sardica passed a canon in retrospect giving the bishop of Rome the right to hear appeals from the decisions of local church synods.[1] The later bishops of Rome cherished this grant of authority, but it carried little weight when it was only the canon of a partisan council. So they tried to pass off their new-found right as a canon of the great Council of Nicaea.[2] Easterners were never deceived by this, but it was widely canvassed in the West, and eventually was backed up by further enactments. But this beginning of the paramount power of the Roman church in fact began as an attempt to rationalize an otherwise unprecedented action.

## The return of Athanasius

The events of 343 at Sardica were perhaps the necessary explosion to clear the air. When everyone had said all the harsh things they wished, tempers cooled down and both sides became ready to compromise. Athanasius and the westerners were induced to abandon their support for Marcellus of Ancyra. He remained in exile as the theological bogy-man of the East, and long after his death his opinions were still solemnly anathematized at many eastern councils. The easterners tried to clear themselves of suspicions of unorthodoxy by sending yet another creed to the West. This was the 'Long-lined Creed' (so called because it was written on paper of exceptional width), and its main aim was to disavow any allegations of worshipping three gods. Altogether, the political climate in the East was becoming more favourable for a settlement. The emperor Constantius was involved in heavy fighting on the Persian frontier, and was quite willing for a compromise peace. Gregory, the intruded bishop in Alexandria, had just died. So the way was open for Athanasius to be formally reinstated as bishop of Alexandria.

Athanasius returned to frenzied rejoicing in Alexandria. His

[1] The canon and a discussion of it, together with other documents from Sardica, are collected in E. Giles, *Documents Illustrating Papal Authority* (SPCK, 1952), pp. 99–107.

[2] *E.g.* in the famous appeal of Apiarius, a North African presbyter, who appealed to Rome against his deposition by a North African council. Details in *CCC*, pp. 227–33.

seven years of exile had done nothing to diminish his popularity, and the final rumblings of the Melitian dissidents seem to have died away. Athanasius was soon busy, preaching to his congregation, outlining the doctrine of the deity of Christ. He travelled much in Egypt, gaining the support of the Coptic-speaking peasants who had previously been largely pro-Melitian. Although he was back in Alexandria, Athanasius knew full well that the struggle was not over. He was still in the part of the Empire ruled by a pro-Arian emperor, and Arianism was still flourishing. The capital, Constantinople, in particular, was an Arian stronghold. Antioch was occupied by a pro-Arian bishop too, although the splinter group under the presbyter Paulinus continued to meet. Arianism was also making headway in the Balkans where Valens of Mursa and his colleague Ursacius of Singidunum (modern Belgrade) were leaders of the heresy. Athanasius knew the battle would be joined again soon, and so he made as sure as he could that in Egypt at least, Christians knew the issues involved and were doctrinally orthodox.

## The rise of state-supported Arianism

The storm became imminent in 350. The western emperor, Constans, though not personally a very admirable character, had given his support to the Nicene party. But in 350 a German officer in the Roman army, called Magnentius, raised a revolt against him. Constans was murdered, and Magnentius then moved against Constantius. The two armies happened to meet each other outside Mursa, the very town where the Arian Valens was bishop. Valens seized the opportunity. He met Constantius and suggested that it would be best if he remained in the church at Mursa and prayed while the battle was being fought. Constantius agreed. The cunning bishop then arranged relays of messengers from the church to the edge of the battlefield, so that he would be the first to have news of the outcome. After a protracted struggle, Constantius' troops were victorious. Valens' messengers brought the news to their chief. Immediately he entered the church, and announced to the praying emperor that God had given him the victory, and that the Almighty had revealed this to Valens. Official confirmation soon came. And Constantius, believing that Valens was a man of vast sanctity with special communication with God, was henceforward willing to follow any and every suggestion of that scheming prelate.

It took a couple more years before Magnentius was finally

**Constantius II, emperor 337–361.** A gold medallion in the British Museum, London.

crushed. Then, in 353, Valens and Constantius were ready to impose their Arian creed on the churches of the Empire. They did not attack Athanasius immediately. First of all, they proceeded against the church leaders of the West, almost all of whom were strong supporters of the Nicene Creed and highly suspicious of anything that came from the East. So Valens organized a council at Arles, where he induced the bishops to condemn Athanasius yet again. But one man defied the imperial threats. He was Paulinus, the bishop of Trier, who had been host to Athanasius during his exile. Constantius could not bear defiance. He determined to be present himself at a fresh council, held in Milan in 355. Thither were summoned not only Paulinus, but also quite a number of other bishops who were know to be strong supporters of the Nicene Creed and of its main defender Athanasius.

The Council of Milan gave Constantius what he wanted, but at a price which was far too high. Constantius found out that he was not dealing with subservient orientals. In fact, if it had not been for the fact that he was the emperor, and had all the imperial power at his command, his own pet bishop Valens would have been the one to be condemned.

To start with, Paulinus of Trier would not recant. Then Eusebius of Vercellae declared that Valens was a heretic, and demanded that all the bishops present should give their assent to the Nicene Creed. Dionysius of Milan got up, said that he would gladly sign, and took out his pen to do so. There followed an undignified fight as Valens forcibly intervened to stop him. Constantius decreed exile for one bishop after another, but the list was ponderously long. Eusebius of Vercellae went into exile in the East, and there joined up with Athanasius.[3] Another bishop who went east into exile at this time was Lucifer, the bishop of Cagliari in Sardinia. He was a violently spoken cleric who wrote pungent pamphlets in the vernacular Latin, and was not afraid to insult Constantius personally. He was also an extreme rabble-rouser, and we shall hear of him later on in the East causing yet more trouble. Another much milder cleric who went into exile at this time was Liberius, the bishop of Rome who succeeded Athanasius' old friend Julius. He fared rather better than some, because the city mob at Rome caused such trouble that Constantius was eventually compelled to let him return for the sake of peace. During his exile, however, Constantius had induced him by threats of violence to sign some kind of compromising document. Even the extreme old age of Hosius of Cordoba was no protection against the viciousness of Constantius and Valens. The old man, now over a hundred years old, was exiled. But from exile he wrote a stinging letter to Constantius. He rebuked the emperor for his interference in church affairs, and handed out plenty of grandfatherly reproofs. The rejoinder from Valens and Constantius was to threaten to beat up the old man if he did not sign some kind of heretical document. In the end they managed to get the old man's signature, but he stubbornly kept declaring, 'I won't condemn Athanasius.' Within a few months the aged bishop who had been the last survivor of the era of the great persecution was dead.

## Athanasius in danger

The news reached Athanasius that Constantius had silenced opposition in the West. He knew that his turn was coming. But ten

[3] This Eusebius is also known to history as the scribe of the oldest surviving copy of the Latin Gospels, the *Codex Vercellensis*.

years in Alexandria as bishop had mellowed Athanasius. Egypt had taken him to its heart, and from the lowliest peasant to the high officials there were few who were against him. Constantius knew that he must act swiftly if he were to defeat the powerful pope of Alexandria. Imperial troops rushed to the main church at Alexandria one Sunday morning. Athanasius was in church presiding at worship. He instantly sized up the situation. If he gave the word, the crowd would take on the soldiers, and the carnage would be terrible. His friends urged him to flee. After calling on the congregation to disperse quietly, he made a dash for a side door and escaped in the crowd. Even though a bishop, he dressed no differently from most of his congregation, and it was easy for him to slip away. For the next five years Athanasius organized his flock while on the run from Constantius' agents. Sometimes he slipped back into Alexandria unnoticed. More often he hid in the cells of the hermits of the Nitrian desert. Here he was made very welcome, although there was one friend of his who was no longer in the desert. Old Antony had died just before Athanasius had been forced to go on the run. The aged hermit (he was over a hundred when he died) left his most valuable possessions, his sheepskin cloak and mantle, to Athanasius. Athanasius must have been deeply touched by such a vote of confidence by the man whom most of Egypt viewed as the greatest saint of their era. Such was Athanasius' own admiration for Antony that he set himself to write a biography of the hermit, and this is our main source of knowledge about the first great Christian hermit.

While hiding in the desert, Athanasius had time to write. And although secluded, he did not fail to keep in touch with the outside world. Detailed reports of the latest manoeuvres in the theological battle were brought to him, and Athanasius kept abreast of the current events. He wrote prolificly himself, detailing the progress of the Arian controversy and arguing out the various theological points raised in debate. Meanwhile, on Valens' advice, the emperor Constantius had put in an Arian as bishop of Alexandria. But he had to keep troops in the city to protect his nominee. This man was called George, and his main claim to fame was that he had been a pork butcher in Asia Minor before being appointed bishop. He was a heavy-handed, loutish man, who was disliked by Christians and pagans equally. And although he tried to hunt down Athanasius, he was totally unsuccessful.

# The triumph of the Arians

At their moment of seeming triumph, the Arians met to publish their own creed. This was the decisive point at which they lost the support of the moderate easterners, and their cause became hopeless. Only hatred for Athanasius and dislike of the Nicene creed had kept the two parties together. But the main body of the eastern bishops, however suspicious they were of the Nicene Creed, were in no mood to underwrite the extremes of Arianism. Quite a number of easterners would have been willing to have described Christ as 'of the same sort of essence' as the Father (Greek, *homoiousios*), which was only a short step from saying that He was 'consubstantial' (Greek, *homoousios*). But in 357, when Valens and a small group of his friends met at Sirmium, they issued a document[4] which not only outlawed 'consubstantial' but even condemned the eastern discussion of 'essence' as unscriptural! It was a nakedly Arian document in which God the Son is unequivocally treated as a secondary and second-rate deity with little or no connection with God the Father. It shocked not only Athanasius and friends but also a whole crowd of people who had hitherto been his enemies. It fully merited the name given to it by a western theologian, Hilary of Poitiers, when he called it the 'Blasphemy of Sirmium'.

Hilary, the bishop of Poitiers, was the western theologian who did most for the cause of orthodox Christian doctrine in the West. He came from an educated pagan family, and was already married and well into middle life when converted. Not long after his conversion he was elected bishop of Poitiers. In spite of being a Christian for only a short while, Hilary was well versed in theology, and he was an avid learner. He avoided being present at the Synod of Milan in 355 when Constantius took tough measures against the western bishops. But he did not escape imperial displeasure, for he was soon caught agitating against Arianism and trying to get the pro-Arian bishop of Arles deposed. Constantius exiled Hilary to Asia Minor. But Hilary was an enterprising man who was not going to waste his time while in the East. He was probably the only western bishop who really managed to understand the easterners' outlook. He travelled round, debating and arguing in the East, and in the end made such a nuisance of himself to the Arians that to get some peace Constantius sent him back to Gaul.

[4] *CCC*, pp. 35–7.

## The 'Dated Creed'

Watching from his hideout in the Egyptian desert, Athanasius must have been surprised to see the way things were moving. The 'Blasphemy of Sirmium' had alarmed many even of his former enemies. One of the leaders of the new protesters was Basil of Ancyra, the very man whom the Arians had put into the see once occupied by Athanasius' one-time associate Marcellus. When such a man became worried over Arianism, it was a sure sign that things were changing. Basil of Ancyra summoned a council of like-minded people, and issued a statement which, while still condemning the Nicene Creed, also outlawed the now fashionable Arianism which declared the divine Christ to be 'unlike the Father'. Valens and his clique were frightened at the new turn of events. So they determined to hold a major council which would officially promulgate a creed that would tolerate Arianism. With Constantius' help they summoned two parallel councils, one for the eastern bishops at Seleucia and one for the western bishops at Rimini. The official creed which was put to both councils is usually called the 'Dated Creed', because it begins with the official date of the councils. Later on a good joke went around about this creed, to the effect that this was the belief invented on the date shown, in contrast with the timeless truth of apostolic belief.

The 'Dated Creed' left wide loopholes for Arians, and condemned only the most extreme forms of Arianism. The most it would do to define Jesus' relation to God the Father was to say that He was 'like the Father'. Few people liked it. The westerners clamoured for the Nicene Creed. The easterners demanded that Jesus should at least be described as 'like the Father in all things', and expressed a preference for the creed of the Council of Antioch of 341.[5] It was only imperial pressure that overrode the objections. Many bishops with widely differing theological opinions, including Basil of Ancyra himself, found themselves in exile. And nowhere was there more consternation than at Antioch.

The church at Antioch was already split between the Arian majority and the minority group of orthodox Christians led by the presbyter Paulinus. Just around this time a new bishop was appointed, a safe, unexciting cleric called Meletius. He was seemingly loyal to the official creed of Arianism, and when he preached he

[5] See above, pp. 55–6.

usually kept clear of controversial doctrinal subjects. Imagine the consternation of all present when he began to preach on the Nicene Creed, and when he started to support orthodox doctrine instead of Arianism. People took more notice of sermons then than nowadays, and one of Meletius' fellow clergy, an ardent Arian, rushed up into the pulpit and tried to silence him. He got his hand over Meletius' mouth, but Meletius held up first one finger and then three to make his point. There was uproar. The whole affair was reported to Constantius, and he deposed Meletius. But many of the congregation went with him and refused to accept the new bishop. Paulinus and his orthodox group, however, would have nothing to do with Meletius, on the grounds that he and his party had been baptized by Arian heretics and so were 'guilty of heresy by association'. So there were three rival congregations at Antioch, each claiming to be the true church!

## The collapse of state-supported Arianism

It is strange that the collapse of Arianism was probably hastened most effectively by a man who was not even a Christian. Julian, a nephew of Constantine the Great, had been almost the only survivor of the bloody purge which followed his uncle's death. For years he had lived in fear of his life. He had been tutored mainly by Arian court bishops, whom he detested. In secret he managed to gain access to the classical literature of Greece and Rome, and he became an ardent disciple of the ancient gods. As he grew older he managed to go to Athens to study, and he lived there in comparative obscurity until he was suddenly summoned by his cousin Constantius. Barbarian tribes had burst across the Rhine frontier and had occupied large tracts of Gaul. Julian was commissioned to lead the imperial forces against them. From 356 to 360 he campaigned in the West with signal success. Meanwhile, on the eastern frontier, Constantius decided that with the help of Julian's victorious troops he might be able decisively to crush the Persians. But Julian's troops were not at all keen on a desert campaign. They mutinied, and demanded that their general take over as emperor. Once more the armies of the East and West moved on to a collision course. But as he hurried through the mountains of Asia Minor, Constantius caught a fever. In a few days he was dead, and Julian entered Constantinople unopposed as emperor of the whole Empire.

We shall deal later with Julian's abortive attempts to restore paganism.[6] He was no friend of the Christians, and as a stroke of malice he decided to allow all exiled bishops to return home. He hoped that the Christians would thereupon tear themselves to pieces. The effect of this move, however, was to deal Arianism its death blow.

While Julian was still marching east, Hilary of Poitiers was back in the West leading the overthrow of Arianism there. In the East the bishops returned to scenes of confusion. Lucifer of Cagliari, still in eastern exile, contributed to the confusion at Antioch by taking it upon himself to ordain Paulinus as bishop, and the church was left with two orthodox bishops. Athanasius and the westerners tended to support Paulinus, while the rest of the East supported Meletius. Not content with having caused this much damage, Lucifer then proceeded to form his own rigorous sect who refused to hold communion with those who had associated with the Arians.

At Alexandria the populace had not waited for Athanasius' return before moving against the loathsome George. This prelate had incited his followers to burn down a pagan temple in Alexandria. This brought out a pagan mob. The Christians joined in, and together they literally tore George to pieces, and murdered a number of other city officials for good measure. This was to be the first of many times when the mob of Alexandria ran amok in support of its bishop. When Athanasius actually returned to Alexandria, he there met Eusebius of Vercellae, one of the western bishops still in exile, and they summoned a small council to try to unite the various anti-Arian groups. At last the fiery pope of Alexandria was extending the olive branch to some of his former opponents. It was the three newcomers mentioned below, however, who did most to bring about the final agreement on doctrine which destroyed Arianism for ever within the confines of the Empire.

Basil the Great had been a student at Athens with the future emperor, Julian. With his brother Gregory of Nyssa, and his friend Gregory of Nazianzus, Basil had been drawn to cultivate the ascetic life in his native Cappadocia (Eastern Asia Minor). As well as being one of the greatest names in eastern monasticism,[7] however, Basil was also bishop of Caesarea in Cappadocia. From this

[6] See below, pp. 74–9.
[7] See below, pp. 103–5.

vantage point he was able to strike at the strongholds of Arianism. He and his two associates preached and wrote tirelessly. Starting from the traditional eastern standpoint, they succeeded in showing that only the creed of Nicaea was an adequate safeguard against Arianism. Basil corresponded with Athanasius, and together they fought out the later battles against Arianism. Athanasius was not left in peace even during the short reign of Julian. The ardent pagan emperor was outraged when Athanasius was baptizing many prominent ex-pagans in Alexandria. But Athanasius' fourth exile was of short duration (less than a year), and he was soon back in Alexandria when Julian died fighting the Persians on the eastern frontier (363).

## The latter years of the Trinitarian controversy

Julian the Apostate died in 363 and was succeeded by the emperor Jovian, who reigned for only eight months before dying of asphyxia due to fumes from a coke stove. On Jovian's death the Empire was divided between two brothers, Valentinian and Valens. Valentinian ruled the West, and although nominally a Christian he took little notice of church affairs except when disorder upset the public peace. With the exception of the Arian bishop of Milan, orthodox Christians took over as leaders of all the western churches. In the East, Valens, the emperor, still tried to support the 'Dated Creed';[8] and he even succeeded in forcing Athanasius to go into exile for the fifth and last time (only for a few months). But the crowds at Alexandria went wild and refused to be calmed down until Athanasius was allowed to come back. The emperor Valens would also have liked to get rid of Basil at Caesarea. But Basil stood out against him and dared him to do his worst. Valens' nerve failed, and he left Basil unmolested. When Valens died in battle against the Goths at the catastrophic Battle of Adrianople in 378, the eastern Christians heaved a sigh of relief, and attributed his death to his heretical leanings.

## The Council of Constantinople in 381

Three years after Valens' death, the final demise of official Arianism took place with the hearty support of the emperor Theodosius.

[8] See above, pp. 64–5.

Gregory of Nazianzus had been appointed bishop of Constantinople, and he preached orthodox doctrine with great success. A council of the eastern bishops was convened, with Meletius of Antioch as president. The last Arians in the East were deposed. A few old traditionalists tried to hold out against the full deity of the Holy Spirit, which is the reason why in our present Nicene Creed there is a long section on the Holy Spirit.[9] The Nicene Creed, as revised at this Council of Constantinople in 381, was accepted by the great majority as the standard of Christian truth.

Athanasius died in 373, undefeated and in possession of his see in spite of the pro-Arian emperor Valens. His personal destiny had been inextricably bound up with his whole-hearted belief in the full deity of Jesus. He had progressed from the hot-headed zealot to the mature and wise theologian without losing his deeply held convictions. Although he did not live to see the final victory, it was obvious by the time he died that the decisive battles had been won. Arianism within the Empire was never afterwards a force to be reckoned with, although small groups of Arians existed well into the fifth century.[1] Outside the Empire, however, Arianism had been received as normal Christianity by many barbarian tribes, notably the Goths and Vandals.[2] And in its barbarian form it was to come back to trouble the churches later on. But this is a story which will be told in another chapter.

There are lessons for today to be gained from the Trinitarian controversy, even though it was fought in the fourth century AD. First, the whole controversy highlights the need for clarity in theological statements. The same set of words may mean two utterly different things to two different sets of people.[3] Second, it is

[9] It is remarkable how little controversy there was over the deity of the Spirit: Athanasius mentions some people in Egypt who denied His deity, but these are the only others known apart from the dissidents of 381. This group of eastern bishops are sometimes called 'Macedonians', after Macedonius (bishop of Constantinople, deposed 360), but in fact he was never known to have held this opinion. The leader of the dissidents of 381 was Eustathius of Sebaste, and their objections seem to have been that Scripture did not explicitly call the Holy Spirit God. In spite of the considerable support which they had in 381, they formed no lasting party.

[1] The Arian church historian Philostorgius flourished *c.* 420, and there were Arian congregations at Constantinople in the time of Nestorius (deposed 431).

[2] See below, pp. 93ff., 128f., 166ff., 172ff.

[3] Hence the misunderstandings at Sardica in 343.

not enough for a theological statement to be orthodox. It must also explicitly rule out the heresy under discussion. All the well-intentioned creeds issued by the easterners in the earlier phases of the controversy were inadequate because they did not expressly tackle all the points of Arius' heresy. Any doctrinal statement tends to be a fence set up to mark out the limits of acceptable belief. The fault of the easterners was that they were busy erecting a fence on one side of their field against the dangers of Sabellianism, and then hopefully imagined that this same fence would do duty against the encroachments of Arianism on the opposite side of the field! Third, and most important, the Trinitarian controversy shows how necessary it is for Christians to have a clear notion of the deity of Jesus. Well-worn, traditional phrases are not enough. It is impossible that Jesus should be a reliable revealer of God and an effective Saviour unless his relation to God the Father is one of absolute equality. The Arian error, in trying to detract from this equality, could open the way for thinkers who would state openly that Jesus was merely an inspired man and utterly different from God. Fourth, the Trinitarian controversy shows the danger of imposing a foreign system of thought on the biblical data.[4] Arius was considerably influenced by the Neo-Platonic idea of God and the world, and this coloured his theology and made him incapable of seeing just how the eternal and unknowable God could totally communicate Himself to humanity. Arius' rigid logic, coupled with an alien philosophical system, forced the biblical data to give erroneous conclusions. Thanks to his unscrupulous political friends, Arius' doctrines caused havoc in the churches, and it took over sixty years to repair the damage.

[4] In more recent times we can see parallels to this in the imposition of Hegel's system of thesis–antithesis–synthesis on the New Testament documents, and in the influence of existentialism on the theology of Bultmann.

# 4

# The fading of the old order

It would be a great mistake to assume that once Constantine had declared himself in favour of Christianity, Graeco-Roman paganism just vanished overnight. In actual fact, for most of the fourth century, paganism remained a live option for some people, and Christians still had to address themselves to the task of converting Roman citizens to Christ.

Constantine the Great had done little to attack paganism, and the situation did not change too much under his sons. Constantius did issue some edicts against pagans, possibly at the prompting of over-zealous Christians;[1] but they were applied only in a very limited way, if at all. Certainly, the future emperor Julian found no difficulty in obtaining all the pagan learning which he desired.

Christian attitudes to paganism varied. Most viewed their non-Christian neighbours as unfortunates outside the holy fellowship of God's people. And many Christians spent considerable time trying to persuade their non-Christian friends to throw their lot in with the churches. But there was a growing group who viewed pagan religions as enemies of the truth of God, and therefore institutions which had to be positively repressed. Strange to say, some of the most vocal demands for repression came from ex-pagans who were recent converts. One such man, a former astrologer called Firmicius Maternus,[2] wrote to the emperor Constantius demanding that all non-Christians be forcibly 'rescued' from the error of their ways. It is to the credit of Constantius that he took little notice of such vicious ideas.

[1] See *CCC*, pp. 2, 3.
[2] Extracts in *CCC*, pp. 3, 4.

**The tomb of Caecilia Metella** on the Appian Way outside Rome. It was used in the Dark Ages as a fort.

It was in Rome itself, especially among the Senators and the intelligentsia, that there was one of the greatest centres of resistance to Christianity. It was a resistance based on reverence for the traditions of Rome, buttressed by a conservatism that viewed the current trends as a terrible degeneration from Rome's past glory. The learned classicists of the Roman Senate secretly despised the dynasty of Constantine, descended from obscure peasants of the Balkan provinces. And although there were a few senatorial families which had embraced the claims of Christ, the great majority were solidly entrenched in their traditional ways.

## Marius Victorinus, a convert from the pagan aristocracy

In such a situation, the conversion of a learned man could cause both consternation and hostile comment. Marius Victorinus, a leading professor of rhetoric, was viewed as one of the pillars of the ancient learning. But for some time he had been studying the Bible because a friend has persuaded him to do so. Gradually Victorinus became more and more attracted to the Christian faith, and was even ready to admit to his friend that he secretly wanted to follow Christ. But he hesitated from taking the step of open commitment and baptism. With perhaps more wisdom than he knew, he declared that it was not the walls of a church that made a man a Christian. There the matter rested for some years, until suddenly one day Marius Victorinus told his friend that he was going to go to church because he wanted to become a Christian.

The sight of Marius Victorinus going to a Christian church was the talking-point in Rome for many a day, especially as he declared that he wished to be enrolled for instruction for baptism. The Roman Christians were equally amazed as one of the leaders of the pagan establishment patiently learnt the creed along with the other candidates for baptism. The public recital of the creed before baptism was a great ceremony in the church at Rome; and some of the clergy, wishing to spare Victorinus embarrassment, suggested that he make his recital less publicly. But the converted professor insisted that he make his declaration of faith in Christ just like anyone else. He was baptized, and immediately threw his talents into Christian work. He wrote a long treatise in support of orthodox doctrine during the Trinitarian controversy. When the emperor Julian issued a decree forbidding Christians to teach classical literature,[3] Marius Victorinus resigned his professorship. And many of his pagan colleagues, admiring his stand for his convictions, declared that the emperor's decree was a gross injustice. On the death of the emperor Julian, Victorinus was back at his lecturing again. He died some years later, widely respected for his learning and his Christian commitment, and the story of his conversion was widely told even after his death. Among those whom it influenced was the young Augustine, one day to become the greatest theologian of the western churches.[4]

During the reigns of Constantine the Great and his sons, Christianity and paganism existed side by side in relative peace. But in many places Christian propaganda had been very effective in winning the mass of the people away from the ancient deities.

[3] See below, pp. 75–7.
[4] Augustine himself is our main source of the story. See *Confessions* viii.2.

# Map 3

## Italy

Vercellae • Cassiacum • Milan • Pavia • Bobbio • Genoa

Verona

*Fripidus*

Aquileia

Ravenna

Rimini

Busta Gallorum ✗ 553

Faesulae

Split

TUSCANY

Gubbio

Spoleto

Nursia

*Tiber*

Rome

Ostia • *Milvian Bridge*

Monte Cassino

Benevento

Naples • Nola

SARDINIA

Cagliari

CALABRIA

Vivarium (Squillace)

Messina

SICILY

This was especially true of the towns of the East, for the first Christians had mainly been town-dwellers. But even in the countryside, Christian preaching was gradually making headway against the innate conservatism which is found in most country folk. All this was happening without much imperial pressure. But the complacent advance of Christianity was to receive a sharp jolt during the brief reign of the emperor Julian, known to later ages as Julian the Apostate.

## Julian and his pagan revival

Julian is a tragic figure, at one and the same time both noble and ridiculous. The embittered survivor of the bloody purge that had taken place on the death of Constantine the Great, he had seen almost all his relatives murdered, and had lived his earlier life in constant fear under the surveillance of servants of his cousin Constantius (who had presided over the purge). Outwardly he had been compelled to conform to the court Christianity of Constantius, which was both unorthodox and lacking in spirituality. As Julian grew older, he was allowed a little more freedom. He managed to read many of the Graeco-Roman classics, and was fired with a devotion to the old gods. He went to the university at Athens, where classical pagan learning still flourished. Here he met people like Basil the Great and Gregory of Nazianzus, who were one day to be the greatest theologians of the eastern churches. But whereas they were taking Neo-Platonic philosophy as a means of buttressing their Christian belief, Julian was using it to make his veneration of the ancient pagan gods philosophically respectable. In public, Julian still gave lip-service to Christianity, but his heart was elsewhere. It was from Athens that he was summoned by Constantius to take charge of the armies of the West. His achievement in driving the barbarian tribes back across the Rhine was one of the great Roman military victories of the fourth century. As a determined, courageous and successful general, he won the support of his troops; and they were quite willing to make him emperor, whether Constantius wished it or not. In the event, Constantius' death prevented a civil war, and in 361 Julian entered Constantinople as sole emperor.

It was at this point that he revealed himself as an ardent pagan. And he set to work to rejuvenate classical paganism, and to dis-

**Julian the Apostate, emperor 361–363.** A coin in the British Museum, London.

credit and overthrow Christianity. His first move, the recalling of all exiled Christian bishops did not cause the chaos in the churches for which he hoped. So he followed this up with rather more cunning moves. Julian tried to avoid persecutions which would make martyrs. Instead, he aimed at making life difficult, if not impossible, for organized Christianity. Pagan temples which had been taken over as Christian churches were to be returned to their owners. Tax exemptions and other privileges which Christians had obtained were withdrawn. Niggling regulations were made governing Christian assemblies, such as one which prohibited a meeting of both men and women in the same building on the grounds of danger to morality. Julian's most cunning move, however, was to attack Christians through education. He compelled teachers to teach anti-Christian works. A forged *Acts of Pilate*,[5] purporting to be the 'real truth' about the origins of Christianity, was issued for use in schools. Still more dangerous was Julian's decree concerning teachers. He proclaimed that only those people who sincerely believed in the gods of classical Greece and Rome were allowed to teach the classics. And the Graeco-Roman classics (such as Homer, Virgil, Livy and Euripides) were the staple diet of higher education. At a stroke, Julian was aiming to destroy Christian influence in the intellectual world.

But Julian was not content with attacking Christians. He had grandiose schemes for a 'reformed Hellenism'[6] which would consciously ape many Christian institutions. There were to be arch-

[5] There are apocryphal *Acts of Pilate* surviving, but these are Christian versions probably dating from the fifth century.

[6] Julian's normal term for his religion is 'Hellenism'.

priests in each town and village. State susbidies were to be allowed for their support. A considerable number of Julian's letters survive, in which he gives copious exhortations on the moral qualities which should be seen in a 'priest of Hellenism'. All the charitable works which Christians did were to be done even better by the priests of Julian's new religion. When he came to power, one of Julian's first acts was to banish all the hangers-on who had collected around the court of Constantius. Julian's own personal example in life was one of frugal pagan virtue. And this was what he hoped to foist on the whole Empire.

In fact, Julian's attack on Christianity is the model for many attacks by modern dictators. Crippling the machinery of the churches, a crusade against corruption, and a determined anti-Christian educational programme are the main planks in the policy of most present-day anti-Christian governments. The Nazi initiation ceremony for youth consciously aped the Lutheran confirmation service. The Communists have frequently seized power in reaction to a corrupt and inefficient régime. Many modern African dictators like Nkrumah have insisted on the cult of the head of state being enforced in the schools with quasi-religious patriotic songs. It is a formidable method of attack.

## How contemporaries viewed Julian the Apostate

How did people view Julian's actions? From the pagan point of view we possess the testimony of Ammianus Marcellinus.[7] He was born in Antioch, and served under Julian in the army. Although Greek-speaking by upbringing, he came to Rome, learnt Latin, and is the last prose author in the classical Latin tradition. From his writings, we gain a neutral view of both pagans and Christians in this troubled time.

Although a pagan, Ammianus admired much of what he saw in Christians. The uprightness and pastoral zeal of the country bishops earned his heartfelt approval. At the same time, he admired Julian for his moral virtues as a leader of soldiers and a competent emperor. But Ammianus had little time either for the religious eccentricities of Julian or for the internecine quarrels of the

[7] Ammianus, *Res Gestae* xxii.5.1–4; 10.7. A collection of the material on Julian, including much from his own letters, is contained in *CCC*, pp. 61–77.

Christians. He had no love for the nominal Christian Constantius, Julian's predecessor as emperor, whom he censures for confusing the simple Christian faith with all sorts of foolish old wives' tales. Ammianus' reaction to Julian's edict on teachers is interesting. Although a pagan himself, he heartily disapproved of it as an inhumane edict not worthy of being even remembered. At the same time, Ammianus was quick to comment on the sins of professing Christians. When reporting the disturbances in Rome, when Damasus and Ursinus and their supporters fought over who was to be the next bishop,[8] he says, 'I do not deny, when I consider the ostentation that reigns at Rome, that those who desire such rank and power may be justified in labouring with all possible exertion and vehemence to obtain their wishes; . . . And they might really be happy if, despising the vastness of their city behind which they hide their faults, they were to live in imitation of some of the bishops in the provinces, whom the most rigid abstinence in eating and drinking, and plainness of apparel, and eyes always cast down on the ground, recommend to the everlasting Deity and his true worshippers as pure and reverent men.'[9]

The churches' reaction to Julian's attacks was varied. In Alexandria, Athanasius just continued as usual, until his success in evangelizing pagans caused Julian to send him into exile. Julian's reign was too short, however, for many of his regulations directed against Christians to be put into force; he reigned less than three years. Further, some Christians found ways round the edicts. A certain Apollinaris came up with a novel idea.

Apollinaris became bishop of Laodicaea in Syria in 361.[1] Both he and his father had been teachers of the classics. Now he combined his classical and theological talents to foil Julian. Julian had decreed that no Christians should teach the classics, thus aiming to keep Christians out of higher education. Apollinaris replied by producing his own 'Christian classics'. The stories of the patriarchs were rendered into Homeric verse. Paul's Letters were recast as philosophical dialogues in the style of Plato. All the Bible was treated in a similar way, so that a Christian could gain a full education in grammar, stylistics and rhetoric without having to touch

[8] The violence was so bad that over 130 people were killed in one clash, and the city prefect had to leave Rome because of fears for his safety.

[9] Ammianus, *Res Gestae* xxvii.3.12–15, quoted in *CCC*, p. 87.

[1] For Apollinaris' theological peculiarities, see below, pp. 189f.

the pagan classics. Julian's death in 363 rendered Apollinaris' work no longer necessary, and all copies of these 'Christian classics' have been lost. But it was at least an interesting experiment.

The real failure of Julian's pagan reaction, however, was in the religion which he propounded. His 'reformed Hellenism' was dead almost before it was born. To begin with, it tried to produce the virtues of Christian character without the spiritual strength that comes from the Holy Spirit alone. Julian could sermonize, moralize and produce big government subsidies for charity, but there was no spirit behind them. Everywhere, the Christians by their very lives made nonsense of Julian's religion. He was seen to be struggling to imitate what the Christians already did.

## The failure of 'restored Hellenism'

The ideology which Julian tried to propagate had no popular appeal. His Neo-Platonic mysticism might suit an eclectic set of university dons, but it was too nebulous and vague for the masses either to understand or to get excited about. Its austerity contrasted badly with the pageantry of many church celebrations. The pathetic failure of it all is highlighted in Julian's visit to the grove of Daphne outside Antioch.

Julian had wanted this to be a glorious occasion, when 'reformed Hellenism' would outshine Christianity. He had compelled the Christians to vacate the grove, where they had buried the body of their martyred bishop Babylas.[2] A new temple had been built, and on the appointed day Julian went there to offer sacrifice. The place was very quiet as he approached the doors. He looked around for the crowds. There were none. Inside, he demanded where were the animals for sacrifice. The miserable priest on duty replied that he had one goose which he had brought himself, but that the city of Antioch had not made any arrangements. Meanwhile, in the city, the crowds were thronging to celebrate the anniversary of the martyrdom of bishop Babylas. And the new temple of paganism echoed in hollow mockery to the footsteps of the lonely emperor.

Julian was not only deserted by the Antiochenes. They made fun of him, jeering at his beard and his round shoulders. And Julian roundly abused them back, thus descending to their level. His great army, brought to combat the Persians, caused a scarcity of

[2] He had died during the persecution of Decius, 249–51.

food in Antioch, and merely heightened the public outcry against him. He was glad to leave the city of Antioch, and set out for his campaign. Even then, he spent too much time sniping at Christians. He ostentatiously avoided the city of Edessa where there were many Christians, even though it was the chief city in the region just beyond the Euphrates. His expedition against the Persians failed, after achieving some initial success. Julian himself was badly wounded while trying to rally his troops. He died, exhibiting all the stoical virtues of a philosopher. And his 'reformed Hellenism' died with him.

## Christian pressure on pagans: the altar of Victory

The emperors who followed Julian were at least nominally Christian, and the remaining pagans received no encouragement. Furthermore, the toleration which Constantine and his sons had shown was now replaced by a pressure for conformity from Christians. The whole conflict is crystallized in one incident, the controversy over the altar of Victory in the Senate house at Rome.[3]

Constantine the Great had largely ignored the pagan religions of Rome, and although there were in the Senate house a statue and altar to the pagan goddess of Victory, he had let them remain there. His son Constantius continued to leave many pagan institutions untouched, but when he came to Rome late on in his reign he ordered that the altar of Victory should be removed. With the accession of Julian the Apostate, the altar was put back, and under his successor Valentinian I it was left undisturbed. Valentinian I, though nominally a Christian, made it a matter of policy to leave religious affairs alone. His son Gratian, however, who succeeded him in 375, was a more determined supporter of the Christians; and, perhaps moved by the fact that there were now quite a number of Christians in the Senate, he ordered that the altar of Victory be removed again. But Gratian had no sooner done this than he was defeated and killed in a revolt led by a usurper from Britain called Magnus Maximus (383). The pagan elements in the Senate drew up a petition to the new emperors, asking that the altar of Victory be restored.

[3] Sections of the speeches on the subject are contained in *CCC*, pp. 121–5.

**A statue of Victory dating from the third century BC,** in the National Museum of Naples.

It was not a very propitious time for such a petition, for none of the emperors was pro-pagan. In the East, the energetic Theodosius had taken over after the death of the emperor Valens at the Battle of Adrianople (378), and he was a fervent supporter of Christian orthodoxy. In the West, Magnus Maximus was setting himself up as champion of Christian orthodoxy in opposition to the pro-Arian policies of the empress-mother Justina, who was ruling during the minority of her son (a nonentity called Valentinian II). But neither Arians nor orthodox Christians had any love for paganism.

The spokesman of the pagans was Symmachus. He came from one of the most noble senatorial families, and was as blue-blooded a Roman aristocrat as one could find. His antiquarian learning was immense, and his command of rhetoric was masterful. He was the head of all that was cultured and traditional in the ancient city of Rome, and had every right to act as spokesman for the ancient ways. His plea, addressed to Valentinian II and Theodosius, was a model of moderation and reasonable pleading. He reminded the emperors of previous toleration. He recalled the former glories of Rome. He powerfully contended for a policy of 'live and let live'. There was no hint of bitterness against Christians, such as characterized Julian the Apostate. Instead there is the eloquent appeal to allow those who value ancient traditions to be allowed to continue them undisturbed. Thus he sought that the altar of Victory be restored. In spite of the unfavourable circumstances, Symmachus might have won his case. But he was up against a formidable adversary in the bishop of Milan, Ambrose.

We will hear of Ambrose's life story later.[4] He was a recent convert who had changed sides with unbounded zeal. He had been an important provincial governor when the populace of Milan demanded that he become bishop; in fact, he had been baptized one week and consecrated bishop the next. Eleven years had passed since his consecration in 373, and he had brought all of his political expertise into the service of the church. As bishop of Milan, where the emperor Valentinian II and his mother Justina had their court, he was in the right place to hear of Symmachus' appeal. And he went into action immediately.

Ambrose's reply to Symmachus was on two levels. On the historical level, he could fairly easily show that the past successes of the Romans had not been due to their religion. And he had considerable fun mocking Symmachus' claims. For example, when Symmachus claimed that the ancient gods had protected Rome from the Gauls, Ambrose pointed out that in fact it was only the cackling of a goose which had alerted the sleeping sentries to a night attack from the besieging Gauls. And he asked, taunting, if Jupiter had spoken through a goose! But it was on the second level that Ambrose's reply really hurt. Addressing himself to the emperor, who claimed to be a Christian, Ambrose asks how toleration of pagan idolatry can be consistent with his Christian profession. He makes the thinly disguised threat that an emperor who even permits pagan ceremonies to take place will have no place within the Christian church. For Ambrose, truth must be upheld by all means, including state coercion. And failure to suppress error puts the soul of the 'Christian' emperor in jeopardy. It was unanswerable as a weapon of psychological pressure. Ambrose got his way. The altar of Victory was never replaced in the Roman Senate. But justice was probably a casualty.

The clash between Ambrose and Symmachus highlights a

[4] See below, pp. 127–33.

perplexing problem. How far can the state be invoked to support truth and to suppress error? Ambrose declared that the emperor, as a Christian, had a right and duty to uphold and propagate Christian truth with all the means in his power. This is the voice eventually to be heard from the Inquisition and from all state-enforced forms of Christianity of later ages. Symmachus argued for tolerance and individual liberty. But Symmachus and his circle loftily refused even to consider Christianity, and had no thought for the Christians in the Senate who would be outraged at a pagan symbol confronting them every time they came to debate. And Symmachus' plea for respect of tradition could become an excuse for culpable inertia when faced by entrenched vices. Yet the plea of Symmachus was not for unbounded licence, but merely for tolerance. And there is the heart of the problem. Both truth and individual liberty need to be upheld. It is an agonizing choice for a ruler, to decide how far he may allow his subjects to be wrong.

## The twilight of the old gods

After the failure of Symmachus' plea in 384, Graeco-Roman paganism entered its twilight. Pressures for conformity to outward Christianity continued, reaching their climax in 391 when Theodosius passed an edict[5] formally outlawing all forms of non-Christian rites. And it was not only pagans who suffered. All deviant forms of Christianity were formally outlawed. The usurper Magnus Maximus[6] had the dubious distinction of being the first emperor to execute a man on a charge of heresy. The victim was an obscure visionary from Spain called Priscillian.[7] But although paganism was officially outlawed, the spirit of the old classical tradition was a long time dying. Many of the poets of this period, such as Claudian and Ausonius, were more pagan than Christian.[8] In the circle of

[5] *Codex Theodosianus* xvi.10.10. This total ban was somewhat modified by a law of 423 (*Codex Theodosianus* xvi.10.24), which permitted law-abiding Jews and pagans to live unmolested.

[6] Emperor in the West, 383–8.

[7] See below, in the section on Martin of Tours, pp. 110ff. Priscillian was officially condemned for black magic (*maleficium*), but the charges against him were religious in substance.

[8] Some were still overtly pagan; *e.g.* Rutilius Namatianus (*fl. c.* 420), a Latin poet who especially hated Christian monks, and the Greek historian Zosimus (*fl.* after 425).

Symmachus and his friends there was never any mention of Christianity. Instead, the *literati* of Rome met to discuss earnestly the correct text of Livy's great history of Rome, and the origins of antique and long-discontinued ceremonies. Living faith and current politics alike were banished as unworthy interlopers in the sacred world of antiquity.

In this age of the quasi-pagans, nothing illustrates the gap between them and the Christians more than the correspondence (executed in verse!) between Ausonius and Paulinus.[9] Ausonius was born in Bordeaux in about 310, before Christianity was even a tolerated religion. He had a full classical education, and became the most famous professor of grammar and rhetoric in the whole of Gaul. He was appointed by Valentinian I as tutor to his son, the future emperor Gratian, and he filled many of the highest offices of the Roman state. He was already an old man when Gratian was killed, and so he took the opportunity to retire to his country estates near Bordeaux. While at court he had come to accept at least outward conformity to Christianity, and it would be unfair to Ausonius to suggest that this was merely a useful piece of hypocrisy. But the depths of his heart were elsewhere. His poetical works show virtually no trace of Christianity, and his main claim to fame as a poet rests on a long descriptive poem on the subject of the river Moselle.

Among Ausonius' pupils had been a young man called Paulinus. Paulinus came from the same educated and wealthy class in Bordeaux as did Ausonius, and he shared in his master's advancement under the emperor Gratian. But then a change took place. While Ausonius retired to a life of gracious leisure in the country, Paulinus was deeply converted to Christ. He sold up his estates, and with his Spanish wife Therasia he set out to serve Christ in ascetic seclusion. Eventually he went to Campania in Italy, where he became bishop of the church at Nola. And such was Paulinus' sanctity, as he preached and cared for the poor during the death-throes of the Western Empire, that he was venerated as a saint soon after his death.

But when Ausonius heard of his former pupil's change of life, he was both amazed and shocked. He wrote to him trying to dissuade

[9] For a fuller description, see J. Vogt, *The Decline of Rome* (Weidenfeld & Nicolson, 1967) pp. 131–5.

Paulinus from taking so drastic a step. Ausonius' letters and Paulinus' replies give a touching commentary on the gap between a nominal Christianity and a deep devotion to Christ. Ausonius asks why Paulinus should renounce all his classical learning and his rich estates, wondering if he hasn't perhaps made a bad mistake. Paulinus' reply is that Christ is worth far more. Ausonius asks why he cannot be a Christian and still enjoy the old pleasures which they once shared. He pleads that their friendship should not suffer. Paulinus responds by saying that their friendship must be on a new footing with allegiance to Christ as its cornerstone. Ausonius viewed Paulinus with the horror some people have when they see a man or woman with success and position in this country set off to serve Christ in some obscure part of the foreign mission field. Paulinus looks back in pity at an old friend who cannot fully understand his new enthusiasm for Christ. Yet, in the final analysis, it was men like Paulinus who were to carry the cause of Christ successfully through the troubled years ahead.

## Evangelism within the Empire: Cyril of Jerusalem

So far, we have looked at the relations between Christianity and the pagan religions from the legal and official standpoints. But Christians did not limit themselves to waiting until an emperor made further decrees in their favour. Active evangelism went on both inside and outside the Roman Empire.

Inside the Empire Christian evangelism centred around the existing churches. And it was highlighted each year when some weeks before Easter an appeal was made for people to enrol for baptism. This was the pre-eminent sign of Christian commitment, and we are fortunate in possessing several examples of the preaching and instruction given at such a time.

Bishop Cyril of Jerusalem is of special interest, because he was a fairly representative cleric of the period. He became bishop of Jerusalem around 350, and his lectures to the candidates for baptism give a very good idea of what was taught. Theologically, Cyril was a moderate eastern bishop. He had supported the majority who had been suspicious over the Nicene creed, but along with Basil of Ancyra and many others he had suffered exile when the extreme Arians gained the ascendant at the time of the 'Dated Creed'. Reinstated on the death of Constantius, he was exiled again during the reign of the pro-Arian Valens, but later returned and continued as bishop of Jerusalem until his death in 386.

The course of instruction comprised an introductory lecture, five lectures on general topics, thirteen giving a detailed explanation of the creed which candidates had to learn by heart, and an additional five given soon after baptism to explain baptism and the communion service.[1] Cyril's theology is a strange mixture of evangelical earnestness and superstitious ceremonial. For him, baptism is a rite of almost magical power, but at the same time he warns the candidates that unless they receive the rite in the proper frame of mind it will do them no spiritual good.[2] Cyril regards personal righteousness as a prerequisite for baptism. He solemnly warns candidates to give up sinful habits before they come to baptism, basing his doctrine on the parable of the great wedding-feast and the man without a wedding garment.[3] But Cyril does not castigate only open sinners. He warns against coming to baptism for the wrong reason, such as mere curiosity, or the wish to please a business associate or a prospective husband or wife! Baptism is not to be treated in a trivial fashion. Cyril is not merely a moralist, however. He views baptism as a move in a battle against the spiritual powers of the devil. He warns his hearers that only with Christ's help can anyone safely reach heaven and escape all the devil's snares. Candidates are solemnly exorcized, and Cyril regards these exorcisms as potent means of defeating the devil. Usually Cyril bases his teaching on the text of Scripture, but occasionally he uses other means to justify church practices. For example, he justifies praying for the dead on the basis of imperial court ceremonial of the day, when petitions were made to the emperor on behalf of absent friends.

In response to such preaching, each Easter day saw crowds coming to baptism. The effectiveness of the exhortations of men like Cyril was considerably reinforced by the fact that there were obvious advantages in joining the Christian fellowships. By Cyril's

[1] There is some doubt whether the five lectures on the sacraments are the work of Cyril or of his successor John of Jerusalem (died 417). An English translation of the introductory lecture and of the five lectures on the sacraments is available in F. L. Cross (editor), *St Cyril of Jerusalem's Lectures on the Christian Sacraments* (SPCK, 1951).

[2] To illustrate this, he expounds the story of Simon Magus, Acts 8:9–24.

[3] Matthew 22:1–14.

time the Christian world-view was the dominant one within the Empire, and many turned to follow the new direction of the tide of thought. There was a wealth of friendship to be found in the Christian churches, and, furthermore, material help in time of need. As emperors were nearly all pro-Christian, there was some advantage to be gained in espousing the religion that they followed. But even when we have taken this into account, we have not by any means explained away the attraction of Christianity. Those who came forward to baptism were conscious of a spiritual need which they found satisfied only in Christ. Even if it was no longer positively dangerous to become a Christian, this did not mean that all the converts who joined the fellowship were totally lacking in spirituality. Yet, while a majority found the churches of the late Roman Empire spiritually satisfying, there were some who found the atmosphere in these churches not conducive to full Christian discipleship. We shall deal with their story in the next chapter.

So far we have considered the progress of Christianity only within the Roman Empire. To complete the picture, we must now look beyond the frontier of the Empire, to regions where Christians had to work and witness without the overt support of the civil authorities.

## Christians beyond the eastern frontiers

The first area to be considered covers the lands beyond the eastern frontiers of the Roman Empire. Here the Romans faced the Persian Empire. The Persians of the Sassanid dynasty had taken over the old Parthian Empire in the mid-third century, and were to be Rome's bitterest enemies till the rise of Islam. The frontier was usually stabilized on the line of the river Euphrates, but periodically one or other side would try to push the other back, almost always with little lasting success. The situation was complicated by the fact that on both sides of the frontier were people speaking Syriac. There were many people among the Syriac-speakers who were Christians, and the centre of Syriac-speaking Christianity was at Edessa, a city beyond the Euphrates in the debatable land over which both Roman and Persian tried to exercise influence.[4]

[4] For fuller details of earlier Syriac Christianity, see my book *From Christ to Constantine*, pp. 43–5.

# Map 4

## Mesopotamia and the East

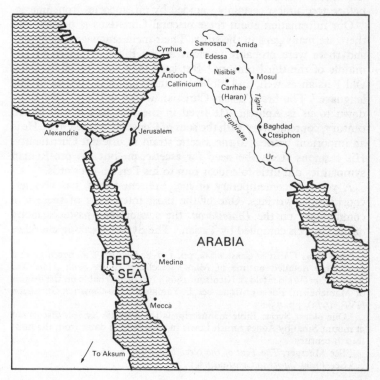

Labels on map: Cyrrhus, Samosata, Amida, Edessa, Antioch, Nisibis, Mosul, Callinicum, Carrhae (Haran), Tigris, Euphrates, Alexandria, Jerusalem, Baghdad, Ctesiphon, Ur, ARABIA, RED SEA, Medina, Mecca, To Aksum

The religion of the Persians was Zoroastrianism. This was based on the teachings of the sixth-century-BC preacher Zoroaster, who taught that there is a system of two equal and opposite forces in the world, one evil and one good. The worship of this religion centred around the sacred fire, and was superintended by the magi-priests. The kings and leaders of Persia therefore viewed Christianity as an alien religion, intruding into their realm to further the schemes of their arch-enemies the Romans. Even attempts to harmonize Christianity and Zoroastrianism, such as the preaching of Mani[5] in the third century, had been bitterly suppressed. And yet, Christianity made headway beyond the eastern frontiers of the Empire. To the north of Persia, Christianity had become the official faith of Armenia even before it was tolerated in the Roman Empire itself. In the Persian Empire itself, especially in the Tigris and Euphrates valleys, there were strong Christian churches well before 300, almost certainly founded by missionaries from Edessa.

Our information about these oriental Christians is patchy, and there are many gaps in the story. Their main language was Syriac, and there were probably versions of the Bible in Syriac by the middle of the third century.[6] But later they were certainly using Old Persian as well, and biblical manuscripts also survive in this language.[7] The first Persian Christian whose writings have come down to us is Aphraat. He lived in the first half of the fourth century, contemporary with the sons of Constantine the Great. He is an important witness to the ascetic strain in oriental Christianity. His sermons stress the need for asceticism, but his pro-Roman sympathies did little to endear him to his Persian overlords.

A younger contemporary of his, Ephrem Syrus, has also left considerable writings. One of the most interesting of these is a commentary on the *Diatessaron*, the scissors-and-paste harmony of the Gospels compiled by Tatian.[8] The Syriac-speaking churches

[5] See *From Christ to Constantine*, pp. 157–8. George Widengren gives a reasonably detailed outline of Mani's teaching in his book *Mani and Manicheism* (Weidenfeld & Nicolson, 1965), but is unreliable on the origins of Manicheism. For a critique, see E. Yamauchi, *Pre-Christian Gnosticism* (IVP, 1973), pp. 73–83.

[6] Our oldest Syriac Bible manuscript is the Sinaitic Syriac, discovered at mount Sinai by Agnes Smith Lewis in 1894, which dates from the mid-fourth century.

[7] See Metzger, *The Text of the New Testament*, p. 86.

[8] See *From Christ to Constantine*, p. 56.

**Part of a Peshitta** dating from the 6th century AD, in the British Museum, London. The page contains part of the book of Job. The Peshitta was the 'Authorized Version' of the Syriac-speaking churches, which had the four Gospels separated out. It finally displaced the Diatessaron (where the Gospel narratives were combined into a single narrative) in the 5th century.

actually preferred this version to the original, canonical, four Gospels, and abandoned it only in the early fifth century when the Old Syriac Gospels were revised into the version known as the *Peshitta*.[9] The *Diatessaron* itself is no longer extant, and Ephrem's commentary is an important means of reconstructing its text. Although he wrote in Syriac, Ephrem was greatly admired by Greek-speaking Christians such as Basil the Great,[1] who considered him the most eloquent man of his age. Ephrem lived as a hermit near his birthplace at Nisibis, but later moved to Edessa, where he founded a school of instruction for Christians. The 'school of Edessa' was to be the power-house for the oriental churches. Ephrem is also noted for his hymns, written in complex Syriac metres, and such was his greatness that many of his works were translated into Greek during his lifetime. This is all the more astonishing because most Syriac writings are dull and tedious.

As already stated, the Christians in the Persian Empire had to endure many bitter persecutions. It was in Aphraat's time (340–350) that the first great persecution came about. It was instigated by the Zoroastrian priests, but was suggested to the Persian king as a patriotic measure against potential friends of the Romans. The Jews in the Persian Empire also helped the persecutors, perhaps because Christians such as Aphraat directed much of their polemics against Judaism.[2] The Persian king, Shapur II, first attacked the Christians with crippling taxes, but later extended his activities to demolishing church buildings and arresting clergy.[3] The chief bishop (called the 'catholicos'), Symeon, was brought before the king; and after refusing to worship either the king or the sacred fire of the Zoroastrians he was beheaded. Many other Christians suffered a similar fate for refusing to deny Christ. Although this persecution eventually lapsed, there were intermittent outbreaks of persecution throughout the fourth century. But they were unable to break the determination of the Christians of the Persian Empire. The early fifth century saw a long period of peace, thanks to the more liberal outlook of the kings of that time, and it

[9] For the story of the various Syriac versions of the New Testament, see Metzger, *op. cit.*, pp. 68–71.

[1] Basil's opinion is given in *CCC*, p. 83.

[2] At this time, Babylon, in the Persian Empire, was the great centre of Jewish learning. Its scholars were responsible for the codification of the Jewish oral tradition in the Talmud.

[3] For details, see *CCC*, pp. 6, 7.

was this time that western thought, and particularly the theology of the church of Antioch, began to reach the oriental churches.

## Nestorians and Monophysites beyond the eastern frontier

We shall deal with the controversies over the doctrine of the person of Christ in detail later on.[4] For the moment, we must confine ourselves to the effect which they had on the oriental churches. One of the great preachers of the Eastern Roman Empire at this time was Theodore, the bishop of Mopsuestia in Cilicia. He was famous as a biblical expositor. He usually explained the Bible in its literal and grammatical sense, as opposed to the currently fashionable allegorical method. But his greatest contribution was his stress on both the humanity and the deity of Jesus Christ. His writings were translated into Syriac, and they filtered eastwards. Among many Syriac-speaking Christians he was revered as 'Mar Theodore the Interpreter'.[5] One of Theodore's disciples, Nestorius, became patriarch of Constantinople. He put such stress on the two distinct natures in Christ that he made it sound as if there were somehow two people inside the one Jesus. His theological and political opponents gathered together and succeeded in condemning him as a heretic at the Council of Ephesus (431). The effect of this condemnation was to divide the oriental churches.

One group, later known as Nestorians, refused to accept the condemnation of their views. They held that Mar Theodore (who had died revered and orthodox in 428) and Mar Nestorius were their greatest teachers, and they even attached their names to two of the liturgies which they used. One of the leaders of this group was Narsai, known by his friends as 'the Harp of the Holy Spirit', and by his enemies as 'the Leper'. He was the head of the school which Ephrem Syrus had founded at Edessa. Like most of the leaders of the oriental Christians, he was an unmarried, austere ascetic. When his theological opponents made Edessa too hot for him, he moved with his disciples and refounded the academy at Nisibis. There he continued his work, and it was from Nisibis that Nestorian Christians set out eastwards, taking Christianity across the Orient as far as both India and China. Narsai's theology is a most strange amalgam of truth and rubbish. He viewed the eucharist

[4] See below, pp. 189–98.
[5] The title 'Mar', Syriac for 'Lord', was given to any notable church leader in the East.

as a quasi-magical re-enactment of the death, burial and resurrection of Jesus. Yet, at the same time, he had a real and heartfelt devotion to Jesus, and this issued in a form of life which astonished many by its single-minded otherworldliness. It was from men like this, victims of a none too creditable church quarrel, that there came a missionary movement which is almost unparalleled in antiquity.

Meanwhile, the anti-Nestorius group among the oriental Christians took their theology to the opposite extreme. They were so much against any suggestion of two natures in Jesus that they ended up viewing Him as totally divine and with only a veneer of humanity. Rabbula of Edessa led this faction, and it was his actions which compelled Narsai to flee from Edessa to Nisibis. But meanwhile, inside the Roman Empire, the theological pendulum had swung again. At the Council of Chalcedon in 451, the ideas supported by Rabbula were condemned. The Monophysites[6] had strong support in Egypt and even some of the later Byzantine emperors favoured them. But they were cut off from mainstream Christianity. They had considerable influence on the Ethiopic churches, but they did no missionary work comparable to that of the Nestorians.

The isolation of the oriental Christians grew during the fifth century. There was some renewal of persecution, but the Christians of the Persian Empire were able to survive this. At the same time, possibly to convince their Persian overlords that they were not a Roman 'fifth column', the synod meeting under the presidency of the catholicos Dadiso in 424 had prohibited appeals to the patriarchates of the Eastern Empire (especially Antioch). Then had come the Nestorian and Monophysite controversies, which had further served to break links with churches in the Roman Empire. Although there still remained some contact, as when Persian Christians gave relief to Roman prisoners of war, the gulf widened rapidly.[7] The oriental churches tended to fossilize. Strange ascetic

[6] So called from their insistence on 'one nature' in Christ. In their Syrian form they were organized by Jacob Baradaeus in the sixth century (see below, p. 202). Some other oriental churches became Monophysite at this time, partly as a reaction against the central power of the Byzantine Empire; notably the Armenians and the Copts.

[7] During the period of the Roman–Persian wars, Christian leaders on both sides distinguished themselves by their kindly treatment of prisoners of war. See for example the action of Acacius, bishop of Amida, in *CCC*, pp. 258–9.

movements sprang up, with their vaguely Christian fakirs gaining much veneration. The mental vigour tended to decline as well.[8] When Nestorian missionaries reached India they did not translate the Scriptures into the Indian languages such as Tamil, but obstinately retained Syriac. At the same time their theology became less Christ-centred. The Virgin Mary and the saints soon achieved high positions, often obscuring the proper place of God and Jesus Christ. It may well have been from fringe groups of such churches that Muhammad acquired his bizarre and misguided views of Christianity.

## The evangelization of the Goths

Leaving the East behind, and turning our attention to the area north of the Danube frontier, we find the barbarian tribes. Along the river Danube, the Romans had been under pressure from the Goths for more than a century. In the third century, the persecuting emperor Decius had died fighting them (251), but the menace had been halted for a generation by the victories of Claudius Gothicus (268–70). But the raiding Goths had taken many prisoners from the Roman territories, and these people remained in Gothic hands as slaves. Most of them never returned to their homelands, but they and their children continued to live among the barbarian tribes. Some of these families were Christians, and it was from one of these that there came Ulfilas, the great missionary to the Goths.

It is difficult to unravel the story of Ulfilas,[9] because we have to depend on various passing references to him in later writers. But even so, the information that we have suggests that he was a remarkable man. He first appears as a member of a Gothic embassy to Constantinople in 340. But by this time he must have been a missionary of many years' standing, for while he was at Constantinople he was ordained bishop by Eusebius of Nicomedia. The Gothic chieftains, too, must have reckoned him to be a man of great influence, if they chose him to be one of their envoys. Of Ulfilas' missionary methods we know next to nothing. Admittedly,

---

[8] This was a slow decline, however, for much of the scientific and mathematical knowledge of the Arabs was acquired from Nestorian Christians, many of whom frequented the court of the earlier Muslim caliphs at Baghdad.

[9] The evidence is collected and assessed in *CCC*, pp. 84–6.

he did not have the disadvantage which oriental Christians faced, where the Persians considered Christianity as the 'Romans' religion'. But we know that Ulfilas was dependent on the support of some of the Gothic chieftains, and that tribal conflicts hindered his work. It seems that if one Gothic tribe decided to accept Christianity, their neighbours (and hereditary enemies) would become ardently pagan. But on one point Ulfilas deserves special mention. He produced the Gothic Bible.[1]

None of the German barbarian tribes was literate at this time, and yet Christianity is very much a 'religion of a book'. Ulfilas seems to have been bilingual from birth, speaking both Greek and Gothic. So, in order that his Gothic converts could have the benefits of the Scriptures, he set about producing an alphabet which could be used for writing the Gothic language. He started off with the Greek alphabet, and added signs for sounds not used in Greek. Then he began the work of translation. By the time he died, Ulfilas had translated all the Bible except the books of Kings (one of our sources says that he left these till last as he felt that the Goths were warlike enough!).

Ulfilas' work among the Goths was interrupted when a civil war broke out. The chief on whose protection he had depended was killed. Persecution broke out, and it seemed as if the Gothic Christians were threatened with extinction. Faced with this situation, Ulfilas gathered together most of his flock and led them in a hazardous march across the frozen river Danube into Roman territory. The date of this 'Gothic exodus' is uncertain. Some of our sources place it in the time of Valens, and connect it with the permanent settlement of Goths in Roman territory by the Danube river, while other sources put it much earlier under the emperor Constantius. Perhaps it is best to assume that Ulfilas and his flock took temporary refuge in Roman territory, and that at a later date he was involved in negotiations about permanent Gothic settlements on Roman territory. Certainly he was back working among the Goths later, although he eventually died while on a visit to Constantinople.

Ulfilas' visits to Constantinople resulted in one unfortunate outcome which was to cause untold trouble later on. He had been ordained by Eusebius of Nicomedia (an arch-Arian), and his visits

[1] For surviving manuscripts of this, see Metzger, *The Text of the New Testament*, pp. 81-2.

to Constantinople coincided with the period of Arian domination. Knowing no different, he readily accepted the milder form of Arianism as at least permissible doctrine. And this spread through the Goths. At first it did not permeate very deeply, and some orthodox Christian leaders within the Empire were quite happy to tolerate Gothic Christianity without any thought that it might be heretical. For example, John Chrysostom[2] often visited the Gothic church in Constantinople (set up for the benfit of Goths serving in the imperial army), and preached there with the help of an interpreter. Especially in the West, however, they were seen by many as a threat to orthodox Christianity. We shall hear later how Ambrose of Milan stood out against Gothic-supported Arianism. And when the Western Empire collapsed, many of the invading tribes (*e.g.* the Vandals) had already acquired the barbarian form of Arianism from the Goths. This caused intense bitterness among orthodox Christians, and made them less willing than ever to come to terms with the barbarians. And it resulted in 200 years of strife before barbarian Arianism finally withered away.

We know next to nothing about the form which Christianity took among the barbarian tribes. They conducted their services in the vernacular, but apart from a few Gothic manuscripts of the Bible no written material survives. From the orthodox side, the Catholic writers viewed Goths, Vandals and other Arian barbarians as heretics needing to be converted; and consequently they had no interest in recording details of their church organization. From incidental remarks we know that clergy in the barabarians' churches were organized on similar lines to those in other churches. Later on, when the Arian Ostrogoths under Theodoric the Great dominated Italy (493–526), they put up many church buildings[3] which survive to this day. But it is impossible from these to determine what Gothic church services were like or what the average Gothic Christian believed.[4] And anyway, by this time all the barbarians were under the influence of the late Roman culture. It was a sad coincidence that Ulfilas' chance encounters with Arians should have effectively cut off his churches from mainstream Christianity

[2] See below, pp. 187–8.

[3] *E.g.* the Baptistry of the Arians at Verona.

[4] In North Africa, despite the long Vandal domination, it has been impossible to identify any church building as certainly Arian. This seems to indicate that in outward forms there was not all that much difference.

and laid the seeds of so much bitterness and mistrust on both sides. Racial, linguistic and cultural barriers between Roman and barbarian were capable of being breached, given time and mutual forbearance. But the theological barrier was different. Christians of the West refused to compromise truth. The Arian barbarians saw no reason to change. The result was tension that lasted until the seventh century, by which time barbarian Arianism had had time to wither and die.[5]

## Other missionary efforts: Ethiopia and Scotland

Two further missionary efforts during the patristic period need to be noted. Apart from the incident of Philip and the Ethiopian eunuch, recorded in Acts, we have no information about Christians in Ethiopia until the fourth century. There were many Christians in Egypt, however, and it is likely that they gave some support to Christian groups in Ethiopia. Athanasius himself ordained a certain Frumentius as bishop of Aksum, the capital of Ethiopia.[6] But during Athanasius' exile under the emperor Constantius, this emperor wrote to the rulers of Aksum insisting that Frumentius return and be reordained by the notorious George, the man intruded into the bishopric of Alexandria. We do not know whether Frumentius did come back, however, or whether he remained in Aksum in defiance of the heretical emperor. Nor do we know anything more about Ethiopian Christians for some while. But it is reasonable to believe that some time in the late fourth century the Bible was rendered into classical Ethiopic.[7] The Ethiopic Bible differs somewhat from normal Bibles in that it includes certain apocryphal works in addition to all the canonical books. This divergence may be explained by the fact that Ethiopia was very isolated, and so its church leaders were seldom able to confer with other Christians and so rectify this anomaly.

The other missionary enterprise took place at the opposite end of the Empire, beyond Hadrian's wall in northern Britain. At some time in the late fourth or early fifth century, a Romanized Celt

[5] It lasted very stubbornly in Visigothic Spain, where the churches did not formally accept orthodox belief until the Council of Toledo (589). The Lombards, who reached Italy during the sixth century, were also Arians, and were not converted to orthodox Christianity until c. 650.

[6] CCC, pp. 34–5.

[7] See Metzger, The Text of the New Testament, p. 84.

called Ninian began preaching in lowland Scotland. His centre of activity was at Whithorn, where he built a small stone building as a place of worship. Such was the novelty of this structure, in an area where almost all buildings were wooden, that it gave to the place the name 'Candida Casa' (the White House). Ninian's work of evangelism is again very difficult to describe fully, since all our informants lived many centuries later.[8] He may well have followed the example of Martin of Tours, having a centre of activity from which he went out on preaching journeys in the surrounding areas. His work of evangelism is all the more remarkable when we remember that Christianity was not very strong in Britain at this time, being limited to the large towns and to a few villas in the southern part of England.[9] His work among the Picts of lowland Scotland left its mark, however, although it did not prevent them carrying on their business of piratical raids against their neighbours. Years later, Patrick wrote a letter to king Coroticus, a Pictish king of this area. He was complaining about a raid on Ireland in which a large group of newly baptized Christians were massacred. Patrick rebukes Coroticus in the language of a bishop castigating a Christian whose acts have fallen far short of his Christian profession. Coroticus and his men in all probability had been originally evangelized by Ninian. Archaeology in the Whithorn area has helped to add a little to the sketchy story of Ninian's mission.[1] Various tombstones with specifically Christian inscriptions or motifs have been found in the Whithorn area. By their style they can be dated to the fifth century. These bear witness to the fact that Ninian's work produced a continuing Christian community, whose members carried on in the Christian life long after the original evangelist was dead.

Inside and outside of the Roman Empire, the old order was fading away. Various factors contributed to the downfall of paganism, but it remained a long time dying. Inside the Empire, for example, the pagan philosophers at Athens continued to lecture until the reign of Justinian in the sixth century. Outside the frontiers, deep in the German forests, pagan rites were not challenged by missionaries until the eighth century. But when confronted by Christianity,

[8] First account in Bede, *Church History*, iii.4.

[9] *E.g.* a church building at Silchester; Christian rooms in Lullingstone Roman villa, Kent.

[1] Archaeological evidence and an up-to-date discussion of Ninian in R. P. C. Hanson, *Saint Patrick* (OUP, 1968), pp. 56–62.

classical paganism was shown to be visibly bankrupt both of intellectual depth and of popular appeal. Imperial decrees tended to follow public opinion. Some injustices were done in the forcible suppression of intellectual paganism at Rome. But by the year 400 no-one could doubt that Christianity was the philosophy and way of life for the future.

# 5

# Drop-outs and communes

From the beginnings of Christianity many individual Christians have wanted to gain a much deeper knowledge of God. The means of attaining this end has taken many forms, some of which are praiseworthy, while others are eccentric if not positively harmful. As the Christian churches spread, such desires became channelled into various forms. People would vow themselves to celibacy, or would devote themselves to prayer and Bible study far beyond what was normally expected of rank-and-file Christians in the churches. But for a long time, such special acts of devotion to God did not necessitate that the spiritual Christians should separate from the normal congregation. What they did was simply in addition to the normal worship and devotion. But as time passed, and the churches became more popular and their spirituality tended to decline, tensions arose for the ultra-spiritual. They felt that they could no longer be 'real Christians' among the barely Christianized crowds. And so a separation took place.

### Antony, the first hermit

Antony was a Coptic-speaking peasant in Egypt.[1] He was also a Christian who was dissatisfied with his own spiritual progress. One day, in the latter part of the third century, he was attending worship in his village church when he heard Christ's advice to the rich young ruler.[2] Antony took this to be God's message to himself. He sold his small farm and retreated into the desert to pray and meditate. It is probable that Antony was not the first hermit in the

[1] Our main source for his story is Athanasius' *Life of Antony*.
[2] Matthew 19:21: 'If you would be perfect, go, sell what you possess . . .'.

desert, but he was certainly the first influential one. He persevered in his solitary life of fasting, prayer and meditation on the Bible, although as time went on he had to retreat further and further into the desert to avoid the visits of friends and curious enquirers. During the great persecution under Diocletian, Antony returned to Alexandria, secretly hoping to be arrested and martyred. He had to content himself, however, with helping the Christians who were then in prison. With the end of the persecution, he returned to the desert, accompanied by many others who wished to follow his example. Groups of hermits came into being, especially in the deserts of Nitria and Scitis. Living in their own separate cells, they met only for Sunday worship, and sometimes not even then. Often they vied with each other in feats of devotion, competing for the length of vigil or the number of prayer rituals which they could perform. The hermits had dropped out of Christian society, judging it to be too contaminated for those who wished to pursue the true Christian life.

Solitude in the desert, however, did strange things to these Christian drop-outs. Antony himself suffered anxiety states when he believed that his cell was full of demons or wild beasts. At other times he believed that he was visited by the devil in the form of a seductive young woman. His defence against all this was the sign

**St Antony being beaten by demons** in the desert. A painting by Sassetta (late 14th century).

of the cross and the memorizing of Scripture (in the Coptic dialect, for Antony spoke no Greek). With other hermits, psychological stresses produced even stranger extravagances. One desired to remain standing all through Lent. Another wished to be devoured by wild beasts, but when he intruded into a den of hyenas they refused to touch him! Some became so controlled by mysticism that they despised both the written text of Scripture and the sacrament of the communion. In the hot climate of the desert, the hermits could exist on little food. They usually had only one meal a day, but often they would abstain from food for days on end.

To the Christians in the traditional churches, the desert hermits were viewed with almost superstitious reverence. Athanasius, the famous bishop of Alexandria, became a great admirer of Antony, and the biography of the hermit which Athanasius wrote helped to popularize the ideal of the ascetic life. In return, Antony gave Athanasius considerable moral support during the Trinitarian controversy, and Athanasius was glad to spend his exile from 356 to 361 in the hermit cells of Egypt. So far from being criticized, the drop-outs of the desert were viewed as the front-line troops in the battle against the devil, and there was a powerful drawing power which persistently called the ecclesiastical statesmen to leave church politics for the contemplative life in the desert.

Although Egypt was the first place where hermits became famous, there were soon similar developments in Syria. Here the extremes of personal asceticism verged on sheer masochism and self-torture. Hermits would wall themselves up in caves, or perch on the tops of pillars. There had always been a strong ascetic streak in Syrian Christianity which had viewed the material world as evil. This was taken up into the ideals of the hermits, who did everything in their power to end what they viewed as the domination of the flesh over the spirit. Some of them would have made Antony look self-indulgent. But it is very questionable whether such extremes of self-deprivation in fact led to spiritual growth. The individualistic drop-outs did not of necessity become closer to God. Soon, wiser men looked for a better way.

## Pachomius and the religious community

Pachomius was a pagan soldier who was converted while serving in Egypt. His conversion was largely as a result of the kindness

**From a Christian Coptic tombstone.** Notice that the inscription is in Greek. A considerable number of Copts spoke both Coptic and Greek.

shown to him by local Christians. During the times of peace under Constantine, he was discharged, and for a while he lived in the desert as a hermit. In response to inner guidance, however, he and a friend set up a commune[3] on the river Nile near Tabenissi.

Pachomius' aim was to form a community where the Christian life could be practised without distraction. In his commune, he had an ordered régime, with one or two meals a day, and regular times of prayer. The members of the commune engaged in work such as making palm-leaf mats or growing vegetables, so that the community should be self-supporting. The members wore a simple version of peasant dress, and were dissuaded from undertaking extreme forms of asceticism. Entry into the community was not easy. The would-be monk had to wait outside the door of the commune for a considerable number of days, to prove that he was in earnest. Then he had to learn by heart about twenty Psalms, as well as other portions of Scripture. If he could not read and write in Coptic, he had to learn. Then, before admission, he had to dispose of all his money as an act of faith and to show that he meant business.

The commune buildings were a compound surrounded by a wall. Each member had his own cell, but meals and worship were communal. As one would expect from an ex-soldier, the discipline was strict and the ideal was for the monk to be a self-effacing and obedient member of the commune. But at the same time, there was a safety and stability which appealed to many. And there was a spiritual atmosphere which was in marked contrast to that prevailing in many of the churches. Small wonder that Pachomius' own settlement soon had over 1,300 members, and that other groups were established under his control, so that when he died in 346 there were more than 7,000 monks living in communes in Egypt.

## Basil and practical service

It would be a mistake to assume that Christians in the fourth century were faced with a choice of either retreating to the desert or of remaining in the traditional churches. It was possible, albeit difficult, to combine the two. But often such a combination was most beneficial, as is shown in the life of Basil the Great.

[3] More details in *CCC*, pp. 102–3.

Basil came from a famous Christian family in eastern Asia Minor.[4] As a young man he went to complete his studies at Athens along with the future emperor Julian. He returned to his home in Cappadocia, extremely learned and with a rather high opinion of himself. It was his elder sister, Macrina, who cut him down to size and impressed on him that spiritual values were of greater importance than worldly success. Fired with enthusiasm, Basil retreated to the mountainous country near his home to live the life of a hermit.[5] but he kept being drawn back into the orbit of church affairs. Along with his brother, Gregory of Nyssa, and his friend, Gregory of Nazianzus, he was instrumental in ensuring the victory of biblical orthodoxy in the latter stages of the Trinitarian controversy. He also made many fruitless attempts to heal the split which had developed in the church at Antioch, where Meletius and Paulinus both regarded themselves as bishop and were each supported by several of the main churches. But Basil's greatest work was his monastic rule, which is still the only order accepted by the eastern churches.[6]

Basil's rule was an improvement on that of Pachomius. He was concerned for the spiritual well-being of the members of the community, and he limited their numbers to manageable proportions (between thirty and forty to a community). In common with Pachomius, he put high value on communal prayer, and the scheme of the monastic hours (the seven[7] daily services of the monastery) was his invention. But Basil's monasteries were to be under the control of the local bishop (he was a bishop himself), and the work they undertook was not only self-supporting manual labour. Under Basil's kindly rule, the members of his commune ran hospitals for the sick, taught in schools set up for local children, and carried out a considerable amount of social relief work.[8] The

[4] For his antecedents, see my book, *From Christ to Constantine,* p. 146.

[5] For Macrina's influence, see *CCC,* p. 104. Basil's own description of his hermit life in Kidd, *Documents Illustrative of the History of the Church,* vol. ii, pp. 87–8.

[6] Extracts in *CCC,* pp. 109–11. Basil did not produce a codified rule like that of Pachomius or Benedict, but rather a series of regulations drafted for particular situations or precepts based on his own methods. His monastic teachings are scattered through many of his works.

[7] The number seven was based on Psalm 119:164: 'Seven times a day I praise thee'.

[8] See *CCC,* pp. 105–7.

harshness of the rule of Pachomius was replaced with a spirit of Christian brotherhood and love. At the same time, Basil was no weak, pious bishop. When the pro-Arian emperor Valens tried to get him to tolerate Arianism, Basil refused point blank. And when imperial officials came, bringing both promises of imperial blessing and threats of dire reprisals if the emperor's will was ignored, Basil told them that such bribes and threats might be suitable for small children but they carried no weight with him. And such was his influence that Valens left him undisturbed.

## The tension between monasticism and church leadership

Basil the Great managed to combine monastic devotion and episcopal office fairly well. His friend Gregory of Nazianzus did not fare so well. Poor Gregory was a timid man, plagued by ill health and much more inclined to devote himself to private prayer and meditation than to enter into the arena of church politics. But he was a firm believer in Christian truth, and he was probably the most gifted preacher of his day. So, when he was persuaded by his friends to become bishop of the orthodox congregation in Constantinople in 380, he reluctantly agreed.[9] Gregory had a hard task. Constantinople had been an Arian city for many years, and even the crowds Gregory met while shopping in the market were well versed in all the Arian catch-phrases.[1] Gregory's church, called the Anastasis (the Church of the Resurrection), was a small one away from the centre of the city. But such was Gregory's eloquence that it was soon packed. He preached in support of orthodox Christian doctrine with great fervour, and his ascetic way of life was a powerful support for his doctrine. With the pro-Arian emperor Valens dead, and with Theodosius deposing the Arian bishop, Gregory would have seemed the ideal choice to succeed as patriarch of Constantinople.

Things then went wrong, however. The patriarch of Alexandria, Peter, decided to fish in troubled waters. The patriarch of Alex-

[9] Details in *CCC*, pp. 143–6.
[1] Gregory of Nyssa, *On the Deity of the Son and the Holy Spirit*, in J.–P. Migne (editor), *Patrologia Graeca*, vol. xlvi, column 557: 'If you ask someone for change, he will discuss whether the Son is begotten or unbegotten. If you ask about how good the bread is, you will get the answer that "the Father is greater, and the Son less."'

andria had never liked the supremacy of the church of Constantinople in the Eastern Empire, and he saw this moment as a chance to get one of his creatures appointed as bishop there, hoping thereby to control the church of the capital city. He supported a charlatan called Maximus, and recognized him as bishop in Constantinople instead of Gregory. When a general council was held in Constantinople in 381, all this trouble came to a head. Many of the court prelates did not like Gregory's ascetic life style, and Gregory could not stand their ostentatious luxury. With the triumph of orthodox Christianity assured, Gregory handed in his resignation to the council. In a bitterly sarcastic farewell speech, he asked his hearers' pardon for being unable to come up to expectation as a court bishop. He said that he was sorry he did not realize that he was supposed to rival the emperors in splendour. Then he bade a touching farewell to his church, his congregation and to the great city which he had longed to see brought to Christian repentance and faith. After he left, the council proceeded to depose Maximus, reaffirm the Nicene Creed, administer a rap over the knuckles to Peter of Alexandria and appoint a new bishop. From then onwards, Gregory resolutely refused to get involved with church politics. A year later, writing to a court official, he states bluntly that in his opinion no good at all ever came from a congress of church leaders, and that all such meetings produced only strife and bitterness. A great number of Christians of all ages would heartily endorse his remarks.

## The beginnings of western monasticism: Jerome

While, in the East, monasticism took root and flourished quickly, western Christians were slower to take the drastic step of completely departing from the world. The asceticism practised in the western churches was normally a régime of fasting, prayer and celibacy observed in an individual's home. When Athanasius had been in exile in the West, two hermits from the Egyptian desert had accompanied him and their sanctity had impressed many.[2] But western Christians were slower to follow their example. In fact, some were openly suspicious of some of the effects of extreme asceticism, and not without good reason. It is against this background that we must view the stormy career of Jerome.

[2] See above, p. 54.

Jerome was born in the Balkans, but came to study literature at Rome, and was baptized there as a young man. He was an ardent admirer of the classical Latin writers, especially the orator Cicero. He himself relates a nightmare he had, in which he dreamt that he had died and was summoned to God's judgment. When he confessed himself to be a Christian, God rebuked him and said that he was a follower of Cicero, not of Christ. Thus condemned, Jerome was about to be consigned to hell when the heavenly court decided that in view of his youth he might be allowed a chance of repentance. At this point Jerome awoke from his dream, and vowed from henceforth to forswear the pagan classics. Although he might forswear the actual writings, however, he took with him a vicious style of invective which he owed at least in part to Cicero, the hero of his youth.

Jerome travelled widely, and among his friends at this time was Rufinus of Aquileia, a young ascetic scholar who translated many of Origen's works into Latin; and who sometimes 'improved' Origen to make him sound more orthodox.[3] Rufinus was a member of one of several ascetic groups with which Jerome was acquainted. Their influence fired Jerome with enthusiasm for ascetic ideals, and so he went east to the desert. But while in the East, Jerome did not only seek to be a hermit. He listened to many of the great eastern theologians, such as Apollinaris of Laodicaea[4] and Gregory of Nazianzus.[5] Having added Greek and Hebrew to his accomplishments, Jerome came back to Rome in 382.

The Roman church to which Jerome returned was not notable for its sanctity. The previous bishop, Liberius,[6] had succeeded in keeping his position during the Arian repression under Constantius, but had been guilty of at least some compromise with Arianism. When he died in 366, all the pent-up tensions came to the surface in the contest for the new elections. The two contestants were Damasus and Ursinus, and they formed rival armies of supporters who did battle with each other in the streets. For a while all civil

[3] Both Origen's original text and Rufinus' translation survive for parts of Origen's great work, *Concerning first principles*, and the alterations are sometimes quite large.

[4] See above, p. 77, and below, p. 189.

[5] He heard Gregory preach during the latter's short and stormy tenure of the see of Constantinople (380–1).

[6] See above, p. 61.

order in Rome collapsed, until finally Damasus came out on top after slaughtering many of Ursinus' supporters.[7] Ursinus retired to intrigue and complain for many years to come. Damasus himself had a charge of murder hanging over his head for ten years before it was finally dropped. Nor was the example of lesser clergy much better. Jerome bitterly complains of the dandy clerics who dressed more opulently than the rich nobles, and who spent their time spreading gossip and angling for gifts from wealthy ladies.[8] Indeed, so rife was clerical greed that the emperor Valentinian I issued a decree making it impossible for any clergyman to benefit under a will.[9]

In this situation, Jerome was in a quandary. He became friendly with bishop Damasus, who was trying to repair his damaged reputation by adorning the tombs of the martyrs in Rome.[1] Damasus was also building up the bureaucracy of the Roman church, and he entrusted Jerome with the task of revising the text of the Bible.[2] While Jerome set himself to this task with considerable zeal, he also began to preach his ideals of asceticism and received considerable support from some of the noble ladies of Rome. Among these patrons was the widow Paula, who eventually followed Jerome in his further travels to the East.

In 384 Damasus died. Jerome had cherished a hope that he would succeed him as bishop. He did not. Then people began to make nasty suggestions about his frequent visits to Paula, and when one of Paula's daughters died as a result of over-enthusiastic fasting Jerome became so unpopular in Rome that he had to leave. He went east again, eventually settling at Bethlehem. Paula and various other Roman ladies followed, and used their wealth to build communities for men and women. Paula ruled the women's convent; Jerome ruled the men's.

---

[7] See above, p. 77.    [8] *CCC*, pp. 179–81.

[9] *Codex Theodosianus* xvi. 2. 70. There were also edicts against clerical immorality (*Codex Theodosianus* xvi. 2. 44); fully justified, according to Jerome's strictures quoted in *CCC*, p. 179.

[1] Many of the fine inscriptions in the Catacombs were put up by Damasus. Further details and illustrations in L. Hertling and E. Kirsch-baum, *The Roman Catacombs* (Darton, Longman and Todd, 1965. This book has a strong Roman Catholic bias and is not always totally reliable.)

[2] Up till now, there had been many versions in Latin of the Bible, and the situation was so confusing that Augustine once said there were as many versions as there were individual manuscripts.

In his self-imposed exile Jerome devoted himself to his literary activity. He had never been the easiest person to get on with, and life in the desert did not improve his temper. He got involved in a bitter controversy over some of the teachings of Origen, in the course of which he spent a large amount of time blackening the character of his former friend Rufinus. When certain Christians in the West, Jovinian and Vigilantius, questioned the value of asceticism, Jerome roundly abused them and kept up the clamour until the church authorities condemned Jovinian as a heretic. Later on he was involved in the Pelagian controversy,[3] where he put his ability to vilify and abuse at the service of Augustine and the orthodox viewpoint. He lived to hear of Alaric's capture of Rome,[4] and he died as an old man in about 420, cantankerous and argumentative to the last. It is noteworthy that when a certain monk, Palladius, visited the Holy Land and wrote an account of the various hermits and monks there, he praises Rufinus as a gracious and godly man, but says that Jerome was so objectionable that no-one would live anywhere near him.[5]

Jerome's greatest work was his revision of the Latin version of the Bible. Since he was learned in Latin, Greek and Hebrew, he was eminently suitable to undertake such a task. He also deserves credit for disentangling the Old Testament Apocrypha from the canonical Old Testament books.[6] Like all revisions, Jerome's new version was not immediately popular, and was bitterly attacked by conservatives; something which did not improve Jerome's temper. It gradually won its way on its merits, however, and although revised several times later on[7] it still forms the basis of the Latin Vulgate today (the term Vulgate was not used of Jerome's version until much later).

[3] See below, pp. 145–7.
[4] In his letters and his commentary on Ezekiel he makes a great deal of fuss about it.
[5] Palladius, *Lausiac History* xxxvi. 6, 7 and xlvi. 5. Palladius was writing a laudatory account of monasticism for the benefit of the royal chamberlain Lausus.
[6] The Apocrypha had received wide publicity because it is included in the Septuagint, the Greek version of the Old Testament, but it is no part of the original Hebrew.
[7] Notably by Alcuin in the eighth/ninth century.

## Martin of Tours, monk/evangelist

While Jerome was pursuing his stormy way to the East, a converted soldier was laying the foundations of the communal life for Christian ascetics in the West. He was Martin, subsequently to become bishop of Tours.[8]

Martin was born of a military family in Pannonia, one of the provinces bordering on the river Danube. We do not know where he first learnt of Christ, but it was not from his family, since they were pagans. He had strong Christian convictions while still in the army. A story is told that one day he was accosted by a beggar. Having no money, he cut his scarlet military cloak in two and gave half to the beggar. That night, in a dream, he saw Jesus wearing the half of the cloak, and telling the saints in heaven how Martin, though not yet baptized, had shown such great Christian generosity. After his military service, he spent some time in south-western France, receiving Christian help from Hilary of Poitiers.[9] After travelling back to Pannonia to try to bring his parents to Christ (his mother was converted, but his father refused to listen to him), he returned to France and retired to be a hermit at Ligugé.

In his cell, he endured visions and delusions similar to those which Antony faced in the Egyptian desert.[1] Many people, however, recognized that Martin was a man close to Christ, and when the bishop of Tours died in 371 the Christians of that place dragged an unwilling Martin from his hermitage to become bishop. Martin had already collected a good number of disciples around him while at Ligugé, and when he came to Tours he built a small cell for himself next to the church building. Around this grew up the first substantial monastery in the West. Martin took many of his ideas from the rule of Pachomius, but put more stress on prayer and less on manual work. He also allowed his monks to copy out manuscripts, however. The result was that his monastery produced many men both godly and learned, who were eagerly sought after as church leaders.

[8] Most material comes from a biography of him written by Sulpicius Severus (363–425?).

[9] See above, p. 63.

[1] Perhaps some of the similarities in the story are due to Martin's biographer, Sulpicius Severus, who may have wanted to make his hero emulate the Egyptian ascetic.

# Map 5

## France and Germany

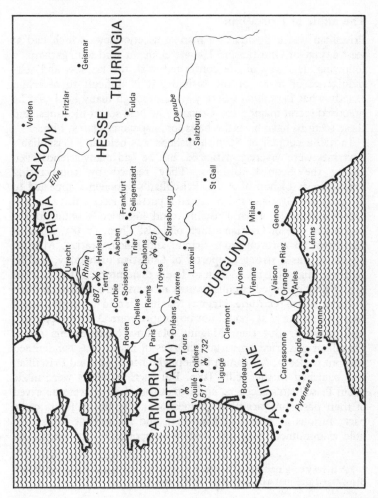

Rural France at this time was still largely unevangelized, and Martin spent much of his time travelling around preaching and combating paganism. He was soon noticed by church and secular leaders, who viewed him with awe and respect. Much to Martin's credit, this did not turn his head. His most famous incursion into great affairs of state was over Priscillian.

## The affair of Priscillian

Priscillian was a Spaniard, a man of ascetic views which had at least a tinge of Gnosticism.[2] He was eloquent, and soon gathered a following. His way of life contrasted with the laziness and self-indulgence of many of the bishops. It is difficult to ascertain exactly what Priscillian's heresy was, although many held that he practised secret magic rites. Certainly he held secret meetings, and these seem to have been the basis for suspicions against him.

In 380 a council of Spanish bishops was held and Priscillian's doctrines were severely criticized, but he had many friends even among the Spanish bishops. They replied by consecrating Priscillian as bishop of Avila. Priscillian's opponents appealed to the emperor Gratian, and obtained a partial success. But this was speedily reversed when Priscillian and his friends obtained the support of one of Gratian's high officials. Then, in 383, Magnus Maximus led a revolt from Britain and killed Gratian. Magnus Maximus was a strong supporter of Christian orthodoxy, and he put Priscillian on trial. Martin of Tours then intervened to halt the trial, partly because Priscillian's own accusers were far from models of ecclesiastical rectitude. Magnus Maximus is said to have promised Martin that the trial should not be a capital one. Martin departed, well satisfied. But then Magnus Maximus changed his mind. Priscillian was tried on certain charges of magic, was condemned and put to death. A Spanish bishop who had supported Priscillian was banished to the Scilly Isles. But then enquiries were made about Priscillian's accusers, and two of their leaders were deprived of their posts for various misdemeanours. Martin of Tours came back, furious at what had happened, and for a while refused to hold communion with the bishops responsible. At length, he

[2] A heresy originating in the second century, which, among other things, disparaged the material world as totally evil.

**Tours.** Martin of Tours (died 397) and the historian Gregory of Tours were both bishops here.

prevented a witch-hunt against Priscillian's supporters[3] in Spain by agreeing to one act of communion with the offending bishops, but this never laid easily on his conscience. Thereafter Martin studiously avoided gatherings of church leaders. He lived on as bishop of Tours until 397, and after his death was revered throughout the western churches. In a few years he became one of the most popular saints of the West; and this in spite of the fact that he did not die as a martyr (he was the first non-martyr to be widely venerated as a saint). The popular devotion which Martin inspired speaks eloquently of his Christ-like character.

## The growth of western monasticism

Martin died at a time when the Western Roman Empire was entering its death throes. The ensuing barbarian invasions gave

[3] The first evidence for the once-famous Trinitarian proof text, the so-called *Comma Johanneum* in 1 John 5:7 (AV only) comes from a work written either by Priscillian or by one of his followers. It probably entered the biblical text from a marginal annotation.

considerable impetus to those who saw the only possibility of living out the full Christian life in terms of a retreat from the world. The monastic movement in the West had its main centre in the South of France at Marseilles and Lérins. On the island of Lérins, off the Riviera coast, a man called Honoratus founded his monastery; while on the mainland at Marseilles, John Cassian, an exile from the East, set up a community which was to be influential as the bridge between eastern monasticism and the West. From Lérins and Marseilles came much of the teaching which would direct western monasticism. They provided the inspiration for Germanus at Auxerre,[4] and thereafter for the later Irish monasteries which doggedly copied many practices first adopted in the Egyptian deserts. On a more practical level, Lérins and Marseilles became spiritual training grounds from which many future church leaders came, and they ensured that at least some of the churchmen of the Dark Ages would be men of God.

John Cassian is noteworthy for two things. First of all, he was one of the leading exponents of so-called Semi-Pelagianism. In reaction to the insistence of Augustine that the grace of God was the sole force involved in converting and guiding a Christian, Cassian insisted that human effort was also necessary. While avoiding Pelagius' fault in thinking that human effort might be all that was required for a man to please God, Cassian held that divine grace was sufficient only if accompanied by human effort. He minimized the extent of the Fall, believing that the human mind and will were still capable of performing good acts. These ideas were particularly popular among the monastic communities of France,[5] and were eventually condemned only at the Synod of Orange in 529. But the Semi-Pelagian protest was not without effect, in that it softened some of the more extreme forms of Augustine's doctrine. For example, the Synod of Orange which condemned Semi-Pelagianism also refused to endorse the doctrine of predestination to damnation.

John Cassian's other claim to fame is as a moral theologian. He made an exhaustive study of human nature and its weaknesses. He

[4] See below, pp. 158–60.
[5] They also seem to have been popular in the British Isles, the native land of Pelagius. One of the strongest supporters was Faustus, a Briton by birth who became bishop of Riez (458) after having been abbot at Lérins from 433. After a chequered career he died c. 495.

is particularly interesting in his acute observations of the ills which afflict people living in close communities. His description[6] of the nervous listlessness (called by the technical term *accidie*) which he saw in certain of his monks is a model of accurate reporting, and his preoccupation with human behaviour may account for the emphasis which he places on human effort in the Christian life.

John Cassian died about 430, and for the next hundred years western monasticism continued to be organized on an *ad hoc* basis. Individuals would feel moved to retreat to form a religious commune, and they would make their own rules as they went along. There was nothing in the West like the rules of Basil or Pachomius in the East.

Around 520 a former hermit called Benedict formed a number of small monasteries in Italy. Although not himself a brilliant administrator, he put his rules down in writing. They were taken up by Gregory the Great[7] (bishop of Rome 590–604) and popularized to such an extent that they gradually became the normal method of organizing a monastery during the next 600 years.[8] Benedict succeeded in making a synthesis between eastern and western forms of monasticism. Prayer and work are the twin aims of the rule, with great stress being put on the monk's remaining in one monastery. Hitherto, it was often the case that a dissatisfied monk would wander from one commune to another, looking hopefully for the perfect one. While Benedict was putting his rule into writing he may well have been influenced in one important detail by a great politician of the day. Cassiodorus was member of the old senatorial aristocracy at Rome, and held many important posts under Theodoric the Great, the Ostrogothic king of Italy. Cassiodorus was a great writer and collector of knowledge, and on his retirement in about 540 he founded his own Christian community at Vivarium in Calabria. His monks there put in many hours of copying manuscripts, and this example may have influenced Benedict when he devoted many hours of his monks' routine to reading and study. It was thanks to the combination of Cassiodorus

[6] *CCC*, pp. 107–8.     [7] See further below, pp. 182–4.

[8] Gregory is almost the sole source for our knowledge of Benedict. The whole story is complicated by the existence of the *Regula Magistri* (*Rule of the Master*), a monastic rule akin to that of Benedict. Scholars are divided over the question of which is the primary document, and there is also considerable discussion as to how far the historical Benedict is responsible for the rule that bears his name.

and Benedict that classical learning survived the Dark Ages. From them, the Irish inherited the tradition of the learned monk, and thereby preserved a heritage which would otherwise have been irretrievably lost in the general barbarizing of the churches.

## Celtic monasticism

Our sources for the history of Christianity in the British Isles during the third to sixth centuries are extremely difficult to evaluate.[9] We shall consider this in greater detail when we come to the barbarian invasions. At the moment, we shall confine our attention to the origins of Irish monasticism.

At the end of the fourth century, Christianity in Britain was similar to that in Gaul. The churches were mainly confined to urban areas, and they were anything but ultra-ascetic. When Germanus of Auxerre visited Britain early in the fifth century, he found a well-organized system with many well-off clerics. There was a notable cult of the martyr Alban (probably martyred during the Diocletian persecution), but little indication of hermits or monks. It is thought that one of the disciples of Martin of Tours (Victricius by name, who was later bishop of Rouen) was the first to introduce monasticism to Britain, but the movement did not immediately become popular. Similarly, when Patrick was in Ireland, he definitely mentions that he encouraged people to take vows of celibacy and to lead ascetic lives, but much of this would still seem to have been in the old tradition of ascetic life lived within the home. In the latter part of the fifth century, we can surmise that a few monastic communities were founded, but they seem to have been neither very strict nor very spiritual (the leader of one establishment is said to have met his death by falling down a well while drunk!). When Gildas wrote, in the early sixth century, monks were still few. Shadowy figures such as Samson, Illtyt and Paul Aurelian were the leaders in a reforming movement in South Wales and the West of England. It also seems that in the far North at Whithorn, Ninian's old centre, there was a revival of life, and some of the earliest Irish ascetics are reputed to have received

[9] A very good discussion of the material is given by J. Morris, 'The Dates of the Celtic Saints', *Journal of Theological Studies,* New Series, vol. xvii (1966), pp. 342–91. For an examination of a specific case, see Hanson, *Saint Patrick*, pp. 72–105.

**Spooyt Vane keeil, near Kirk Michael, Isle of Man.** A typical Celtic hermit cell. Sometimes groups of keeils occur within a boundary wall, an arrangement originating in Egypt.

training there. It is only in the aftermath of the great plague of 540–550 that Celtic/Irish monasticism emerges into the light.[1] And by then it was in full flower.

By means which are far from clear, the Irish form of monasticism had taken the ideals of the Egyptian hermits as its guidelines. The design of the Egyptian monastic settlement, with a group of individual cells surrounded by a wall, was faithfully copied in Ireland. In imitation of Antony and the saints of Nitria and Scitis, Irish hermits sought out remote islands and almost inaccessible caves for their contemplation of God. Even the feats of the Egyptian hermits were copied or improved on. While these feats would have required considerable physical endurance in the warm climate of Egypt, they must have been even more exacting in the North Atlantic winter. Men would stand with their hands extended in the form of a cross all night. Or they would recite the whole Psalter while standing up to their necks in water. Even inside the monasteries, the discipline was harsh. Six lashes were given to anyone who failed to say 'Amen' after grace was said at meals.

[1] Our sources are the *Lives* of various saints.

In sharp contrast to the rule of Benedict, where a monk was expected to remain in one monastery, the Irish tended to roam. Whether this was due to missionary zeal, the 'pilgrim' ideal, or indiscipline is hard to say. But from this there came some of the greatest missionary work of the Dark Ages. And when Celtic zeal was coupled with considerable learning and good organization, the results were often exceptional.

The Irish monastic tradition produced two very different types of person, typified by Columba and Columbanus. Columba[2] seems originally to have been a firebrand, for his departure from Ireland is associated with a bloody battle and censure, if not excommunication, at a church synod. It is alleged that the cause of all this was Columba's unauthorized copying of a book belonging to his abbot, Finnian. Finnian had then demanded the copy, and when Columba appealed to the local king, Finnian's right was upheld. In fury, Columba summoned help from his clan, and although he won the ensuing battle, Ireland was too hot for him. After his case was heard at a synod, he left with some companions and sailed to Scotland. Whatever the truth behind the story, Columba henceforth set his face against all violence. He set up his headquarters at Iona, where he was abbot of the monastery,[3] and from there he successfully evangelized the northern Picts. From here, in due course,[4] missionaries went south and were responsible for bringing most of the kingdoms of northern England to accept Christianity. It is believed that it was Columba's influence which also put an end to internal wars among the Picts and the Irish settlers in Argyll. Certainly, after his coming they managed to live at peace, and their later downfall is attributed to the fact that they broke Columba's command to abstain from wars among themselves.

Columbanus set out from Bangor, Co. Down, a generation later than Columba. He made his way to the continent, straight into the turmoil of the Frankish kingdoms so graphically described for us by Gregory of Tours. Columbanus was a fierce ascetic who feared no-one except God, and who was quite ready to rebuke savage

[2] See Bede, *Church History* iii. 4; further details from the rather unreliable *Life of Columba* of Adamnan, abbot of Iona, 657–69.

[3] Bede mentions as a peculiarity that the abbot of Iona was always merely a presbyter, never a bishop—perhaps in imitation of the founder, Columba, who was never ordained bishop.

[4] See below, pp. 215ff.

**Iona Cathedral and St Oran's Chapel.** The site of Columba's monastery.

barbarian kings to their faces. This was all the more remarkable because it was an age when a king would gladly plunge his battle-axe into the head of anyone who crossed him, and where an enraged queen could order that a bishop be murdered at the high altar of his own cathedral. Columbanus was a preacher of righteousness, and he even wrote to pope Gregory the Great to try to enlist his support in reforming the decadent Frankish churches. Gregory, however, preferred to use diplomacy, enlisting the support even of some of the royal monsters whom Columbanus denounced, in an attempt to put some sort of spiritual order into a terrible situation.

Columbanus' greatest legacy was the monasteries which he founded. On first arriving in France he settled at Luxeuil, and the community which he founded there was soon very influential. Columbanus eventually became so unpopular with the Frankish kings whom he verbally scourged for their sins, however, that he had to move. He wandered east into Germany, and then found his way south to the Alps. He halted with his friend Gallus in Switzerland, where they gathered a community of Christians and founded the monastery of St Gall. Gallus was quite happy to stay there, but Columbanus felt an urge to continue his wanderings. So he travelled on southwards into Italy. By now an old man, he settled at Bobbio, again founding a monastery, and died there in 615.

The wandering Irish monk was in some ways a survival from a previous era. His zeal in devotion to Christ, often coupled with considerable learning, made him a figure which could not be disregarded. But ultimately, the *ad hoc* arrangements of Irish monasteries were taken over by the more ordered rule of Benedict. This combination of zeal and order resulted in a great flowering in the eighth century, when there was a renaissance of learning and spirituality under Charlemagne. But thereafter the Celtic zeal was spent. Monasteries sunk back into a dull routine, from which various mediaeval reformers[5] periodically tried to rouse them. The Irish monks left behind them a varied legacy. There were many churches which could look back to them as founders. Many manuscripts written in their distinctive script had an honoured place on the shelves of monastery libraries. But their zeal also produced a wild superstitiousness, in which saints were credited with all sorts of impossible miracles. Cults of saints and relics were very much part of their stock-in-trade, and Jesus Christ was often in danger of being pushed to one side. The Irish appealed to a spiritual *élite* whose standards and spiritual aims were remote from the needs of the average peasant. They eventually faded away in the face of an organized mediocrity, leaving only a memory, albeit an inspiring one.

## Pilgrimages and hagiography

To drop out as a hermit and to join a monastic commune were the two most radical options open to Christians. For those who did not feel ready to make such a big break, there were less drastic options. Helena, the mother of Constantine the Great, had a made a much-publicized journey to Palestine to see the sites of the biblical events. She was certainly not the first to do so, but her example set a fashion. We possess a list of the stopping-places at which a pilgrim from Bordeaux made his halts when he visited the Holy Land some years later. And from the last years of the fourth century we have a first-person account of the pilgrimage of Etheria.[6]

[5] *E.g.* the founders of the Cluniacs and Cistercians.
[6] Available in English translation; M. L. McClure and C. L. Feltoe (editors), *The Pilgrimage of Etheria* (SPCK, 1898).

Etheria (she is sometimes also called Silvia or Egeria) was a noble lady from somewhere in Southern France or Spain, and the account she wrote was intended for her 'sisters' back home. She possesses all the attributes of an enthusiastic, talkative and determined tourist. She must see everything. And being a fairly important personage, she even had a military escort at one point when she insisted on seeing some sites in a remote and dangerous area. At another point, when she had reached Haran in North Mesopotamia, she was dissuaded from going south to Ur of the Chaldees only by the fact that the Persians (Rome's eternal enemies on this frontier) occupied the area. Whenever possible, Etheria and her retinue took part in the church services of the places visited. She gives a long and very detailed description of the Easter services at Jerusalem, where it seems that special arrangements were made because of the large numbers of pilgrims. There were daily services, special services and processions on every day of Easter week, and at the Sunday eucharist one might begin at daybreak and not finish till noon, because various members of the Jerusalem clergy would all preach in turn, with the bishop preaching last of all. Etheria also visited Egypt and Syria, and her narrative ends as she is travelling through Asia Minor, hoping to be able to visit the tomb of the apostle John at Ephesus.

Etheria was no stranger to monasticism, and she made a point of meeting the various hermits and monks in the places which she visited. About ten years after her pilgrimage, these monks and hermits were carefully catalogued by the monk Palladius.[7] It is he who gives us the interesting estimate of Jerome and Rufinus, and he makes an exhaustive list of all the hermits and holy men that he can find. His *Lausiac History* was following in the tradition of Athanasius' *Life of Antony*, and he wrote consciously to commend the flight to contemplation in the desert. Those who were well enough off, but unwilling to make the complete break with society, could follow his example and visit the hermits. When they reached the holy man, they might sit for days waiting for him to speak some word of wisdom,[8] or they might try to count how many genuflections Simeon Stylites performed at the top of his pillar. For the great majority, who could not afford to travel, sober works like that

[7] See above, p. 109.
[8] There is a collection of the *Sayings of the Egyptian Fathers* which dates from Palladius' time.

of Palladius supplied the information so that they could admire those who were reckoned as the spiritual shock-troops. And when sober reporting failed to excite, there were always the hagiographers on hand to weave fantastic tales of miraculous saints who could manage anything that you might dream of. Too often, the desire to seek to be closer to God eventually resulted in people forgetting their duties in this world and neglecting the works of love and compassion which Christ Himself commanded.

## The lunatic fringe

Foolish otherworldliness, however, was not the greatest sin of the drop-outs and communes. Like most movements founded on enthusiasm, they had a lunatic fringe. Even in the mid-fourth century there were groups who went to excessive lengths. A synod held at Gangra,[9] in Northern Asia Minor, condemned their excesses. They refused to worship at normal church services, fasted on Sundays, despised Christians who were married, and affected superior, ultra-spiritual ways. Those condemned at Gangra may well have been forerunners of the Messalians, a sect which wandered through the cities of the Greek Orient, sleeping rough and keeping up a continual chanting. Jerome speaks scathingly of certain types of monks who were notable mainly for their drunkenness and violence. But while in Syria these tended to be crowds of in-disciplined drop-outs, in Egypt they became organized mobs.

At one time, the church at Alexandria had organized a corps of sick-attendants to help care for the sick during the frequent plagues which broke out in the city. The successors of Athanasius viewed this organization as a powerful political weapon. The emperors were none too keen on such an organization, and there is an imperial decree extant[1] which limited its numbers to 300. But under the able and unscrupulous patriarch Cyril of Alexandria (patriarch 412–444) they became his strong-arm men. They were responsible for the murder of the pagan lady and philosopher Hypatia, and they appeared at church councils with clubs and weapons to support their patriarch. In the Egyptian desert, the Pachomian system of communes produced leaders like the redoubtable Schnoudi. He was abbot of the White Monastery, and lived to be 100 years old.

[9] Perhaps in 340. See *CCC*, pp. 4–6.
[1] *CCC*, pp. 158–9.

His monks were organized into a terrible private army. Under his leadership, which was upheld by savage punishments including the death penalty, the monks terrorized the rural communities of Egypt, burning down any surviving pagan temples and beating up Christtians who happened to disagree with them theologically. Schnoudi himself turned up at the Council of Ephesus in 431, and hurled a large book at Nestorius, the patriarch of Constantinople who was on trial for heresy. When the tables were turned at Chalcedon, and the pope of Alexandria was deposed as a heretic in 451, the monks and the Alexandrian mob murdered his orthodox successor!

But such sins were in the main confined to Egypt. When men and women opted out of society to seek God, they usually remembered that Christ had said that His kingdom was not of this world. Whatever their eccentricities, the first generations of any monastic movement were characterized by a passionate devotion to God. When they failed later, the reasons were most usually the deadening weight of habit and the self-contained complacency which thinks that God is pleased with His own in-group of saints and that the world may safely be left alone.

## Church worship in the last days of the fourth century

The churches which had been left behind still continued their life. What was it like to worship in a church at the end of the fourth century? Perhaps the most immediate impression would be that one was attending a public function. The clergy would be smartly dressed, even if their clothes were little different from those of the wealthier members of the congregation. The church building would be a purpose-built structure, neatly if plainly decorated. At the east end there would be the altar-table, perhaps now the tomb of a martyr containing some of his relics. There would be the seats for the bishop and the other clergy, and perhaps also some elegant curtaining to make this part of the building look more impressive. For it was here that the awesome mystery of the eucharist would take place. When the service began, it would soon be noticed that the old, extempore tradition was being replaced by fixed forms. From Cyril of Jerusalem we can gather that some set forms were used during the eucharist.[2] At Milan, Ambrose could quote from

[2] Cyril of Jerusalem (?), *Mystagogic Lecture* 5.

the great prayer of the eucharist when preaching about the sacraments,[3] and from Egypt we have a papyrus fragment of a prayer
which later formed part of the Alexandrian *Liturgy of St Mark*.[4]
But although written prayers were being increasingly used, the
form of words varied widely between churches. From sixth-century
Egypt we have evidence of at least six or eight different forms of the
eucharistic rite;[5] therefore it is likely that in the fourth and fifth
centuries there were many more forms used, even if they were now
written forms instead of extempore ones. There was no move
towards liturgical uniformity yet; merely a solidifying of older
forms.

In some places, such as Milan, congregational hymn-singing
was just beginning,[6] but the congregation usually participated only
in certain fixed responses and in the receiving of communion.
Preaching was normal, and in many churches the sermon would
provide the main talking-point for the rest of the week. Eloquent
rhetoricians gave out polished sermons from the pulpit, and
combined Christian teaching with public entertainment. At the
centre of all was the mystery of the eucharist. The average Christian
believed that something of quite phenomenal importance happened
during the eucharistic rite, so that when he came to receive the
bread and wine he actually received Christ. The eucharistic bread
and wine were referred to as 'the body and blood of Christ', as well
as the 'spiritual food' and the 'medicine of immortality'. More
acute theologians would distinguish between the spiritual reality
and the bread and wine which were received, but this distinction
would be lost on the average worshipper. Superstitious reverence
soon became attached to the elements. People believed that all
sorts of things might be gained during the 'great sacrifice'. Long

[3] Ambrose, *De Sacramentis*, book 4, v. 21–7.

[4] The Strasbourg papyrus, edited by J. Quasten, *Revue des sciences
réligieuses*, vol. viii (1928), pp. 489–515.

[5] (1) Archduke Rainer Papyrus 19937 (a fragment of the great eucharistic
prayer of the *Apostolic Constitutions*, viii). (2) Rylands Greek Papyrus 465
(part of the *Liturgy of St Mark*). (3) Berlin Papyrus 13918. (4) *Coptica
Lovaniensia* 27 (a Sahidic eucharistic prayer). (5) Two fragments of the
Coptic version of the *Liturgy of St Basil*. (6) Various Coptic fragments of
uncertain date. To these should perhaps be added the Der Balyzeh Papyrus
and Heidelberg Greek Papyrus 2.

[6] See Augustine, *Confessions* ix. 7. Augustine quotes two stanzas of one
of Ambrose's hymns at ix. 12.

prayers were offered for the living and the dead in the hope that Christ who was present in the eucharist would specially bless them. All this was a far cry from the simple memorial service in the upper room.

At this time, too, there began the development of weekday services. This received especial encouragement in two places; Jerusalem and the monasteries. At Jerusalem, the many pilgrims and the ultra-pious gathered for daily worship, while in the monastic communities there were seven special times for prayer each day. The Psalms were used extensively, and there were Bible readings and prayers. This regular worship ensured that the more spiritual were closely in touch with God. It was only later on, with the collapse of learning in the West, the cessation of regular preaching and the swift growth of rank superstition after the barbarian invasions that such practices became little better than the turning of prayer wheels.

By the end of the fourth century, also, there was a development in the Christian calendar. For the pre-Constantinian church, Easter had been the greatest festival, and almost the only big church occasion. Now Easter still retained its pre-eminent position, especially as it was the time when there were the baptisms. But Pentecost, or Whitsun, also came into prominence as the festival at the end of the Easter period of rejoicing. Good Friday was also observed as a separate holy day, and Christmas was beginning to be celebrated. In the celebration of Christ's birth, East and West began to diverge. The western churches fastened on 25 December. This may have been popularized by the fact that in his early years Constantine seems to have identified Jesus with the Unconquered Sun, whose day was celebrated on 25 December. But it is certain that Constantine's whims were not the main reason for the selection of this date, because no early mentions of this date for the nativity connect it with the Unconquered Sun. The eastern churches preferred 6 January, calling it the Epiphany (or appearing) of Jesus. Mainly due, however, to the advocacy of John Chrysostom at Constantinople in the last years of the fourth century, the eastern churches accepted the western date for Jesus' birth, while the western churches took up Epiphany.[7] Saints' days were celebrated,

[7] The present-day celebration of Christmas on 6 January by the eastern Orthodox churches is due to a calendar divergence and is not a continuation of ancient practice.

but not in great numbers. It was only the Celtic influence which later introduced many saints. A church would probably celebrate the anniversary of any local martyrs, and perhaps the day of one or two of the apostles, but widespread saints' days throughout the church were not yet celebrated.

As one looks at the churches at the end of the fourth century, one can clearly see the turn that things were taking. The spontaneous enthusiasm for Jesus has departed from the monasteries and hermitages, and, although there were some who returned to pastor churches, the old spirit had gone. While there was still regular preaching, people would have some idea of Christian truth, but already alien ideas were creeping in. Worldly prelates were gaining charge of many of the leading churches, and their influence reflected itself in the congregations. When the great crash occasioned by the barbarian invasions took place, the West swiftly became superstitious and barbarized. The East remained intellectual and theological, but theology became a political toy while loyalty to Christ and loyalty to the state became synonymous in many minds. The era of the first drop-outs and communes was one of loss for the Christian churches.

# 6

# The last flowering in the West

In 374 the Arian bishop of Milan, Auxentius, died. For a considerable time he had been the only heretical blot among the otherwise orthodox churches of the western part of the Empire. The western emperor, Valentinian I, a man whose declared policy was not to interfere in church affairs, had refused all approaches from outraged bishops and synods who were trying to have Auxentius deposed for heresy. Now, apart from Milan, Arianism was virtually dead in the West, but it was still continuing in the East, under the protection of the pro-Arian emperor Valens. Furthermore, Valentinian's wife, the empress Justina, and many of his Gothic mercenaries were Arians as well. Orthodox Christians wanted to see an orthodox bishop appointed to the church at Milan. But the Arian party at Milan had much to lose, and were not likely to give up without a struggle. So it was a tense assembly which met to vote for a new bishop.

## Ambrose of Milan

The civil authorities were taking no chances. The governor of the area was present in person to see that there was no disturbance. He was a small man, with a sharp face and piercing eyes (at least, this is the impression given by a contemporary mosaic portrait of him). He himself was not a baptized Christian, although he was very sympathetic towards Christians. He was at that time, in fact, under instruction for baptism. Also, he was a member of a family where high office was normal. Both he and his brother were eminent and efficient administrators in the imperial service. He also possessed considerable classical learning. But at the present time he was there to ensure that the scuffles between Arians and orthodox Christians which had already taken place should not erupt into a riot. Governor Ambrose would certainly not stand for that. There was considerable argument and shouting among the crowd, and in such a situation almost anything might have happened. Then, amid all the hubbub; a high-pitched voice called out, 'Ambrose for bishop!' And everybody took up the cry. Both factions united in agreeing that this was God's leading. The astonished governor was elected by acclamation, baptized that very Sunday, and ordained and consecrated bishop within the week. In such a way Ambrose of Milan, one of the key figures of the western church, became a bishop.[1]

Ambrose learnt most of his theology from a church elder called Simplicianus, a man who later was to have a decisive influence on Augustine, and who eventually succeeded Ambrose as bishop at Milan. When Augustine knew Simplicianus, he was an old man, but a gentle and patient teacher who inspired confidence in those who knew him. But the theology which Simplicianus taught Ambrose was anything but weak. The absolute truth of Christ was contrasted with the half-truths of Arianism and the untruths of paganism. And Ambrose deployed his political powers to ensure the victory of the truth.

We have already seen[2] how he intervened to prevent the pagan Senators from restoring the altar of the goddess Victory to the Senate house at Rome. The uncompromising spirit which Ambrose showed then characterized his whole life. Before this incident he had been pursuing a policy of outright war against Arians. Time and again he put pressure on various emperors to enforce decrees of church synods against Arian bishops, and he effectively uprooted Arianism from the Balkans, where for a long time it had been almost unchallenged. His anti-Arian stand, however, had made him enemies.

The emperor Valentinian I had died in 375, shortly after Ambrose had become bishop. He was succeeded by his sons Gratian and Valentinian II who divided the Western Empire between them. Valentinian II was only a small child, and his mother, the empress Justina, was the effective ruler. And she had her court at Milan. Then, in 378, the Arian emperor of the East, Valens, was defeated and killed at the Battle of Adrianople. He was

[1] Paulinus, *Life of Ambrose* 6, cited in *CCC*, p. 120.
[2] See above, pp. 79–82.

succeeded by the orthodox and energetic Theodosius. Five years later, Gratian was killed in a revolt led by the governor of Britain, Magnus Maximus. Justina and her young son Valentinian II were left sandwiched between two orthodox and determined emperors. Justina was an Arian, and she had the support of many Gothic mercenaries who were also Arians. But there was no place of worship for them in Milan. So she proposed to take over one of the church buildings, and thus came into collision with Ambrose.

Ambrose adamantly refused to concede anything. For him there was no doubt over the rights and wrongs of the matter. He was a servant of God, and therefore responsible for all the church buildings, for they were God's property. Futhermore, as a vigorous defender of truth against error, Ambrose was not going to assist the progress of Arianism by conceding its supporters one of his own churches—which in any case were fully used. Ambrose's anger, however, was against the cause of Arianism, not its individual members. When an Arian cleric was seized by an angry mob of Ambrose's supporters, Ambrose himself intervened to ensure that the man was released unharmed.

The empress-mother Justina and her son, however, were not easily put off. When Ambrose refused to comply, they threatened him and his supporters with fines and imprisonment. It was hinted that he was committing treason by resisting the emperor, who was absolute lord of all property. To this, Ambrose bluntly replied that the emperor owned the palaces, but that the bishop was the custodian of the church buildings. The imperial reply was to send in the troops. But this was not easy. With the exception of the imperial household and some Gothic mercenaries, most of the soldiers were at least nominally orthodox Christians. When they came to the churches, they found them already filled with people. And Ambrose was there, conducting worship, and preaching sermons with pointed references to the troubles caused by women such as Herodias and Jezebel. Justina must have understood the reference, and also her peril; for the orthodox Magnus Maximus was just across the mountains, and it was only on Ambrose's intercession that he had not come across after the death of Gratian to sweep her and her son into oblivion. Inside the churches, Ambrose effectively organized a sit-in. The soldiers shrank from massacring most of the population of Milan. It was in this situation, which lasted for several days, that antiphonal hymn-singing was first used in a church, as Ambrose's supporters kept up their spirits. Ambrose himself was fully convinced of the rightness of his cause. In fact, he even said that he was willing to suffer martyrdom rather than give way on this point. In the end it was the imperial party that had to climb down. Valentinian II gave orders that the troops should leave the churches. High officials told Ambrose that they would have his head for defying the emperor. Ambrose could afford to treat such empty threats with contempt. Valentinian knew the real situation better when he complained to his own officials that if Ambrose commanded them they would have handed himself over to Ambrose in chains!

Although Ambrose had won, the battle continued in desultory fashion. An attempt was made to proclaim Arianism officially tolerated. Ambrose refused to have anything to do with it, and consequently was summoned to appear at court and debate the question with an Arian bishop. But Ambrose was strong enough to refuse to come. He refused on the grounds that the state had no right to arbitrate in affairs of faith. Instead, Ambrose proposed that a synod of bishops be summoned to debate the issue. He knew full well what the western bishops thought of Arianism. And the upshot of the matter was that nothing was done.[3]

The issue was more than just a case of two strong-minded people fighting each other. This was to be the heart of many quarrels up to and beyond the Reformation. Basically it is the question of church versus state. Should the secular authorities have absolute power over Christian doctrine and practice? Or should the church be in a position to dictate to the civil powers? And what happens when the ruler is a professing Christian? How far is he also a loyal 'son of the church'? Ambrose's struggle with Justina and Valentinian II was merely a prelude. The definitive struggle, which was to set the pattern for future church–state relationships in the West, was soon to come.

### Ambrose versus the emperor Theodosius

In 388 Theodosius, the orthodox emperor of the East, finally defeated Magnus Maximus and gained effective control of the whole Empire. He did leave Valentinian II theoretically in charge

[3] The most significant documents concerning Ambrose's struggle against Arianism are collected in *CCC*, pp. 125–34.

**Theodosius I, emperor 379–395.** A coin in the British Museum, London.

of the West, but the substance of the power was with Theodosius. Ambrose realized this. Soon he was also to come into conflict with Theodosius.

Callinicum was a town on the far eastern frontier of the Empire, on the river Euphrates.[4] The local bishop, leading a rabble of 'holy men', had burned down a local synagogue and also the meeting-place of a congregation of Valentinian Gnostics.[5] The local governor had ordered that the bishop and the church should repair the damage which they had caused. But an appeal was made to Theodosius. Ambrose was present, and was in no doubt about what should be done. He viewed any reparations as tantamount to forcing the bishop to commit apostasy, and as allowing unbelievers to fleece Christians. Ambrose picked his ground for the showdown carefully and quite unscrupulously. With the emperor in his congregation as he preached in Milan, Ambrose worked his way around to the subject. With a perversely tendentious use of Nathan's parable against David, Ambrose hinted that God might withdraw his favour from Theodosius if he proceeded against the rioters of Callinicum. When Ambrose came down from the pulpit, prior to beginning the celebration of the eucharist, the emperor remarked that he had been preaching against him. Ambrose agreed. Then Theodosius offered a compromise. He would not enforce the decree about the rebuilding of the synagogue, but he was not happy about the monks getting away scot free. Ambrose did not move. He threatened, in a thinly veiled manner, that he could not offer the eucharist with a clear conscience, if Theodosius would not concede

[4] Details, from Ambrose's own letters, in *CCC*, pp. 137–40.
[5] A heretical group whose origins date from the second century.

everything. It was an intolerable position for a devout and super-stitious man like Theodosius. He promised to drop the whole matter. Ambrose walked up to the altar to continue the service, triumphant. But it was a most despicable triumph.

Ambrose had the power, but it should be mentioned to his credit that he did not always use it so despicably. Two years after the Callinicum episode he was in action again. Riots had broken out at Thessalonica[6] after the arrest of a popular charioteer (chariot races were the occasion of many brawls and riots in many cities, just like football hooliganism nowadays, but on a far greater scale). In these riots, one of Theodosius' senior army officers had been killed. Theodosius, out for revenge, proposed to massacre the rioting citizens. Ambrose got to hear of the plan, and immediately wrote to the emperor. The message authorizing the massacre had already been dispatched, but a second, countermanding the order, was sent. It came too late. The troops had gone in, and about 6,000 people were dead.

Ambrose was not a man to confine himself to rebuking the emperor verbally. In spite of Theodosius' protests (he foolishly invoked king David, guilty of murder *and* adultery, who was yet loved by God), Ambrose insisted that Theodosius do public penance. He refused to officiate at worship otherwise if the emperor were present. Theodosius certainly made some sort of public confession of his sin before Ambrose was satisfied. And for an emperor to acknowledge his sin in such a violent age was no bad thing. Ambrose was certainly wrong over the Callinicum episode. He was within his rights over Thessalonica. One can see how such a victory laid the foundation for papal tyranny during the Middle Ages (although it should be noted that it was the bishop of Milan, not the bishop of Rome, who disciplined the emperor here). Yet the tyranny of the churchman was one of two options; the other was the tyranny of the king or emperor. Often there was no middle way between the two.

Although Ambrose and Theodosius might not have realized it, the Western Empire was coming to a close. Theodosius I was the last effective emperor of the West. But even his last years were not free from trouble. Two years after the Thessalonica massacre, in 392, one of his generals, a Frank called Arbogast, raised a revolt

[6] See *CCC*, pp. 140–2.

in the West. The miserable Valentinian II was killed, and a puppet emperor called Eugenius was set up. It is significant that Eugenius had considerable support from the pagan Senate at Rome, who were still unyieldingly hostile to Christianity, especially that kind seen in Ambrose and Theodosius. Theodosius hurried West, and defeated the rebels in 394 at the battle of the river Frigidus. It was his last act of any importance. Early in the next year he died, while in Milan. Ambrose survived him by only two years. The Empire was divided between Theodosius' two sons, who were equally incompetent. The year 395 marks the point where the Western Empire ceased to be a real force. The massing barbarians broke in, and although shadowy emperors lingered on until 476, the substance of power was now in other hands.

The decline of the Western Empire after the death of Theodosius proceeds unevenly. The Rhine frontier was breached by a torrent of barbarians in 406. In North Africa the barbarians, the Vandals, did not arrive until 429. The crumbling façade of Roman authority survived just long enough for the career of the greatest theologian of the West, a younger contemporary of Ambrose of Milan, whose name was Augustine.

### North Africa from Donatus' time onwards

Augustine's native land, North Africa, had suffered a great deal during the fourth century. The most notable reason for its sufferings was the unremitting conflict between official Christianity and Donatism.[7] We left the story of Donatism with the death of Constantine in 337, with the redoubtable Donatus organizing his followers into a rival church with branches even beyond North Africa.[8] Then, in 347, the Western emperor Constans decided to intervene and settle the dispute. His officials, Paul and Macarius, came to Carthage with money, ostensibly to help the poor, but probably also with the intention of weaning away powerful support from Donatus. The governor, Gregory, was almost certainly involved as well. But when they approached Donatus they realized

[7] For a complete history of Donatism, see W. H. C. Frend, *The Donatist Church* (OUP, 1952). Some of the most important documents are given in *CCC*, pp. 26–8, 202–3, 210–11.
[8] He corresponded with eastern church leaders, and there was a Donatist congregation at Rome.

that they had underestimated their adversary. Donatus asked them acidly, 'What has the emperor to do with the church?' It was a historic question, because it became the slogan of the Donatists from then onwards.[9] Donatus made his low opinion of the imperial officials quite clear, and was openly rude to the governor. He rejected their advances and their money with considerable vehemence. The emperor replied by sending Donatus into exile.

With the leader out of the way, the imperial officials decided that they could safely proceed against the Donatists. Troops were called out to evict them from their buildings. Donatists formed armed bands to resist, and many were killed. The imperial commissioner Macarius took a leading part in the repression, and long afterwards the Donatists still referred bitterly to the troubles of 347 as 'the times of Macarius'.

Although repressed, Donatism was undefeated. Until his death in 355 Donatus led the movement, although in exile. And gradually the situation polarized in North Africa, with Donatism becoming the creed of the rural areas while official Christianity remained strong mainly in the towns and among the landed gentry. On the accession of Julian the Apostate in 361, Donatist leaders were allowed back, and they returned to exact vengeance. Churches belonging to their opponents were burnt down, and armed Donatists beat up and even killed members of the official (or 'Catholic') churches. But after the worst extremes of the return, wiser counsels prevailed. Parmenian, who was Donatist bishop of Carthage from 363 to 391, was a man of peace who refused to countenance violence. But, as so often happens, the moderate leader of a popular movement cannot control his extremists. The 'Circumcellions', as they were called, bore some resemblance to the rowdy groups of quasi-monks of the East, but they were infinitely more dangerous and fanatical. They terrorized rural areas, especially directing their attention to the great landowners who were supporters of official Christianity. One of their more amusing tricks was to stop a landowner's coach and force him to run alongside it while his slaves rode on the coach in comfort. But they also burnt down farms and churches, robbed and killed, and if any of their number died during such episodes they were regarded as

[9] There was an inconsistency here, because the Donatists had appealed to the emperor to intervene on their behalf in 313 and 346, and did so again in 361.

martyrs. Indeed, they were even involved in a revolt against the central Roman government, when they supported the revolt of Firmus in 372.

Mainstream Donatism, although enthusiastic, was not without its learned men. Foremost among these were the lawyer Petilian and the biblical scholar Tyconius. But perhaps it is worth noticing that Petilian was in fact a convert from official Christianity, and that Tyconius was eventually excommunicated for heresy[1] by bishop Parmenian. Yet it is also symptomatic that Tyconius never considered joining any of the Catholic churches. Donatist and Catholic were viewed almost as different species of men.

## The young Augustine

Augustine was born into this stormy situation in 354, at Thagaste. We have a vast amount of information about him and his spiritual pilgrimage thanks to his autobiography, the *Confessions*,[2] which covers the period up to his conversion and his return to North Africa as a Christian in 388. Even allowing for a certain amount of pious hindsight, Augustine's testimony is a most frank and detailed account of how God dealt with one man in the dying days of the Western Empire.

Augustine's account of his life is shot through with a preoccupation with his sins and God's indescribably marvellous grace to him. This is the key to understanding Augustine. His consciousness of personal unworthiness served to make God's love all the greater, and he never tires of marvelling that God, who is so pure and holy, could ever love such a sinner.

Augustine begins by tracing his sinfulness right from infancy. His home was nominally Christian, although his father Patricius was not converted until very late in life. His mother, Monica, was a devoted Christian, and by all accounts a pretty formidable character. She had had to contend with a hostile mother-in-law, and had received little encouragement in her Christian faith. It was perhaps

---

[1] His 'heresy' was that he considered that there might be both saved and condemned people in the visible churches; thus denying the original basis of Donatism which was that the church should be a company of perfect people.

[2] An English translation by R. S. Pine-Coffin is available in the Penguin Classics series (1970).

these stresses which at one time turned her to drink, but after being called a drunkard by one of her own serving-maids she became teetotal. It was due to her influence that the young Augustine was enrolled as a candidate for baptism; and it was due to his lack of spiritual inclination that he did nothing further about it.

Augustine admits that he was lazy at school. He put up with the Latin classics, and even enjoyed a certain amount of success at rhetoric. But he loathed Greek, and was never any good at it, and his Roman hatred of things Greek persisted throughout his life. One more admission of Augustine deserves special attention. From early life he desired to love and to be loved. This might be put down to deprivation in his home, but it certainly explains quite a lot of his subsequent actions. The quiet and sensitive young man from rural North Africa was to do many things in his search for a love that was satisfying to him and which would completely engage all his powers.

Augustine's home was at Thagaste, but he studied first at nearby Madaura and then went to the capital, Carthage, for further education. His father footed the considerable bill (this is about the only good thing Augustine says about his father, but he mentions him seldom). It was while still at school that he and his friends got up to a prank which showed Augustine the senselessness of sin. He and some other boys raided an orchard and stole some pears. But even when they had them, they merely fed them to some pigs. Years later Augustine remembered that act, and for him it pinpointed the utter destructiveness of sin, and the memory of it probably influenced him in his theory that evil was in fact a negation of existence.

In spite of his protestations of sinfulness, Augustine had to admit that he was a fairly well-behaved student. He enjoyed reliving the joys and sorrows depicted in the emotional theatrical shows of his day, and it was in Carthage that he began his search for something to give meaning to his life. The experience which saved him from merely living a life of self-indulgence was the reading of a dialogue by Cicero, called *Hortensius*.[3] This pagan work set Augustine off on his search for wisdom and truth, a search which he did not conclude until he had found Christ.

[3] No longer extant.

## Augustine the Manichee

The pagan classics, the staple diet of education, were not the only books which Augustine read. He turned to the Bible. But the arrogant young littérateur found the Gospels poor in style when compared with the pagan writings. There was no beauty in the Old Latin versions of the Scriptures such as now gives an aura of holiness to the King James version. And so Augustine looked elsewhere. With a temperament such as his, he was a likely prospect for cults (today he might have become an ardent Mormon or Jehovah's Witness). And it was among the Manichees that he found a spiritual home. His conversion was emotional, not intellectual, for from the beginning he had plenty of awkward questions to ask about Manichean doctrine. But in this sect, secretive and despised, Augustine found a place where he was somebody, and an ideology to follow. Needless to say, his mother was terribly upset, and in her anxiety she went to see the bishop of the local church. In response to her pleas that he should go and speak to Augustine, he replied that she should pray for him, adding, with considerable insight, that it was impossible that a son who was wept for so much should be lost.

Meanwhile, Augustine went on his own wayward way. Since only the *élite* of the Manichees (the elect) were under severe discipline, it was possible and allowable for Augustine to indulge himself. He had become a teacher of public speaking at the university, and not content with Manicheism he also dabbled in astrology. At the same time he took a mistress and by her had a child called Adeodatus. We do not know the name of this girl, but it is obvious that Augustine loved her. They lived together for fifteen years. Then, to Augustine's eternal shame, he turned her out, keeping the son she had borne him. The anonymous girl returned to her home in North Africa, vowing she would love no-one else, and that is the last we hear of her.

It was only at the age of twenty-nine that Augustine began to break with the Manichees. He had been studying the best science of his day (works in Latin translation emanating from the school of Aristotle). His intellectual doubts over Manicheism now came to the fore. The Manichees in Carthage, however, assured him that a certain Faustus would settle all his queries. This Faustus was one of the leading Manichean teachers, and Augustine awaited his arrival eagerly. But when he came he was a great disappointment.

Augustine quickly found out that, although a pleasant person, Faustus had only a smattering of education. Much worse, the statements of the Manichees about the visible world conflicted with the best scientific observations of the day. Augustine's doubts were increased when the Manichees consistently refused to enter into debate with Elpidius, a Christian controversialist who repeatedly challenged them to public debate. Augustine continued to be friendly to Faustus, even lending him some of his own books, but the spell of Manicheism was broken. Still, Augustine was not going to desert his safe harbour among the Manichees until he found something to take their place.

## Augustine leaves North Africa for Italy

At this time, fed up with the rowdy students at Carthage, Augustine decided to go to Rome. His father was by this time dead; and his mother did not want him to go. But he managed to slip her careful watch and board a ship for Italy. On reaching Rome, he found friends among the Manichean community there, but he suffered from a very dangerous illness. Intellectually, he flirted with agnosticism. But he still found a need for something more solid and definite as a basis for life. Then came a crucial event. The pagan city prefect Symmachus, whom we have already met during the controversy over the statue of Victory in the Senate house,[4] got Augustine appointed to a post of public teacher of rhetoric at Milan. So Augustine's household moved to Milan, and in Milan he was joined by his mother. But by coming to Milan he came within the influence of Ambrose.

Ambrose was then in the middle of his conflict with the empress Justina,[5] and was a man of immense authority. Augustine's mother Monica was very impressed with him. She took part in the sit-ins which Ambrose organized to prevent the Arians taking over one of the churches of Milan, and she even submitted to the bishop's command that she should give up making nightly visits to pray at the tombs of martyrs.[6] Augustine went to listen to Ambrose, not because he expected spiritual help but because he had heard that

[4] See above, pp. 79–82.
[5] See above, pp. 129–30.
[6] A North African practice which the stern Ambrose considered not respectable.

Ambrose was an eloquent man. And Augustine was pleasantly surprised at what he heard. In particular, Ambrose spiritualized those parts of the Old Testament which the Manichees claimed were proof that God could never create a material universe. Augustine's intellectual resistance to Christianity weakened. He admired Ambrose, not only for his eloquent wisdom, but also for his strict self-control and celibacy. But admiration was one thing; following the example was quite another. The scheming Monica was planning an advantageous marriage for Augustine, and therefore his beloved mistress had to go, even though Augustine had lived with her faithfully for years in a union which was marriage in all but name. But Monica's plans misfired (we are not told how), and Augustine had another liason to satisfy his cravings for love. He was at sea not only morally but intellectually. His faith in astrology was broken when two of his friends carried out an experiment. They knew of a nobleman and a slave born exactly at the same time. The horoscopes were identical, but the lives of the two were utterly different from each other (as one might expect). Then, at another time, Augustine and some of his friends proposed to form a philosophical commune, but it never even got started. Augustine was finding that his weak will was the greatest barrier to his idealistic aims, and he searched almost everywhere for a remedy. He went back to the Christian Scriptures, and began to read the Gospels. He found much to admire in Jesus as a 'philosopher'. At the same time he was reading Platonic literature, in which God was described as the 'ultimate good'. His Manichean background still bedevilled his ideas of God, but here in Plato at last there was the idea of God as a spiritual being, rather than the physical demigod of the Manichees. At this time, too, Augustine began to read the writings of the apostle Paul. He was now prepared to receive help from Christian teachers.

Augustine had not found Ambrose very approachable. Ambrose was reserved, and he puzzled Augustine and his friends by reading silently.[7] But Ambrose himself had been greatly helped by a church elder called Simplicianus. Augustine approached him and got the help he wanted. Among other things, Simplicianus told Augustine about the conversion of Marius Victorinus, the man who had translated into Latin the very Platonic works which Augustine had

[7] In Roman times most reading was done aloud, even when it was only for one's own benefit.

been reading. Augustine was confronted with the example of a man with a post like his own, who had found no insuperable difficulty in becoming a Christian. The only problem was Augustine's own inability to make the decisive step.

## The conversion of Augustine

From this point onwards, everything conspired to thrust the choice upon Augustine. Two of his friends, Alypius and Nebridius, pressed him to go to the house of a certain Ponticianus. Both these two friends came from North Africa. Nebridius had already been a major influence on Augustine, helping to destroy his faith in astrology. Now he helped Augustine to the final step. Ponticianus told them of the story of Antony, the hermit of Egypt, and how his example was compelling men to abandon the rat race of the world in favour of a life spent in prayer and contemplation of God. Augustine was driven almost to distraction by his inability to do

**A street in Ostia,** the town where Augustine's mother Monica died.

likewise. He was now thirty-one (it was 386), and he wanted to believe, but he was torn apart by a most terrible inner conflict. He went out into the garden with Alypius, and then managed to be alone. After a period of mental anguish, he heard a child's voice saying, 'Take it up and read it.' He returned to where Alypius was sitting. Beside him was a copy of Paul's Letters. Augustine opened the book at random, and read, 'Not in revelling and drunkenness, not in debauchery and licentiousness, not in quarrelling and jealousy. But put on the Lord Jesus Christ, and make no provision for the flesh.'[8] Augustine himself said that at that point the light flooded in and all difficulties to accepting Christ were dispelled. He knew himself to be converted, and his first act was to go and tell his mother about it. It was summer time, and Augustine felt an urge to give up his teaching post in order to attempt something more spiritual. He had long been dissatisfied with his work, and later even remembered how one day he had met a tipsy but happy beggar and had contrasted that man's gaiety with his unhappiness and lack of satisfaction. As it happened, a fresh attack of lung trouble forced him to give up his post, and for a while he went with his family and friends to stay at a villa outside Milan at Cassiacum. He wrote to Ambrose, asking for instruction for baptism the following Easter. His friend Alypius and his son Adeodatus were baptized at the same time. Then in 387 they set out to return to North Africa. Late in the year they reached Ostia, the port of Rome, There, Augustine's mother Monica died suddenly after a short illness. Augustine was shaken, but his new-found faith enabled him to bear the loss. Monica knew she was dying, and told him that she was thankful to have lived to see him become a Christian. She was only fifty-six when she died.

Augustine returned to North Africa, put into effect his plan for forming a Christian commune in his home and reluctantly agreed to ordination. He hoped for a quiet life, but he was soon needed in the busy world of Christian administration. The elderly official bishop of Hippo, Valerius, pressed him to become his assistant. Augustine tried hard to avoid this, but in the end in 395 he allowed himself to be appointed. Within a year Valerius was dead, and Augustine found himself bishop of Hippo and in the centre of the storms of North African church life.

[8] Romans 13:13, 14.

## Augustine, church leader and controversialist

Augustine was a voluminous writer. By 423, by his own counting, he had already written ninety-three literary works, apart from sermons and letters which are often long and detailed. And he continued work unabated until his death in 430. His theology was based in controversy, and his life revolved around five great controversies. The result of a great spiritual intellect facing five very different sets of opponents was the production of a theology which set the tone for western Christendom for centuries to come. Augustine's opponents were the Manichees, Donatists, Pelagians, Arians and pagans, and we will consider each in turn.

Manicheism was the last of the Gnostic sects to emerge. We now know[9] that Mani, the founder, had originally been a member of the Elchesites along with other members of his family. The Elchesites were a Gnostic sect fairly far out on the Christian fringe, and received their name from the angelic being who, they alleged, had given them special revelations. But Mani broke with them and set himself up as a spiritual teacher on his own account. While most Gnostic sects aimed to reform Christianity to what they considered was its original truth, Mani consciously proclaimed a new religion. Nevertheless, there were many points upon which Mani and other Gnostics would agree.

The basic premise of Mani's doctrine was that there were two principles in the world, God and matter. God was all good, matter was all evil. This idea Mani may have derived from Zoroastrianism, the religion of Persia where he was born, but the depreciation of the material universe also occurs in Gnosticism. By means of a complicated mythology, Mani taught that particles of light from the good God had been embedded in the material world, and the task of Manicheism was to release them so that they could ascend to the source of light once more. Human beings were considered to be part light, part matter, and although the Manichean 'elect' might expect a direct passage to the realm of light, most people would have to undergo many thousands of transmigrations before they were released from the world of matter. Finally, it should be said that Mani's own opinion of himself was vastly inflated. He considered himself to be the ultimate revealer of the truth, akin in personality to the Holy Spirit. He viewed the founders of the other

[9] New evidence in Yamauchi, *Pre-Christian Gnosticism,* pp. 80–1.

religions, Buddha, Jesus and Zoroaster, as forerunners of himself. His disciples called him 'the Lord', and he based his system on his own 'revelations' rather than on any system of logic.

Augustine had been attracted by Manicheism because it seemed to offer an attractive answer to the problem of evil. When he became a Christian, he attacked Manichean teaching by holding that evil was not a positive force, but rather an absence of goodness. Augustine also had to grapple with the problem of how God, who is good and spiritual, could create a material universe in which there was evil. In his attack on Manicheism, Augustine could rely on the previous experience of Christian writers combatting Gnosticism. Like them, he insisted that there was no disparity between the Old and New Testaments.[1] He also put great stress on the real humanity of Jesus Christ, which was the strongest refutation of the claim that God could have nothing to do with the world of matter. Yet, at one or two points, Augustine still kept a tinge of Manicheism even after his conversion. His view of sexual intercourse as somehow sinful, his rigid determinism and his later preference for revelation rather than reason may be vestigal remains of his Manichean period (certainly his opponents would charge him with this). But, at the same time, these could have been the result of his particular spiritual experience. His mistrust of sex could be a revulsion against his own pre-conversion excesses. And his view of God, as seen throughout the *Confessions*, draws considerably from Platonism, and thereby makes Him seem so lofty as to leave little room for human choice or human reason.

## Augustine and Donatism

When Augustine turned his attention to Donatism,[2] he was facing a very different kind of opponent. Here was a Christian movement which was theologically orthodox, and yet which stood in opposition to official Christianity. The keystone of Donatist theology was its view of the church. To the Donatist, the church was the congregation of holy people. In particular, no sinner could effectively conduct baptism or communion. And sin was contagious, so that all who consorted with sinful clergy were immediately cut off from

[1] Gnostics believed that the God of the Old Testament was an inferior creator, and not the ultimate source of deity.

[2] Examples of his anti-Donatist writings in *CCC*, pp. 201–6, 209–13.

143

the true church themselves. With perfect consistency, Donatists rebaptized any who joined them from the official church. The burning issue in this debate, therefore, was the question, 'What is the church?'

Augustine attacked the Donatists in several ways. On a very superficial level, he could show without much difficulty that Donatists were not the saints they claimed to be. Their behaviour was frequently not only sub-Christian but also illegal. The Donatist bands who burnt and pillaged in the North African countryside were bad advertisements for their type of Christianity. On the theological level, Augustine argued that until the judgment day the church must be a mixed multitude, with both good and bad in it. Admittedly, when he appealed to the parables of Christ for support, he often uses them to speak of the church when they are, in fact, talking about the whole world.[3] He was on stronger ground when he insisted that the unworthiness of a clergyman does not mean that the faithful Christian receives no spiritual benefit when he attends such a man's worship services. Augustine rightly insists that it is the faith of the recipient, not the moral character of the officiating minister, which makes the communion a blessing. When he succeeded in obtaining a public debate with the Donatists in Carthage in 411, Augustine was also easily able to show that the original Donatist objections against the ordination of Caecilian (an event which was then nearly a hundred years in the past) were groundless.

Augustine and the Donatists still failed to agree, however, because there were more deeply seated differences which kept them apart. Donatists regarded Augustine and his friends as representatives of the official and persecuting church. There was a social divide which kept them separated, for the Donatist peasant viewed the Catholic landowner as almost a different animal. It was true that by the time of the great conference of 411 the Donatists had been involved in the unsuccessful revolt of Gildo against the central Roman government, and had therefore suffered when that revolt was crushed. But it was not politics alone which made Donatist bishops at the conference of Carthage hail their Catholic rivals to bishoprics with the words, 'I recognize my persecutor.' Many towns had both Catholic and Donatist congregations. Violence, when it

[3] *E.g.* the parable of the wheat and the tares.

occurred, was not confined to the Donatist side. Official churches often called upon the civil power to support their religious claims. It is to Augustine's great shame that he eventually fell in with such ideas. Exasperated by Donatist intransigence, he took the lord's command at the great banquet ('Compel people to come in'; Luke 14:23) as an excuse to force Donatists to give way. And such was the prestige of Augustine in later ages that his example was invoked as justification for many forms of ecclesiastical oppression. The Donatist schism in North Africa needed the efforts of a peacemaker, not of a controversialist. Sadly, Augustine was not of that mould. Nor was there anyone who could have brought the two warring sides together.

## Augustine and Pelagianism

Today Augustine is perhaps best remembered for his part in the controversy over free will and predestination—a controversy to which the name of Pelagius has been attached. The heart of the problem was whether a man could fulfil completely the righteous demands which God made on him. Pelagius, a Celtic ascetic from somewhere in the British Isles, asserted that it was possible, and that God's grace consisted in enlightening man to know what was God's will. Pelagius addressed his moralistic sermons to the none-too-holy churches at Rome (the ones which Jerome had castigated for their worldliness[4]), and moral rebukes were needed there. But Augustine, from his own experience, knew that sin was more than just ignorance of what was good and that man needed more than merely turning over a new leaf. From this initial debate sprang a whole host of related questions. Was man by nature able to please God? If not, on what grounds did God accept some people and reject others? Was man's sinful tendency learnt or inherited? And if inherited, what happened to babies who died in infancy?

Augustine's solution began with his concept of God. God was totally good, and none could argue with God or demand satisfaction from Him. Man was by nature sinful, because all human beings were descended from the first sinner, Adam. In his unbounded mercy, God had chosen to rescue a certain number of people from the death and hell that they otherwise merited. Man could not please God by his own efforts; he needed the grace of

[4] See above, pp. 107-8.

145

God given through Jesus Christ if his sins were to be forgiven. From this basic idea, Augustine then brought in some ideas which were distinctly unpleasant. For instance, he held that unbaptized babies would go to hell, because they inherited guilt from Adam. He also viewed sex and human procreation as the means of passing on the guilt of Adam, and so in some way as sinful. Such was Augustine's prestige as theologian in the West, that he could gain the support of the bishop of Rome and secure an imperial edict condemning Pelagius and his supporters. In the East, Augustine's views commanded less support. This was partly because East and West were drifting away from one another, and partly because official interpreters often failed to convey the niceties of theological discussion.[5] In the East it was Jerome who did most to secure the condemnation of Pelagianism, turning his theological knowledge and invective against the Pelagians with great success.

[5] One of Augustine's friends, Orosius, complained that the interpreters at the Synod of Diosopolis, where the eastern bishops discussed the issue, were incompetent.

**The Roman theatre, Orange.** A church synod here in 529 ended the Semi-Palagian controversy.

Even if Augustine won the day on the main point, the fact that man was utterly dependent on God's grace if he were to be saved, there were quite a number of western churchmen who did not like some of his ideas. Dissent was centred among the monastic groups in the South of France, where John Cassian and Vincent of Lérins were the main spokesmen. They contended that while no man could please God by his own unaided efforts, it was necessary that man should have some good works so as to make some contribution (albeit an inadequate one) towards his salvation. Most important of all, Semi-Pelagians (as supporters of this viewpoint were called) held that the human will could make the first move towards God without the prior help of divine grace. As people who were foremost among the activist movements to promote sanctity, they felt that Augustine was too pessimistic. The Semi-Pelagian controversy was to continue until 529, when Caesarius of Arles presided at a synod at Orange where Augustine's main points were upheld, but certain peripheral ideas (e.g. predestination to damnation) were rejected.

## Augustine's other disputes

Although in Augustine's day Arianism was dying within the Empire, his great dogmatic treatise on the Trinity was in fact to be of great use when western Christians were later confronted with the Arianism of the barbarians. Augustine is firmly in the western theological tradition in beginning his theology from the idea of the unity of God, and then proceeding to explain the threefold nature of the Godhead. He rejects the eastern view that saw Father, Son and Spirit as three separate entities of the same substance (as with three human beings sharing a common humanity). He avoids the danger of blurring the distinction between the Persons, however, by describing the differences in terms of function (e.g. the Father is the Father because He begets the Son). Augustine's most important and original contribution to the doctrine of the Trinity is his use of analogies with the human soul to describe the relationship of the Persons. He uses a variety of analogies to describe this, although he recognizes that all are severely limited. Father, Son and Spirit are at one time likened to the One who loves, the Object of love, and the Love which unites them. On another occasion he describes the Trinity in terms of being, knowing and willing. It is here, in searching for a description which will illuminate the already agreed orthodoxy, that Augustine made his greatest contribution to Trinitarian doctrine.

The controversy which evoked Augustine's greatest work was the clash with paganism. Even in Augustine's day pagan criticism of Christianity was far from dead, and it was given added stimulus when Alaric the Visigoth captured Rome in 410. People openly asked why, when the Roman Empire had only recently adopted Christianity as its sole official religion, the God of the Christians had failed to protect the capital city. The nostalgic intellectuals looked back to the days of Rome's greatness when the pagan deities were assiduously worshipped. Augustine was stirred to reply, and over a period of fourteen years he produced his greatest work, called *The City of God*.[6]

Augustine begins by going back into history. He shows that the greatness of Rome was not due to its worship of the gods of paganism. He goes further, and even questions whether the Roman desire for world domination was in fact good. Augustine would have had no patience with someone like Eusebius of Caesarea, who viewed the Christianized Empire under Constantine as God's kingdom come on earth. Indeed, he would be more in line with the Old Testament prophets when he viewed the barbarian invasions as God's judgment on sinful society. But even when dealing with Alaric's capture of Rome, Augustine points out that it was an example of God's mercy, since He allowed a fairly restrained Arian Christian to enter the capital city for three days, having a year or so previously saved the city from the attack of the pagan hordes of Radagaisus.

Having dealt a blow against those who felt that Christianity should be an insurance policy against all perils, Augustine then goes on to outline where the real battle in fact lies. It is a moral battle between the forces of good and evil. It has taken place since the beginning of the world, and will be terminated only with the destruction of the devil and his servants at the time of the last judgment. Until that time, the two states are intermingled and cannot be extricated from one another. Followers of God and followers of the devil are mixed up together, and even in the Christian church there is no certainty that all church members are also members of the 'city of God'. In this point Augustine avoided the pitfall into which many

[6] Several editions, including a one-volume edition (1972) in the Penguin Classics series.

Apologists fell when they made the 'city of God' to be coterminous with the visible church.

Within this clear-sighted vision one can see various elements of Augustine's theology. The mixed nature of the church reflects his clash with Donatism. The cosmic battle between good and evil has echoes of his controversy with the Manichees. When he rejects an equation of the 'city of God' with the church, one can hear echoes of the Pelagian controversy, and the fact that God saves whom He will. But above all, this work saved western Christianity from becoming the preserve of Roman nationalism. Augustine's theology and the collapse of the Western Empire ensured that western Christianity would be a faith capable of transcending national barriers and giving a spiritual unity to believers of many different backgrounds.

## The collapse of the Western Roman Empire

Although Augustine lived in a Roman world till his death in 430, the collapse of Roman power in the West in fact dates from the death of the emperor Theodosius in 395. Before that year was out, the Danube frontier had been irreparably breached. In the Western Empire it was the barbarian general Stilicho (a Vandal by race), who was most effective in preserving even some territory for the feeble emperor Honorius (son of Theodosius). But Stilicho could not prevent the great barbarian influx across the Rhine on New Year's Eve 406. He did, however, halt the invading hordes of Radagaisus when they descended into Italy, scattering them with great slaughter at the Battle of Faesulae. For these benefits he was accused of treason and executed by his despicable imperial master (408).

With Stilicho dead, there was nothing left to prevent any barbarian chieftain who wished to do so from taking Rome. But the barbarians who had invaded the Empire were far from savages, and they were far more interested in settling on fertile lands where they could live in peace than in destroying ancient monuments like Rome. When Alaric, king of the Visigoths, eventually entered Rome in 410,[7] he stayed only three days, because he had come to an already starving city which could not feed his large army. The damage

[7] Further good discussion of the end of the Western Empire in S. Perowne, *The End of the Roman World* (Hodder, 1966) pp. 56ff.

**Flavius Stilicho, Roman general under the emperor Honorius.** He was executed by Honorius in 408.

which he did was strictly limited. His soldiers were mainly Arians, and they fraternized with the Christians in Rome. One Gothic officer, finding an elderly Roman lady trying to conceal some of the church plate in her house, insisted on escorting her and the treasure to the safety of a church outside the walls. Quite a bit of the murder and looting, in fact, seems to have been done by Roman slaves who seized on this opportunity to take vengeance on their masters.

Alaric soon left Rome and headed southwards, making an abortive attempt to cross to North Africa. North Africa was the great source of grain for the city of Rome, and was the obvious place where Alaric could settle his hungry tribesmen. Failing in this aim, his people returned north through Italy and thence to France and Spain. Alaric himself died later that year in North Italy, and was succeeded in 410 by another chieftain called Athaulf. This man had attempted to give his position some legitimacy by marrying Galla Placidia, the daughter of the late emperor Theodosius. Athaulf, and most of the invading barbarians, were aiming to take over rather than to destroy the Roman Empire. Hence they settled,

The mausoleum of Galla Placidia, wife of Constantius II, in Ravenna.

usually only partially dispossessing the Roman landowners, and taking over much of the imperial machinery. Meanwhile, Honorius, the western emperor, continued in nominal power; although it was usually the general-in-chief, known as the 'master of the soldiers', who exercised the real power. Athaulf might have forged a union between Roman and Goth, but he died in 415, after only five years in power. Galla Placidia returned to Rome, and there married the 'masters of the soldiers', Constantius. He played off one set of barbarians against another with some success, and on his death in 425 Galla Placidia became regent for their son, Valentinian III, who was still only a small child.

At this point in time, the Western Empire was divided among the barbarians as follows. The Visigoths held the South of France and part of Spain. The remainder of Spain was being contested between the Suevi and the Vandals, until the Vandals crossed over to North Africa and the Suevi were pushed into the northern corner by the Visigoths. Northern France was in the hands of the Franks, while the Saxons were beginning to gain a foothold in Britain. Much of the Balkans was occupied by the Ostrogoths and other tribes who had been pushed westwards by the pressure from the Huns.

It is not often realized how small in fact were the forces of barbarians who invaded the Western Empire. Even when they settled down they would form only about 10% of the population. When Gaiseric the Vandal took his tribes over to Africa (429) and completely subdued it in 439, they totalled only 80,000, including women and children! Second, it should be realized that with a few exceptions the barbarians were reasonably friendly towards Christians and were often partially Romanized themselves. Their law codes contained an admixture of Roman and barbarian law, and as time went on the Roman elements came to predominate. So after the initial shock of invasion, many areas found themselves with two different sets of people living side by side in relative harmony. There were two exceptions to this, however. In Britain, the Angles and Saxons effectively obliterated Roman civilization in the eastern part of the islands. In North Africa the trouble had a slightly different source. The Vandals under Gaiseric were Arians, and they persecuted orthodox Christians most savagely. There is some reason to believe that certain of the Donatists threw in their lot with the Arians against the 'Catholic' Christians.

**Mosaic decoration inside the mausoleum of Galla Placidia.** Notice the bookcase in the bottom left-hand corner.

Before the barbarian kingdoms could settle down, however, there was one more great threat facing all of Europe. The first invaders were mainly dispossessed peasant tribes who had been driven westward by the nomadic Huns. Now the Huns came westwards themselves. Unlike the Goths, Vandals and Franks, who were Germanic tribes, the Huns were Asiatic. They were horse-riding nomads who originated from the steppes of central Asia, and they inspired horror even in the other barbarians. Typical of this feeling is the description of their leader Attila:[8] 'Short in stature, with a broad chest and largish head, tiny eyes, a thin beard flecked with white, a flat nose and repulsive colour, showing signs of his (Asiatic) origin.' Repulsive as they were to civilized people, they were greatly valued as soldiers. The Roman generals Stilicho and Constantius had earlier hired Hun contingents as mercenaries to ward off barbarian invaders from Italy, and Aetius, the 'master of the soldiers' who succeeded Constantius, was the son of a Roman father and a Hunnish mother.

In the earlier years of the fifth century, the Huns had exacted ruinous tribute from the Eastern Roman Empire as the price for not invading. Then, under their leader Attila, they turned westwards through the Balkans and South Germany. As the horde crossed the Rhine, Aetius struggled to gather together sufficient troops to meet them. He had formerly used Huns to restrain the growing power of the Visigoths. Now he formed a hasty alliance with the Visigoths and Franks to halt Attila the Hun. In 451 the combined forces of the Romans and Goths and their allies clashed with Attila's horsemen on the Mauriac plain near Chalons, in central France. The Huns were defeated. Aetius could have annihilated them there and then, but he left them in their weakened state, hoping to use them as a counter-balance against the still-present threat of the Visigoths. Aetius miscalculated, however, for Attila still had the strength to cross the Alps and invade Italy. He was dissuaded from attacking Rome only by an embassy led by the bishop of Rome, Leo the Great. This was the Huns' last success, however, for their power was swiftly waning. Before the year was out, Attila was dead (he died of an apoplectic fit during his wedding celebrations). The remnants of the Huns retreated back across the Danube, where they were torn to pieces by various barbarian tribes. The West could breathe again.

[8] Jordanes, *Getica* xxxv.

**Valentinian III, emperor 425–455.** A coin in the British Museum, London.

Though he returned with his army to Italy, Aetius did not live to enjoy the fame of his victory at Chalons for long. The feeble Valentinian III had him murdered in 453, whereupon Aetius' soldiers murdered Valentinian III. With him the dynasty of Theodosius ended, and also any effective Roman rule in Italy. By 455 government in Italy was so weak that Gaiseric the Vandal was able to come over from North Africa and plunder the city of Rome. Various ephemeral emperors came and went, while the real power was wielded by various 'masters of the soldiers' of barbarian origin. Eventually Odoacer, a Herulian general, deposed the last emperor (Romulus Augustulus) in 476.

The final major shift in barbarian power occurred in 493, when Odoacer, who had made himself king of Italy, was killed by Theodoric the Ostrogoth, who had come from the East and who then set up the Ostrogothic kingdom of Italy. The Western Empire, for much of the fifth century a name rather than a reality, was now officially extinct.[9] In its place were various kingdoms of Germanic barbarians, most of them nominally professing Arian Christianity. In the next chapter we shall see how the orthodox Christians of the Empire reacted to the world-shattering upheavals of the barbarian invasions.

[9] Theodoric did give nominal acknowledgment to the emperor in Constantinople as his overlord. This had been his pretext for invading Italy to depose the 'usurper' Odoacer. But for all practical purposes he was an independent monarch.

# 7

# Christians in crisis

When the Western Roman Empire eventually collapsed,[1] those alive at the time did not immediately realize the full meaning of events. For 150 years there had been sporadic invasions and crises, but always there had been someone who could retrieve the situation. The realization only gradually dawned that this time there would be no rescue act. And one can hardly underestimate the shock of such a realization. For it was inconceivable that there could be any world that was not a Roman world. Rome had existed for (traditionally) 1,150 years, and for the last 450 years had dominated Western Europe. For the last 200 years everyone in the Empire had been Roman citizens.[2] Now all this was collapsing. It was the unthinkable catastrophe.

For a while, some refused to believe the worst. At Rome the poet Claudian could celebrate Stilicho's victories and look forward to a revitalizing of Rome. It is unlikely that Claudian lived long after Stilicho's fall in 408, so he was spared the sight of Alaric's capture of Rome. The Christian poet Prudentius, in Spain (died 405), had similar hopes that Rome would recover and remain mistress of the world. Even after the capture of Rome by Alaric, some could hope for a revival of Roman power. But soon it dawned on them that this would not happen. Some continued to struggle for the survival of the old order. Others, perhaps more wisely, set about the task of living with the new conditions.

[1] For further reading, see J. M. Wallace-Hadrill, *The Barbarian West 400–1000* (Hutchinson, new edition 1967); R. W. Southern, *The Making of the Middle Ages* (Hutchinson, new edition 1967).
[2] Since the emperor Caracalla had extended citizenship to all free men in the Empire.

**A silver bridal casket, dating from about 400.** The inscription on the lip starts with the Christian Alpha and Omega and chi-ro symbols. The inscription reads: Secundus and Projecta live in Christ'. This is possibly one of a number of silver things which were hidden before the barbarian invasion of Rome.

### Salvian: a Christian Jeremiah?

The reaction to the barbarian invasions was varied, but at least some saw these invasions as the judgment of God on their corrupt society. Such was the opinion of Salvian, a presbyter of Marseilles. With the zeal of an Old Testament prophet, Salvian castigates his contemporaries for their many vices. Then, in a spirit reminiscent of Tacitus romantically admiring the 'noble savages' of Germany four centuries previously, he eulogizes the virtues of the barbarian tribes. But Salvian had a short-sighted vision. He might see the barbarians as the 'scourge of God', but he did not give much consideration to them as people needing to be converted.[3] In his outlook there is something of the literary man admiring the 'noble savage' at second hand, while wincing at the prospect of having to deal personally with them. Yet even so, his view has more to commend it than the bankrupt idea that the kingdom of God and the Empire were coterminous.

[3] He saw the need theoretically, when he called them pagans and heretics. *CCC*, p. 345.

### Germanus of Auxerre

Another outstanding Christian leader, Germanus, bishop of Auxerre, reacted in a more typical way to the barbarian invasions. Germanus was born in Gaul in 378,[4] and went to Rome to study law. It was only when he returned home in the turbulent times after the barbarian invasions that he was called on by the people of Auxerre to become bishop. In spite of the fact that a horde of barbarian tribes had crossed the Rhine and flooded right across France and into Spain, Germanus found that in Gaul there was a considerable amount of the Roman civil structure left. His early administrative experience stood him in good stead as he grappled with doctrinal, political and even military problems. Germanus was an enthusiastic supporter of the monastic movement, and from 418 (when he became bishop) he encouraged his fellow clergy to live in a Christian commune along with him. With great wisdom he managed to combine the devotion to God characteristic of the desert fathers with the practical zeal needed in these troubled times.

Soon he was in demand. Legations came from Britain, seeking

[4] Our main source for Germanus is the *Life* written by a certain Constantius in the latter part of the fifth century.

**A mosaic picture of Theodoric's imperial Byzantine palace,** in the Church of S. Apollinare Nuovo, Ravenna.

help from the Gallic bishops to stem the spread of Pelagianism. Germanus and Lupus of Troyes were sent. The Britain to which they came was still relatively untroubled by the barbarians. Rich and powerful churchmen, both orthodox and heretical, met them. The two Gallic bishops were able to preach widely and to hold synods to deal with the heresy. But soon Germanus' other talents were called for, and the theologian turned soldier. A sudden raid was made by a combined force of Saxons and Picts. Germanus took charge of the local forces, successfully ambushed the invaders in a narrow valley, and scattered them into headlong flight with shouts of 'Alleluia!' from his army (most of whom had only recently been baptized).

Despite such success, Germanus needed to return to Britain later on to fight the doctrinal enemy, Pelagianism, again. He also travelled widely in France, going as far south as Arles, where he was warmly received by the bishop, Hilary. He also successfully intervened to prevent a barbarian force from ravaging Armorica (modern Brittany). In this episode, he found himself dealing (with the help of an interpreter) with a barbarian commander who was acting under the orders of Aetius, the commander of the Roman troops in the West. Aetius had sent this contingent of barbarian

mercenaries to suppress a revolt of the Armoricans against the central Roman government. Germanus succeeded in persuading the barbarian general to take his forces back home.

Late in life, in his sixties, he set off on his greatest journey of all. He went to Ravenna in North Italy on behalf of his people. The journey was protracted because all along the way church leaders insisted that the famous preacher should stay several weeks with them. At last, however, he reached the imperial court at Ravenna (Rome had long since been abandoned as too dangerous for the ineffective western emperors). The redoubtable Galla Placidia and her weak son Valentinian III listened to his plea for no reprisals to be taken against Armorica. Before Germanus could get a favourable response, however, a fresh Armorican revolt broke out against the Ravenna government. Soon after, in 448, he died. Such was the veneration in which he was held that his friends embalmed his corpse and carried it back to Auxerre for burial.

Germanus of Auxerre, the energetic fighter against heretics and barbarians alike, became the most popular saint of the Dark Ages along with Martin of Tours. Nonetheless, in some ways Germanus was still a man of the Roman past. Yet it is at least possible that he met as a visitor to the monastery at Auxerre a man who was to be an effective evangelist among the barbarians; none other than St Patrick himself. For Germanus merely resisted barbarians on a military level, but Patrick went among them to lead them to Christ.

## Patrick: evangelist among barbarians

The story of Patrick is bedevilled by a mammoth accretion of later legend.[5] Fortunately, we do possess two works which he himself wrote. There is his *Confession*, written near the end of his life to justify his work, and also the *Letter to Coroticus*. A later *Life of Patrick* by a certain Muirchu (*fl. c.* 675), may contain some additional useful information among a vast amount of hagiographical invention. The remaining material (such as the *Life* by Tirechan, and many later legends) is evidence for the widespread cult of Patrick later on, but is useless for historical purposes.

Patrick came from a nominally Christian family who had estates somewhere in the West of England. His father and grandfather

[5] For an up-to-date, if somewhat pessimistic, assessment of the sources for Patrick, see Hanson, *Saint Patrick*, pp. 72–105.

both held office in the local church, but their spiritual stature seems to have been small. Patrick passed his childhood in this peaceful environment Then, while in his teens, he was captured by Irish raiders, and sold as a slave in Ireland. It was while in Ireland that he came to a personal knowledge of God. While working as a shepherd he had time to think over the Christian teaching he had received as a child. As a result, he was deeply converted; and the marvel of God's goodness to him, a sinner, became the theme for all his life. Subsequently he escaped from slavery by joining the crew of a ship, and after being shipwrecked on the British coast he eventually returned to his family. It is possible that he then joined some monastic community, and as we have earlier mentioned, he may have travelled abroad to Auxerre for training.[6] But Patrick was the first to admit that he was not a great scholar, and the only book that he knew well was his Bible.

After some years, Patrick had a vision, in which some of his former friends in Ireland begged him to come over and preach the gospel to them. Patrick responded by going back to Ireland. He seems to have had the backing of the churches in Britain, although there was some opposition from those who considered him unsuitable for the task. At all events, he seems to have been ordained as bishop, and sent to work in the North of Ireland.

The picture is made more complicated because the chronicler Prosper of Aquitaine, an official in the bishop of Rome's administration, states that in 430 pope Celestine sent a certain Palladius 'to the Irish who believed in Christ'. We do not know if Patrick and Palladius met, or if (as some later writers suggest) Palladius found the task too hard and gave up. At all events, Patrick seems to have worked on his own for many years. This, however, did not mean that he was out of contact with mainland Britain. His letter to Coroticus is a stinging rebuke to a nominally Christian king of lowland Scotland. Coroticus, while on a piratical raid on Ireland, had attacked a group of Patrick's newly baptized converts, killing some and enslaving others. Patrick threatened the erring king with ecclesiastical discipline. A hint of Patrick's contact with mainland clerics is contained in Muirchu's tale of a certain McCuil, cast adrift by Patrick and two other clerics to find the place where he

[6] Later legends concerning his visiting Lérins or Rome are quite worthless, and some (e.g. Hanson) doubt whether he ever travelled even as far as Northern France.

should be bishop. Behind this story may be the truth that Patrick and two British colleagues consecrated McCuil or Maughold as the first bishop of the Isle of Man. Further, the writing of Patrick's *Confession* was occasioned by a demand that he return to Britain to face some kind of church synod, a demand that he declined on the grounds that he could not leave the work in Ireland.

How did Patrick operate? From his own writings, we have hints that he gained the co-operation of the various tribal chiefs in Ireland, on occasion with gifts of money. Then he preached freely, gathering his converts into small groups, and ordaining clergy to pastor them. He mentions with considerable pride that some people of noble birth had been converted. Although it is not certain whether Patrick was a monk or not, he certainly approved of Christians who took on themselves vows to live specially ascetic lives, though in his writings he does not mention the founding of any monastic communities. The inspiration for Irish monasticism seems to have come later on, from people who were fired by the examples of the hermits of the Egyptian desert.

Patrick died somewhere around 460 to 470. His deep faith in God was his sole support in an arduous struggle. In spite of occasional imprisonment and frequent unpopularity, he stuck to his task of telling the harsh barbarians of the graciousness of Christ. His small stock of learning was entirely centred in the Bible. But in that book he read of God who graciously receives sinners, and this God marvellously used Patrick for over thirty years in Ireland. Patrick, as we hear him speaking in his own writings, is one man who really merits the title 'saint'. Small wonder that succeeding generations in Ireland loaded him with all sorts of fantastic miraculous powers, credited him with appointing hundreds of bishops and made him founder of virtually every Christian community in the land.

## Leo and the rise of the Roman papacy

While Patrick was carrying out his lonely toil in Ireland, the church in Rome, at the centre of the Empire, gained a leader who was to be the architect of that church's greatness. Under the 'Christian Empire', the church at Rome held great prestige, as being the chief patriarchate in the Western Empire. Members of that church could look back to Peter and Paul as the traditional founders. Even though that story was unlikely to be fully true, Rome in the fourth century stood alongside Alexandria, Antioch and Constantinople as one of the four great patriarchates of the Empire. As the Western Empire came to its last flowering in the reign of Theodosius, the bishops of Rome strengthened their position as the court of appeal for disputes within the western churches. They held synods to give judgment on doctrinal issues (such as Pelagianism). In this they were simply like the other great patriarchates. Early in the fifth century, Innocent felt within his rights to tell a neighbouring bishop how to arrange certain church ceremonies so as to be in accord with the practice of Rome.[7] But the power of the church at Rome was not unchallenged in the West. In particular, the North African churches resisted Roman directives when disorderly North African clerics had tried to get support for their causes by appealing to Rome. With the departure of the imperial court to Ravenna, however, and with the general collapse of the Western Empire, the bishop of Rome found himself stepping into a power-vacuum. The man who exploited this situation to the advantage of the see of Rome was pope Leo the Great.

Leo came from Tuscany, and had long been involved in ecclesiastical affairs before he became bishop of Rome in 440. By this time, not only were the barbarians settled in much of the Western Empire, but a rift had opened up between the Greek-speaking East and the Latin-speaking West of the Roman world, so that the churches of the two parts of the Empire had little meaningful contact with each other. This meant that there was in the West no effective counterbalance to Rome, especially since the North African churches were effectively prevented from acquiring an independent position because they were under the domination of the Arian Gaiseric, king of the Vandals.

Leo's aim was to enhance the power and prestige of the see of Rome. His theological justification for this was the scattered group of references to Peter's leadership of the apostles in the New Testament.[8] Leo took this to mean that all the succeeding bishops of Rome were inheritors of Peter's primacy over all Christian churches. Even when dealing with his colleagues in the eastern

[7] Innocent's letter to Decentius, bishop of Eugubium (Gubbio); extracts in Kidd, *Documents Illustrative of the History of the Church*, vol. ii, pp. 162–3.

[8] He made great use of Matthew 16:18: 'You are Peter . . .', putting much greater reliance on this proof-text than anyone before.

patriarchates, Leo assumed that he was acting for Peter as leader of the apostolic band. As a buttress to his theological views, Leo was also ready to use legal decisions of church councils. He used the canon of the Council of Sardica about appeal to Rome,[9] passed it off as a decree from the ecumenical Council of Nicaea, and tried to give it a universal application. He also invoked the support of the secular powers, when he obtained a decree from the emperor Valentinian III granting him primacy over the churches in Gaul;[1] although it must be said that such a decree was not very effective in practice. But Leo's aim was clear. In the face of the barbarian inroads and general social collapse, he intended to build a spiritual empire with the church of Rome as its head.[2]

Leo used his position as hearer of appeals to restrain the power of the church at Arles. When the bishop of Arles, Hilary, had deposed two bishops, these men appealed to Rome. With the help of Aetius, commander-in-chief of the Roman army, Leo had them restored, and used the opportunity to get an imperial decree to limit Hilary's powers of intervention in the affairs of the other churches in Gaul. When Leo tried to influence events in the East, however, he was less successful. In 431, the Council of Ephesus had condemned Nestorius for his views on the Person of Christ.[3] In reaction against Nestorius, however, there had been a move in the East towards a view of Jesus which almost discounted His humanity. The leader of this movement (later termed Monophysitism) was the pope of Alexandria, Dioscorus. His principal opponent was Flavian, pope of Constantinople. In spite of Leo's dislike of the pretensions of the see of Constantinople, he gave his support to Flavian. But the eastern emperor Theodosius II and the chamberlain Chrysaphius were on Dioscorus' side. The result was that at the Synod of Ephesus in 449 Flavian and his supporters were condemned for heresy. Leo had sent a lengthy doctrinal statement to the council, but it was ignored. Dioscorus was supported by a violent rabble, who beat up Flavian so badly that he died shortly afterwards. Leo could only fume with rage, and declare that the Council of Ephesus was a 'Robber Synod'.

[9] See above, pp. 57–8.
[1] Giles, *Documents Illustrating Papal Authority*, pp. 286–8.
[2] Specimens of Leo's opinions in Giles, *op. cit.*, pp. 279–84.
[3] See above, pp. 91–3, and below pp. 191–3.

Leo's righteous anger, however, was soon appeased. Theodosius II died in a riding accident. Chrysaphius fell from power. And the new emperor reopened the debate. Leo was unable to attend the new council at Chalcedon in 451, because the Huns were at that moment bursting into Western Europe. But his doctrinal statement was read and loudly applauded by the bishops at Chalcedon. They decided in favour of a formula admitting two natures in Christ.[4] Next, however, much to Leo's fury, the bishops at Chalcedon officially decreed that Constantinople should have precedence over Alexandria and Antioch, so making its church equal in importance to the church of the old imperial capital, Rome. Leo had to be content with the fact that the eastern bishops had officially decided to agree with his orthodoxy.

Meanwhile, in the West, Leo was having to deal with the full impact of the barbarians. In 451 Attila the Hun had been defeated, but he moved into Italy with his army. Leo found himself as the chief civil representative in Rome, and as such he led a deputation to Attila. We do not know what happened when they met, but Attila turned back northwards and Rome was spared from being ravaged by the Huns. Later hagiographers make much of this incident, as though Leo by his spiritual power had overcome the barbarian. It is much more likely that he told Attila that if he came south his army would only starve, as there was already insufficient food in Italy for the people who lived there.

A few years later, Leo had an even more formidable enemy to face. Valentinian III was murdered in 454, and in the next year Gaiseric, the Vandal king of North Africa, calmly sailed up to Rome to plunder the city. Leo's pleas managed to save the city from the full horrors of Vandal pillage, but even so the Vandals stripped the city of all the valuables they could seize (even to the gold roof tiles of the Pantheon) and they carried many of the Romans away as slaves. But although the Vandals might pillage the physical city of Rome, Leo's spiritual edifice was such that it would endure this and many more similar disasters. Leo the Great died in 461, having used his time as bishop of Rome to transform the Roman see from being merely one of the four great patriarchates to being the potential leader of Christendom. The foundations of the mediaeval papacy had already been laid.

[4] As against the views of Dioscorus and his friends, who insisted on one nature, the divine, and were hence called Monophysites.

**The Pantheon at Rome.** Gaisaric the Vandal stripped the gold tiles from the roof in 455.

## The Vandal persecution in North Africa

The Vandals who troubled Leo's latter years had become a great power within the Empire. In 429 they crossed from Spain to Africa under their king, Gaiseric. Although numbering only about 80,000 in all, the Vandals speedily conquered North Africa as far as Libya. This happened during the last years of the great theologian Augustine, who actually died while they were beseiging his city of Hippo in 430. Soon they had established an independent Vandal kingdom, and they ruled not only North Africa but also Sicily, Sardinia and Corsica. Unlike most of the other barbarians, the Vandals were both anti-Roman and strongly pro-Arian. Their effect on the people of North Africa was therefore devastating.

Much of our information comes from the writing of Victor of

Vita,[5] a Catholic bishop who was exiled by the Vandals. Writing about sixty years after the first invasion, he chronicles the trials of the orthodox Christians in North Africa. The Vandals made a determined effort to exterminate the orthodox churches of North Africa, and to set up in their place an Arian hierarchy. Many clergy fled at their approach. Some were enslaved, and life was made difficult for the remainder. Churches refused to appoint new bishops while the existing bishops were still living in exile. Meanwhile, Gaiseric gave all his support to state Arianism.

At Carthage, the bishop Quodvultdeus was sent into exile. There was an interregnum, until in response to pleas from Valentinian III Gaiseric allowed the orthodox Deogratias to be appointed bishop. Deogratias managed to hold things together, and even ransomed captives taken during Gaiseric's famous raid on Rome in 455. But the Arians hated him, and when he died three years later he had to be buried in secret to avoid pro-Arian riots. Victor of Vita says that there were 164 bishops in Africa,[6] but by the time he was writing there were only three of these surviving. It is probable that there was no orthodox bishop in Carthage after the death of Deogratias until the eastern emperor Zeno (474–491) interceded for the Catholics and Eugenius was appointed—a period of twenty years!

By this time the ruthless Gaiseric was dead. But his son Huneric was an equally determined persecutor. And apparently the Arian hierarchy was fairly well versed in theology, for Huneric summoned both sides to a staged debate, afterwards issuing a decree setting out as official doctrine Constantius' 'Dated Creed' of 359![7] This was followed by fresh persecution, and many exiles (Victor of Vita among them) fled east to Constantinople, where they agitated for help to be sent to their persecuted brethren.

Although the Vandals were so set on destroying the North African churches, they could not afford to disrupt the Roman administration of the region. A series of wooden tablets (the *Tablettes Albertini*)[8] dating from the Vandal period show that civil and social life continued in its normal Roman way, even under the

[5] In his work *On the Persecution of the Vandals*.

[6] He must be counting only orthodox ones, and not Donatists.

[7] It is quite astonishing that barbarians with only vague links with Latin culture should be conversant with a creed issued over 100 years previously in Greek!

[8] Details in Susan Raven, *Rome in Africa* (Evans, 1969), pp. 155–8.

barbarians. How far the Donatists co-operated with the Vandals is a moot point. Huneric was certainly helped by one ex-Donatist, a certain Nicasius. But there is remarkably little to suggest that Vandal Arianism was whole-heartedly welcomed by the Donatists. Repeated persecution coming on an already weakened church, however, could do only harm. The North African churches did not recover from the Vandal repression, even though North Africa was ultimately reconquered by Justinian, the sixth-century eastern emperor. The end of the Vandals is very instructive. They had come to North Africa as vigorous barbarian conquerors, and they settled to live off the province, as overlords keeping themselves separate from the existing inhabitants by a rigid apartheid. They lived off the other civilizations by piracy, without making any positive contribution themselves. Such a situation was enervating, and when in 533 Belisarius brought Justinian's forces over to North Africa the Vandals could put up only a token resistance. His forces swept them away without trace, and the further challenge to Roman rule in North Africa was to be only from the desert tribes, not from the alien barbarian invaders.

## Sidonius Apollinaris: Roman gentleman turned bishop

When the barbarian tide swept into France and Spain it did not flood over everything equally. The numbers of the barbarians were not large enough to overrun every area, and some places remained surprisingly undisturbed. One such area was the Auvergne, in central France, the home of Sidonius Apollinaris.[9]

Sidonius was a strange mixture of Roman man of letters and godly Christian bishop. He was born in 432, when the barbarian invasions had already passed their first stage. He received a traditional Roman education in classics and rhetoric, and his family seem to have been cheerfully oblivious of the chaos around them. In 455, after Gaiseric's sack of Rome, he went there in the entourage of the ephemeral emperor Avitus, and was involved in public life until 461, when he retired to his estates in the Auvergne. By this time France had been broken up into various separate

[9] C. E. Stevens, *Sidonius Apollinaris and his Age* (OUP, 1933), gives a good idea of the man and his work. Specimens of his letters, our main source of information, in Kidd, *Documents Illustrative of the History of the Church*, vol. ii, pp. 323-7.

dominions. In the North the Franks had settled on both sides of the Rhine. A sub-Roman kingdom ruled by the Gallo-Roman nobles Aegidius and Syagrius had its centre at Soissons. Brittany was a separate and dissident area, while Euric the Visigothic king ruled most of South and West France. The Auvergne and parts of eastern and Mediterranean France were still nominally part of the Western Empire. Sidonius lived the life of a country gentleman, corresponding with his friends, writing poems and surveying his estates, with a bland unconcern for what was happening. His Christianity was quite nominal and bothered him little. Then, in 467, he went as emissary from the Gallo-Roman nobles of the Auvergne to Rome. There he found himself called on to pronounce a panegyric on the emperor, and was made city prefect for a year. All this after Rome had been occupied twice by barbarians; it speaks well for the resilience of Roman institutions. Sidonius basked in this illusory glory until his return to the Auvergne in 469.

Then occurred the event which changed his life. Euric, the Visigothic king, moved against the Auvergne. The church at Clermont was without a bishop, and the citizens elected Sidonius to the post. The elegant, literary country gentleman turned himself to his new task with commendable vigour. His grasp of Christian theology may well have been limited, but he was not unacquainted with the classical virtues of justice, diligence and even courage. He visited the outlying districts, exhorted the clergy, and also took on the tasks of civil administrator, judge and church treasurer. His eloquence was such that when he came to one church and found that the service book had been removed, he extemporized the whole service, to the amazement of the congregation.

Sidonius was a man who knew his limitations. He refrained from comment in the Semi-Pelagian controversy because of lack of theological know-how, and he was even known to call for a break during prayers in order to have refreshments. In practical matters, however, his generosity was such that he would even give away his domestic silver plate to help the poor, much to his wife's annoyance. He took great pains to see that the churches in his area were well pastored, even if at times he appointed able organizers rather than holy monks.

In 471, war came to Clermont. Euric's forces attacked, and for the next four years Sidonius organized the defence. He had only local levies to help him, and strategically Clermont was a poor site to defend. But in spite of some of the outlying houses of the town being burnt by Euric's troops, Sidonius contrived to keep the barbarians at bay for four years! He even slipped off to Lyons on one occasion, in order to get famine relief for the starving citizens.

Then, in 475, came the bitterest blow. The nonentities at Rome ceded the Auvergne to Euric over Sidonius' head, in exchange for the barbarian king's promise not to invade Italy. Sidonius was furious, especially since he had been betrayed by those whom he had tried to serve. Euric took over in Clermont, and Sidonius was exiled to Carcassonne. He was imprisoned for a while, but his greatest complaint about his confinement was that he had to endure the interminable gossip of two old Gothic women right under his window! After going to Euric's court and making his peace with him, Sidonius was allowed to return to his church at Clermont. But he returned a prematurely aged and broken man. Further misfortune was to come when his son went to Rome and joined in an abortive revolt against the emperor, and was subsequently executed. Sidonius remained in Clermont, preparing his letters for publication, and trying to keep order in his church. The well-intentioned Roman man of letters had thrown in his lot with the Christian church, and in so doing had been called to serve in a most heartbreaking time. He saw clearly the decline of Roman learning, and in one letter bitterly lamented that 'no-one ever writes good Latin nowadays'. In a period of chaos he did his best for his congregation and his fellow countrymen. Although he died a disillusioned man some time in the 480s, he was soon widely regarded as a saint. Perhaps to Sidonius Apollinaris, rather than to anyone else, belongs the title 'the last of the Romans'.

## The 'conversion' of the Franks

Sidonius died during what was the darkest period for the western churches. In 486 Clovis, the pagan king of the Franks, destroyed the last Roman enclave when he defeated and killed Syagrius, the king of Soissons.[1] Italy was by that time under Odoacer the Herulian. If the barbarian kings made any pretension to religion, they were Arians. This was a time when Christians had to hold on and hope for better times. But the tide was turning in strange directions.

[1] Most of our information comes from Gregory of Tours, *History of the Franks*.

Clovis was married to a Christian, Clothilde, a Burgundian princess. In fact, much of the progress of Christianity among the barbarians must be credited to the influence of Christian women who eventually won over their barbaric husbands. Clothilde had spent many years trying to convince Clovis that he should become a Christian. But Clovis preferred to trust in his ability with his battle-axe. He successfully conquered all of northern France, and then turned his attention eastwards to the Alemanni. This was a much tougher proposition, and during one particularly tense battle he vowed to serve the Christian God if he won. After his victory, Clovis kept his promise. He went to Remigius, the bishop of Rheims, and along with a great crowd of his warriors asked for baptism. One can dimly imagine the feelings of the bishop. Here he had a crowd of completely illiterate barbarians, volunteering to support the Christian cause. And he already knew that Clovis was a ruthless man. For, after the capture of Soissons, Clovis had wanted to return a special chalice to the church. But one of his warriors had claimed it as part of the normal booty, and had split it in two to prevent Clovis having his way. Clovis' rejoinder had been to wait for the next muster of the Frankish warriors, and then to bury his battle-axe in the head of the recalcitrant soldier, adding, 'That's what you did to the chalice at Soissons!'

Remigius took the only course open to him. He tried to instruct Clovis as much as he could, and prepared to baptize him. Clovis' understanding of the Gospels is illustrated by his reaction on hearing of Jesus' crucifixion. He was heard to remark that if he and his Franks had been there, it would have been a very different story. Remigius, for his part, had no illusions. When Clovis and his men came for baptism, Remigius addressed him with the words, 'Bow your head, Sicambrian;[2] adore what you have burnt, and burn what you once adored.' Such was the way in which Clovis became an 'orthodox Christian'.

The baptism of Clovis had an effect much larger than its spiritual content. Because he had aligned himself with orthox Christianity, he now had a network of supporters in many neighbouring territories. Catholic clergy looked upon him as a champion of the 'true faith' against the errors of Arianism, and Clovis readily saw himself in this new role. It should be said, however, that such a role had little

[2] The Sicambri were Clovis' clan.

if anything to do with New Testament Christianity. Having consolidated his position at home, Clovis moved against the Visigoths, and posing as the champion of orthodox Christianity he defeated them decisively at the battle of Vouillé in 511. An incident just before the battle shows Clovis giving vent to his real feelings. One of the soldiers seized a bale of hay from a farm belonging to the monastic community at Tours. Clovis had the man executed, on the grounds that he did not wish to anger St Martin just as he was going into battle.[3] Clovis drove the Visigoths back into Spain, leaving them only a small foothold along the Mediterranean coast. He would have siezed this too, but for the intervention of Theodoric the Ostrogoth, the powerful king of Italy. The Arian Theodoric viewed with concern the rise of Frankish power, but after his death the Ostrogoths were unable to prevent further Frankish expansion. Under Clovis' sons, the Franks conquered the kingdom of Burgundy, although on this occasion they could not pose as champions of Christian orthodoxy. Thanks to the efforts of bishop Avitus of Vienne, supported by many ladies of the Burgundian royal house, the kings of Burgundy had abandoned Arianism for orthodox Christianity. But this did not spare them from being overrun by the expansionist Franks, who were combining a profession of Christian orthodoxy with naked imperialism.

## Theodoric the Great

At the same time, in Italy, a strange alliance between Theodoric the Arian Ostrogoth and the Christian Roman nobles produced a final brief flowering of classical culture. Theodoric was by far the greatest of the barbarian kings who flourished in the days after the collapse of the Western Roman Empire. He had been brought up at Constantinople, and was both a skilful soldier and a consummate diplomat. His ability was such that eventually the eastern emperor, fearing his growing power, had seized on the excuse of sending him westwards, ostensibly to reconquer Italy for the Byzantine Empire. Theodoric had invaded Italy, and had treacherously murdered Odoacer, the ruling barbarian king, at Ravenna, after they had agreed to be co-rulers of Italy. With no rivals, he speedily became the king of all Italy, while still nominally owing allegiance to the eastern

[3] St Martin being the much venerated patron saint of Tours, where he had once been bishop. See above, pp. 110–13.

emperor. But although Theodoric was a ruthless king, he brought peace to Italy, and he even obtained the grudging admiration of the nobility of Rome. This was all the more amazing, since there were two factors, either of which alone might have provided an inseparable gulf between barbarian and Roman. He was a barbarian, trying to mingle with the blue-blooded Roman aristocracy. And he was an Arian, ruling over orthodox Christians.

Yet, in spite of these disadvantages, Theodoric's kingdom flourished. His erudite chief minister, Cassiodorus, wrote . a history of the Goths in order to commend the new ruler to the Romans. Under Theodoric the literary men of Rome flourished, and the church even tolerated its Arian overlord. Theodoric himself is credited with the extremely 'modern' statement that he could not compel belief by law. He refrained from persecuting his theological opponents, and interfered in the affairs of the church of Rome only when there was a disputed election for bishop. Even then, all he did was to ensure that an orderly election was held, and he then supported the candidate elected by the majority. Meanwhile, in

**The Basilica of S. Apollinare in Classe;** a typical Byzantine church interior.

Northern Italy, new churches were erected, classical in design; and at Ravenna in particular, attempts were made to rival the splendour of Byzantine mosaic decorations of churches. It was a brief, halcyon period. Two things caused it to end tragically.

First of all, the eastern emperor Justin (517-27) issued an edict against Arians. Second, Theodoric had no male heir to succeed him. These two facts combined to destroy his realm. On the receipt of the edict, Theodoric peremptorily ordered John, the bishop of Rome, to go to Constantinople and get the edict rescinded. With no enthusiasm, the bishop went. And although he did succeed in getting the harshest points of the edict modified, its main provisions in banning Arians from public office remained unchanged. Theodoric, now growing old, was infuriated. Thus the division between Arian and orthodox came back into the open. The Roman nobility found themselves viewed as a potential fifth column. Theodoric accused Symmachus[4] of plotting with Byzantium for his overthrow. Boethius, the most learned man of his day, declared that if Symmachus were guilty then so were all the Roman Senate. The vengeful Theodoric took this as a confession of guilt. Boethius was imprisoned for a year, and then tortured to death in 524. It was during his imprisonment that he wrote the classic *On the Consolation of Philosophy*. Cassiodorus retired some years later to his monastery on his Calabrian estates. Boethius and Cassiodorus were the very last in a line of classical scholars which lasted for 500 years since the reign of the first Roman emperor, Augustus. Meanwhile, Theodoric prepared to persecute the orthodox Christians out of existence. But he died before his edicts could be put into effect.

Theodoric was succeeded by his daughter Amalasuntha. But anarchy soon broke out, and she was deposed and murdered. This gave the signal for the eastern emperor Justinian to send his general Belisarius (535) and begin the reconquest of Italy which effectively destroyed not only Theodoric's kingdom but almost everything of value in Italy.

Theodoric is a truly tragic figure. Except for the last few years of his life, he might have been a model king. In the Germanic *Nibelungenlied*, indeed, he appears as the virtuous great king Dietrich von Bern.[5] He had been fast approaching a position where

---

[4] The great-grandson of the Symmachus who had pleaded for toleration of paganism against Ambrose (see above, pp. 80-1 ).

[5] Old German for 'Theodoric of Verona', so named after his capital city.

**The mausoleum of Theodoric the Great,** who died in 526.

church and state could co-exist as separate institutions, when circumstances beyond his control shattered the fragile concordat. That he had no male heir was an even greater disaster, for this condemned Italy to be a divided country for centuries to come.

## Caesarius of Arles

As we move into the times of Clovis and Theodoric the Great, a deep change has overtaken the western world. In a generation we have left the Roman world for the mediaeval. A comparison between Sidonius Apollinaris and Caesarius of Arles makes this point clear.

Caesarius is definitely the mediaeval churchman, even though he is in only the next generation after Sidonius. Born about 470, he went to Lérins as a monk in 490 (he never seems to have even thought of any other way of life). From Lérins he went to Arles, where he joined the bishop's special clerical entourage, and he became bishop of Arles in 503. Caesarius was an enthusiast for the strict monastic life, on one occasion becoming very unpopular with the monks of a certain monastery where he was cellarer because he was so grudging in his issue of wine. But although he had his own monastic community when bishop, Caesarius was anything but an otherworldly recluse. He was by turns pastor, politician and theologian, according to the needs of the situation.

When he became bishop, Arles was under the control of the Visigoths, and Caesarius had to visit their king in an effort to gain exemption from tribute for his city. Relations with the Visigoths were none too good, and he was even exiled for a short time on the charge of favouring the Catholic Burgundians rather than his Arian overlords. Although he had hoped, however, that the Franks might take over in Arles (they actually besieged the city in 507–8), Caesarius eventually found himself a subject of Theodoric the Great. Under Theodoric, Caesarius was in better favour, and had his 'diocese' extended; but with the collapse of Theodoric's kingdom he finally came under Frankish rule in 536, six years before his death.

Caesarius the theologian drew his learning from the western church fathers, and was active both against Arians and in the Semi-Pelagian controversy.[6] One of his anti-Arian moves was to persuade the Council of Vaison (529) to put certain Trinitarian additions into the liturgy (*e.g.* the threefold recital of 'Lord, have mercy upon us'). In 529 he presided at the Council of Orange, which condemned Semi-Pelagianism. Caesarius in the main favoured Augustine's view that faith was a free gift of God, unattainable by human effort. He diverged from some of Augustine's more extreme statements, however; in par-

[6] See above, pp. 114 and 147.

ticular he rejected Augustine's idea of predestination to damnation.

Caesarius as pastor turned his hand to many things. From 506 onwards, when he presided at the Council of Agde, he was active in getting some order into the multiplicity of church laws. At the same time, he was concerned that country clergy should be free to carry out their duties without hindrance. Some of the conservative clergy felt that only the town bishop should be allowed to preach and to administer church funds. Caesarius upheld the right of the country clergy to do these things, so making the beginnings of the parochial system. He himself was a great preacher, but he spoke in the low Latin vernacular of his day, not in the polished phrases of classical rhetoric. In fact, Caesarius' sermons were so popular that on occasion he had to remonstrate with his congregation, many of whom would leave the church after the sermon and before the celebration of communion, leaving Caesarius and his fellow clergy with only a handful to say the responses.

Caesarius frequently went out into the villages around Arles preaching. He encouraged private Bible reading, and also laid down rules for the organization of monastic communities. For the benefit of unlearned clerics, he compiled a homiliary (a book of sermons) so that their congregations should not be without instruction. In Caesarius' day the churches were still in a state of flux. There were both married and unmarried clergy, and both adult and infant baptism were practised at Arles in his time. But the barbarizing influences of the time were biting deep. Caesarius himself had to teach some of his clergy how to read. The monastic settlement was increasingly becoming the only place where piety and learning could be found. Hand in hand with the cultural decline was a spiritual decline, and church leaders in France were seldom men of great spiritual stature. Caesarius had to look elsewhere for support from like-minded Christians. This he sought in Italy. When he visited Ravenna in 512, to appear before Theodoric, he also took the opportunity to visit Rome; and there he was made papal representative in Gaul. At the time this meant little. Caesarius was merely allying himself with spiritually alive Christians, and hoped for their moral support as he tried to bring life into the churches in his area. But such an alliance laid the foundation for later papal dominance. With Caesarius, as we have said, we move perceptibly into an era that can be called mediaeval. Caesarius of Arles is an example of how a keen Christian could adapt to this new situation.

## Gildas: hope in Britain

While Caesarius was working in Gaul, far away in Britain a younger contemporary of his wrote of the troubles of the British churches. This man was Gildas (*fl.* 530–40) a churchman, and possibly an abbot, living in the Romano–British area in the West of Britain.[7] Gildas writes in a transitional period. He tells the tale of how the British Isles finally became separated from the central Roman rule in the 440s, and how the Saxons came, first as allies against other invaders, and then as conquerors. But the Saxons did not overrun the whole country, for a Romano-British leader called Ambrosius Aurelianus led the resistance and inflicted a crushing defeat on the Saxons at Mons Badonicus. Writing nearly 100 years after the event, Gildas has no further Saxon encroachments to report. The unity of the Romano-Britons under Ambrosius Aurelianus had, however, gone.[8] Gildas mentions five kinglets by name, some Roman and others definitely Celtic, but he denounces them all for their various sins. Internecine war seems to have been going on, and the cities ruined by the Saxon invasions had never been re-populated. But Gildas reserves his strongest denunciations for the churchmen. He slates their gluttony, laziness and deceit. People were buying church posts, and the kings were responsible for appointing unworthy men. Some clergy were going overseas for better posts. If one were to believe everything that Gildas said, it would appear that the British churches were totally without spiritual power. But it was in the breathing space gained by Ambrosius Aurelianus that the British churches came alive. Gildas himself, along with other Christian leaders like David, Illtyd and others were beginning a reform of the British monasteries. From these seed-beds of spirituality men were going westwards to Ireland, to capitalize on the pioneer evangelism of Patrick, and to lay the foundations for the great Irish monastic culture.[9] Irish clergy were coming to Britain for education, and they went back to strengthen the monasteries which would send out men like Columba, who were eventually to train missionaries who would bring Christ to the Saxons. Gildas himself was a keen monk, and he was also a

[7] Known from his work *On the Destruction of Britain* and from a few letters.

[8] It is probable that Ambrosius is the 'king Arthur' of later legend, and his knights were originally the heavy-mailed Roman cavalry.

[9] See above, pp. 116–20.

learned man who knew and quoted his Bible extensively.[1] Although a pessimist about his own times, Gildas was in fact living on the threshold of a revival.

## Gregory of Tours and the barbarizing of the churches

While there was hope in Britain (even if in the event it was long in reaching its full promise) the picture on the continent in the sixth century is one of swift decline into barbarism. And in a period where records are extremely scanty, the decline is fully chronicled in the *History of the Franks* by bishop Gregory of Tours. Gregory was the last link with the old Gallo-Roman aristocracy centred around Clermont, but he appears in his writings as a totally mediaeval churchman. His great historical work is a mixture of fairly sober chronicling and extravagant reports of miracles and prodigies. When he became bishop of Tours in 573,[2] he was definitely a mediaeval bishop among barbarians.

Part of the trouble in the kingdom of the Franks was the ancient and disruptive custom of partitioning the country among all the surviving sons of the king. This led to almost unrelieved civil war. Occasionally the sons might ally together for some external adventure, or one strong son might defeat all other rivals and become sole king. But the normal state of affairs was one of warring factions. And it was not only the men who engaged in war and intrigue. In Gregory's time the two main factions were led by two queens, Brunhild and Fredegund, who used all their powers to ruin each other.

As bishop of Tours, Gregory was the proud owner of a fine church building with fifty-two windows, 180 columns and eight doors (he also mentions with approval the fine cruciform church at Clermont). He was also the custodian of the shrine of St Martin, which was probably his most useful possession. For although the various Frankish kings were violent and bloodthirsty men, they were also intensely superstitious. The threat of the displeasure of St Martin, especially towards those who might violate the rights of sanctuary at his shrine, was often the most potent means of restraining a violent monarch. Church and state were closely inter-

[1] He quotes so much that he is one of the main patristic witnesses for the Old Latin version of the Bible.
[2] He was born within a year or two of the death of Caesarius of Arles.

twined in Gregory's days. Bishops were accounted great magnates, and their wergild (the compensation money payable if they were killed) was 150% of that of a courtier. But bishops were frequently appointed directly by the kings, and consequently there were some who were no better than brigands. At the same time, kings often took over the leadership in church affairs. They summoned councils and gradually exerted such an influence that there was little or no effective voice of the churchmen as distinct from the monarch. Not only bishops, but even kings, composed prayers and masses.[3] There was also a much darker side to royal dominance in the churches. Queen Fredegund, whom Gregory of Tours considered long overdue for hell, had bishop Praetextatus of Rouen murdered at the high altar of his own cathedral. Her arch-rival, queen Brunhild, whom Gregory tended to support, caused the bishop of Vienne to be stoned to death. Even the better kings, such as Guntramn the Good, were only slightly restrained barbarians. In such turmoil, Gregory of Tours struggled to maintain some sort of order. But his spiritual power over the kings was limited, and apart from the intervention of Gregory the Great with Brunhild[4] there was little outside support. Columbanus did rebuke the savage Brunhild, but the strident denunciations of the Celtic wandering prophet were spectacular rather than lastingly effective.

When Gregory of Tours died in 594, the feuds were going on as wildly as ever. The detestable Fredegund (whose crimes had started when as the king's mistress she had his rightful wife strangled, and who had led a life of intrigue and murder for thirty years) eventually died in 597. Her rival Brunhild survived, but was eventually so detested as queen-grandmother that she was brutally executed in 613 by being tied to the tail of a wild horse. From 629 to 639 king Dagobert, known afterwards as 'good king Dagobert', ruled as sole king of the Franks and gave them a short period of

[3] The sixth and seventh centuries were the period of the flourishing of the Gallican rite. In this rite no two service books would be identical, although popular prayers might be found occurring in many books, often drawn originally from very diverse sources (including a few prayers of eastern origin). In the eucharist, the Gallican rite was composed of variable prayers, with only such things as the *sanctus* and the institution narrative remaining constant from week to week. By contrast, the Roman rite, which displaced the Gallican rites in the eighth century, was largely invariable.

[4] See above, p. 119.

tranquillity. Although he followed the example of many former kings, who by lavish gifts of land to the churches had hoped to atone for their sins, his gifts are remembered as pious benefactions. He was also responsible for the great cult of St Denis at Paris. But he died young (he was only thirty-six), and after his death there were no more effective kings. The Merovingian dynasty was in fact afflicted with hereditary weakness. Most of Dagobert's successors either died young or were insane, and the 'mayors of the palace' (the king's chamberlains) increasingly took charge in the name of their colourless and ineffective overlords.

## Gregory the Great, the first mediaeval pope

While the Frankish monarchy declined, the Frankish church became increasingly degenerate, and it was only outside stimulus which could eventually revive it. Even while Gregory of Tours was writing his history, there was in Rome a bishop who was to provide the first real impetus for reform in the churches of the

**Aurelian's Wall, Rome.** It was erected in the third century AD and repaired many times afterwards.

continent. Gregory of Rome, afterwards called Gregory the Great,[5] was descended from a family which was both politically illustrious and also deeply religious. He was a direct descendant of Felix III, who was bishop of Rome from 483 to 494. His family was also the one from which the famous scholar Boethius had come. He was born in 540, and during his childhood and early manhood Rome was sacked no less than five times. He rose to high office, becoming city prefect in about 573. Even after all the wars, Rome was still a great city, even if a rather cavernous ruin of past glory. But its central force was now the church.[6] The civil power of the church was rather precarious because of the invasion of the Lombards in 565, when Byzantine holdings were limited to Ravenna, parts around Rome and Naples and the extreme South of Italy. The Lombards were the last of the barbarian invaders, and although officially Arian Christians they had in fact retained much of their pagan background. They were to be an ever-present threat to Rome until the middle of the eighth century.

In 575, Gregory's father died. Gregory sold up his possessions, made provision for his mother and sisters and retired to a monastery. But such an able man was not allowed to retire to the contemplative life, much as Gregory himself would have liked to have it so. He was made one of the seven deacons at Rome, and then appointed papal representative at Constantinople. Although he was in Constantinople for six years from 580 to 586, Gregory never learnt Greek, and he epitomizes the wide rift which had come about between East and West. Paradoxically, however, through contacts he made in Constantinople, Gregory was able to make the first determined efforts to spread the actual power of Rome throughout the western churches. While in Constantinople he met Leander of Seville. This was just at the time when the Visigoths of Spain were finally discarding Arianism in favour of orthodox Christianity.[7] Gregory gave his support to Leander and his brother Isidore, who was the writer of the first great encyclopaedia of the

[5] A good, short biography of Gregory can be found in G. S. M. Walker, *The Growing Storm* (Paternoster, 1961), chapter 1.

[6] When Justinian, the Byzantine emperor, had reconquered Italy, he had given considerable civil powers to the bishop of Rome under the Pragmatic Sanction of 554.

[7] This was done at the third Council of Toledo, at the instigation of the Visigothic king Recared.

Middle Ages. After he became pope of Rome in 590, Gregory encouraged the mission of Augustine to England, where the king of Kent had a Frankish Christian wife and was ready to receive Christian preachers. Gregory also received appeals for reform in Gaul from Columbanus, and tried to use his influence to better the condition of the Frankish churches by corresponding with queen Brunhild. He even wrote rebuking the Byzantine emperor Maurice because he refused to allow soldiers or civil servants to be ordained. Nearer to Rome, Gregory was both bishop and politician. He tried hard to restrain the advancing power of the Lombards, and he was continually trying to get the Byzantine exarch (governor) at Ravenna to take military action against the Lombards. He also tried to heal the schism between the church of Rome and the churches of northern Italy.[8]

But Gregory was not merely a church politician. He had shrunk from accepting the episcopate because he feared that all its cares would prevent him from keeping close to God. He longed to return to the quiet of the monastery, where he could devote himself to worshipping God without distraction. While seeing the needs of the present world he was very aware of the next world as well. During the plague at Rome, he led processions of penitence through the streets, calling on people to repent before they were summoned to meet God. All his energies were bent on advancing the kingdom of God. This explains why he quarrelled with the determined and virtuous emperor Maurice, who wanted to stop the drain of men from the army needed to defend the Byzantine empire; and why he disgraced himself by rejoicing when the brutal and incompetent Phocas led a revolt which ended in Maurice's murder. To Gregory, the kingdoms of this world were nothing when compared to the kingdom of God. The care of the churches was more important than empire-building, even ecclesiastical empire-building. Gregory himself chose as his title ' servant of the servants of God', and there is no reason to believe that he was hypocritical in assuming it.

[8] This schism, called the Three Chapters schism, was the result of the emperor Justinian's condemning certain writings of eastern theologians as heretical in an attempt to reconcile the Monophysites in Syria and Egypt. The bishops of Milan and Aquileia felt that this compromised the statement about Christ defined by the Council of Chalcedon (451). While Justinian eventually gained the grudging acceptance of his decree at Rome, Milan and Aquileia stood out and broke off communion with the other churches. The schism was not ended until 700.

Intellectually he was a preserver of hallowed tradition, although he is probably responsible for some liturgical reform. He is also notable as the first preacher to insist on the doctrine of purgatory. But as combiner of old traditions with an overriding desire to glorify God, his epitaph is extremely apt, when it describes Gregory the Great as 'God's Consul'.

## The transformation of the western churches

The churches in the West had undergone vast changes in the 200 years or so from the death of the emperor Theodosius to the death of Gregory the Great in 604. To begin with, there was no longer a general literacy or education. With the exception of the clergy, few could read or write; indeed, even some of the country priests were almost illiterate. With this came a vast lack of knowledge both of the Bible and of Christian theology. In place of this knowledge

**A marking-post on a Roman racecourse, Vienne.** In the Middle Ages it was thought to be Pontius Pilate's tomb.

there had arisen a vast amount of superstition. A comparison between Eusebius of Caesarea's *Church History* and Gregory of Tours' *History of the Franks* shows this notably. Eusebius records very few miracles, and assiduously quotes documents for evidence. Gregory of Tours loads his work with miracles and prodigies, and recounts gossip and hearsay at great length. In consequence, by the year 600 few people would doubt that the baptismal water made a man a Christian, and that Christ's body and blood were conjured up at the eucharist. Saints were viewed as powerful allies, and they often received almost greater veneration than Christ himself. It is true that the clergy still had a regard for orthodoxy (the 'Athanasian Creed' is a production of the time of Caesarius of Arles[9]), but few other people could understand the issues involved. Meanwhile, the churches had become great landowners, and the bishops were often ministers of state. Church appointments were often a means of rewarding a loyal courtier. Needless to say, such procedures tended to drive out those whose main concerns were spiritual. Keen Christians considered it almost axiomatic that they should leave the world for the cloister. With most churches utterly under the domination of the secular powers, it needed an international force to reform them. In an attempt to gain a counterpoise to the power of a local king, church leaders were beginning to look to the prestige of Rome and the lead that the pope of Rome could give to halt the worst abuses. By the start of the seventh century all the lineaments of the high Middle Ages were present.

[9] The *Te Deum* also dates from *c*. 500.

# 8

# The rise of Byzantium

When we look at the churches of the Eastern Empire, we see a
radical difference between them and the churches of the West.
In the West the Christian churches grew up with very little
dependence on the state; they were at first societies apart from the
Empire, then standing on an equal footing but separate from it;
and in the high Middle Ages they were to be over and above the
civil power. In the East, by contrast, church and state had always
been closely linked, ever since Constantine had proclaimed toleration
for Christians. Eusebius of Caesarea had viewed Constantine as 'the
Lord's anointed'. When Constantine's son Constantius tried to
impose his own ecclesiastical and doctrinal preferences on the
bishops of the western churches, he was heard to say in exasperation,
'Why don't you obey me, as the bishops in Syria do?' The
emperor Valens exerted so strong an influence in favour of Arianism
that it was only after his death that a council could be held at
Constantinople to condemn the Arian heresy. And when the
orthodox faith was defined at that council, it was mainly the
support of the orthodox emperor Theodosius which ensured
enforcement of the canons of the council. Admittedly there were
rugged individualists among the bishops, such as Athanasius of
Alexandria, who would refuse to bow to any emperor, but in the
East much store was set by gaining the support of the emperor in
theological and ecclesiastical disputes. In the West, Ambrose of
Milan could bend the emperor Theodosius to his will. It was a very
different tale in the East, where only a decade later John Chrysostom,
the patriarch of Constantinople, came into conflict with the
imperial power, and consequently came to grief.

# John Chrysostom

John came from Antioch, where he had for a while been a monk in the desert until ill health had forced him to return to the city. There he speedily became known as an eloquent preacher. In 387, after a disastrous riot against imperial taxation, John used the opportunity to preach searing sermons of repentance, as the citizens of Antioch waited in terror for the emperor to pronounce sentence on their lawlessness.[1] John was also a keen ascetic, and as such would upset many in an easy-going fashionable church.[2] In 397, because of his eloquence and piety, he became bishop of Constantinople. The clergy there soon had reason to dislike him. First he instituted a clean-up campaign, expelling disreputable clergy and tightening church discipline. Then came the affair of the 'tall brothers' from Egypt.[3]

These four men were refugees from persecution initiated by Jerome in Syria and Egypt. The Roman scholar and recluse Jerome had come to dislike many of the views of Origen.[4] So he set out to hunt down all who supported Origen's views, and collected various allies including the able and unscrupulous pope of Alexandria, Theophilus. Theophilus started to investigate and harass the monks of the Egyptian deserts, and a group of fifty, led by four brothers of outstandingly tall stature, fled to Constantinople for refuge. The unkempt holy men of Egypt made a great impression on John, and he endeavoured to persuade Theophilus to receive them back. John interceded for the 'tall brothers' in all innocence, hoping for justice. The unscrupulous Theophilus saw this as an opportunity to gain a controlling influence in Constantinople.

The church at Alexandria had never liked the favour which various emperors had shown to the church in the new capital, Constantinople. Athanasius had defied the Arianism of its prelates when they had forced their creed upon an unwilling Egypt. His successors took the battle on to the home ground of Constantinople.

---

[1] Specimens of these sermons in *CCC*, pp. 233–8.

[2] An example of the moral problems, and the failure to deal with them, is given in *CCC*, p. 239.

[3] Documents for the story of John Chrysostom in *CCC*, pp. 242–51.

[4] *E.g.* the belief in universal salvation, whereby even the devil might be saved; and the idea of transmigration of souls.

At the ecumenical council in 381, Peter of Alexandria had tried to oust Gregory of Nazianzus, the reigning bishop, and have a creature of his own as bishop.[5] Now Theophilus came to the capital. He pointedly ignored John, and set up headquarters at a villa across the Bosphorus where he was technically outside John's jurisdiction. With support from the mob of unruly clerics he had brought with him from Egypt, aided and abetted by all those local clergy who disliked John's reforms, Theophilus held a synod and declared John deposed. And the emperor, swayed by the empress, who disliked John, upheld the decision. John Chrysostom was quickly arrested and taken into exile, while Theophilus returned to Alexandria in triumph.

With Theophilus gone, however, popular pressure mounted for John's return. He was allowed back. Admittedly, his position was badly weakened, but with tact he could have held his own. Technically, he had been wrong in interfering in the affairs of Egypt; but the same could also be justly said of Theophilus' own actions, especially as he had used his mob along with imperial guards to break up church services held by supporters of John. But John 'of the golden tongue' (this is what 'Chrysostom' means) was not a man to keep silent. Soon he was holding forth again. The empress Eudoxia had a silver statue of herself erected in the main square of Constantinople, on the road leading to the main church. All the fun of the fair took place around that statue. John could probably have got the noisy amusements stopped if he had used the usual diplomatic channels. But instead, he spoke out from the pulpit. 'Again Herodias raves; again she dances; again she demands the head of John on a platter.' He had said scathing things about the empress before. Now she flew into a rage, and demanded that John must go. And into exile he went (404). For a year or two he lived not too far away, and his influence still lingered in the capital. But the imperial anger was implacable, and he was violently deported to a remote place on the shores of the Black Sea. Such was the rough treatment he received that he died. Thirty years later, his relics were brought back to Constantinople like those of a martyr. People avidly read his sermons and works of biblical exposition. But the story of John Chrysostom showed plainly that it was the politicians who would rule the eastern churches.

[5] See above, pp. 105–6.

## The rival Christologies

During the fifth century the churches in the East were involved in a series of disputes which are usually grouped under the heading of the 'Christological controversy'.[6] While questions of doctrine were deeply involved in these clashes, it is also fair to point out that the politics of the period played a considerable part. The line-up in the disputes followed closely the main divisions of political parties in the troubles over John Chrysostom. Egypt was always arrayed against Constantinople. Syria was divided, and might favour either side. Rome and the West were sometimes able to tip the balance decisively one way or another. But the trump card was always the favour of the eastern emperor. If the framework was a political one, however, the causes of the disputes were theological. The deep-seated question, 'What sort of a Person was Jesus Christ?', lay at the heart of all the debates. And two distinct and different answers fought for acceptance.

In the Trinitarian controversy, the argument had been over the deity of Christ. All the parties in the 'Christological controversy' would subscribe to the Nicene Creed without any hesitation. The question now was how to accommodate the human side of Jesus. Back in the fourth century, one man had tried to cut the knot by holding that Christ merely assumed a human body. This man was Apollinaris, the famous controversialist from Syrian Laodicaea who had written the 'Christian classics' to foil the emperor Julian's decree against Christian teachers. He had also contended vigorously for the Nicene Creed, and had even helped the theologian Basil the Great to understand the doctrine of the Trinity. Apollinaris held that Christ was merely the Son of God hidden inside a human body, without a human mind. In Apollinaris' scheme, the divine Logos took the place of the human mind of Christ. These views were condemned, but many of Apollinaris' works continued to circulate under other people's names. Writers of unimpeachable orthodoxy[7] were credited with works which in fact propounded his views. And many who felt strongly over the deity of Christ found such views congenial. This was especially so in Egypt, for this was the home country of Athanasius, the great champion of Christian orthodoxy

[6] For a fuller treatment of the doctrinal aspects, see J. N. D. Kelly, *Early Christian Doctrines* (A. & C. Black, 1968), chapters 11 and 12, and R. V. Sellers, *Two Ancient Christologies* (SPCK, 1940).

[7] *E.g.* Athanasius.

against the heresy of Arius. Simple folk here knew that only a divine Saviour could save them. And they viewed the weekly eucharist, in which they believed they received the body and blood of Christ, as the means of infusing divine power into their mortal bodies. On a more intellectual level, Egyptian theologians were suspicious of ideas, emanating from Antioch, which seemed to make Christ not much more than a greatly inspired man. Yet, latent in these views was a tendency to create a Christ of theology who would become almost separate from the Jesus of the Gospels. Few, however, saw this danger in their often frenzied devotion to the Person of Christ, the fully divine Son of God.

The view of Christ which formed the other side of the 'Christological controversy' was a distinctly more scholarly one, and therefore less able to rouse popular enthusiasm. Coming from Antioch, it was especially linked with the names of Diodore of Tarsus and Theodore of Mopsuestia, but its roots may lie further back. During the Arian controversy, theologians had replied to Arian attacks on the deity of Christ by stating that Christ's human attributes (*e.g.* tiredness, suffering, ignorance of the date of the final judgment) were not evidence of a defective deity but were evidence that he assumed a full humanity. Hence came the practice of making minute distinctions between what Jesus did as man and what He did as God. For example, an Antiochene theologian could say that as man Jesus wept at the grave of Lazarus, but that as God He raised him from the dead. Such views were not uncongenial to western minds, either. It also resulted in Nestorius' famous objection to calling the Virgin Mary 'Mother of God',[8] because he wished to avoid suggesting that God could be subjected to human birth and so be liable to change. Nestorius preferred to use the term 'Mother of Christ',[9] which he held to be free from ambiguity. Such were the theological differences which were to be fought out with so much vigour.

## Cyril and Nestorius

The battle between Alexandria and Constantinople had lapsed somewhat after the exile of John Chrysostom. Theophilus had died

[8] This is the traditional translation of the word *Theotokos*, which literally means 'the one who gave birth to God'.

[9] In Greek, *Christotokos*.

in 412, and was succeeded by his nephew Cyril. And Cyril was very much 'son of Theophilus' sister'. He was quite as unscrupulous as his uncle, and in addition possessed a very able theological brain. For a long time he confined his activities to Egypt, being the mastermind behind the demolition of paganism in Egypt by methods which would have made gangland Chicago envious. His 'sick-attendants'[1] helped to burn down the temple of Serapis, and also murdered the lady-philosopher Hypatia. With a blatant disregard for legality he exacted an unofficial tax on linen exported from Egypt, and used the money to swell the funds of the church. And, above all, he made sure that future popes of Alexandria could come to any council assured of a block vote which would be very difficult to out-manoeuvre.

In 428 another reformer from Antioch came to Constantinople as bishop. And as this man, Nestorius, began to cleanse the capital of heretics, Cyril of Alexandria looked for his opportunity to extend his own power at the expense of the church of Constantinople. Nestorius' first moves were against heretics which both sides would condemn. But while Nestorius was closing down an Arian church, the building caught fire and the flames spread to many other houses in the poorer parts of Constantinople—an event which did nothing for Nestorius' popularity. Then Nestorius gave shelter to some refugees from the West. These included Pelagian heretics who had been deposed from church positions by a synod at Rome. Then he began to listen to appeals from dissident Egyptian clerics. Cyril took his chance with both hands.[2]

First of all, Cyril made sure that he would have the help of Celestine, the bishop of Rome. He informed him of some of Nestorius' opinions, and Celestine had them condemned at a synod in Rome. Cyril knew that Nestorius disliked the term 'Mother of God', and he also knew that a lot of popular piety valued the phrase. Cyril also valued the term 'Mother of God' (Greek, *Theotokos*) because it made clear that Mary bore the complete divine–human Christ, and not merely a very inspired man. For these reasons Cyril wrote a lengthy defence of this title, and made sure that Nestorius heard of it and got an opportunity to preach against it. Meanwhile, Celestine of Rome encouraged Cyril to

[1] See above, p. 122.
[2] Material relating to this dispute in *CCC*, pp. 271–88. See also T. H. Bindley, *Oecumenical Documents of the Faith* (Methuen, 1950), pp. 87–148.

pursuade Nestorius to mend his ways theologically. News of this came to the eastern emperor Theodosius II, who summoned a council of church leaders to get to the bottom of the dispute.

Cyril gathered his allies with care. The council[3] was to meet in Ephesus in 431, and so Cyril got Memnon, bishop of Ephesus, on his side. This was fairly easy, since the church of Ephesus jealously guarded its independence from Constantinople, and perhaps still smarted over the high-handed way John Chrysostom had intervened to sort out some internal disputes. Then Cyril made promises of help to bishop Juvenal of Jerusalem, who hoped to have his city made into an independent patriarchate at the expense of Antioch. At the same time, Cyril's own doctrinal expressions were becoming extreme. He was demanding that people should disown any mention of two natures in Christ or the attribution of various acts of Christ either to His manhood or to His divinity.

When Cyril came to Ephesus, he was accompanied by a formidable following, including the redoubtable Schnoudi, abbot of the White Monastery (who distinguished himself by throwing a book at Nestorius), and a whole private army of violent supporters. With overwhelming numbers on his side, Cyril summoned a council, and when Nestorius refused to appear before so partisan a gathering Cyril condemned him in his absence. But at this point John of Antioch arrived, along with a considerable contingent of Nestorius' supporters. They immediately held a counter-synod, which anathematized Cyril and Memnon of Ephesus. Then the delegation from Rome arrived, and gave their support to Cyril. The crowds at Ephesus demonstrated against Nestorius as the man who rejected their title of 'Mother of God' for the Virgin Mary. At last, the emperor himself intervened, and gave his support to Cyril. Nestorius was deposed, and the term 'Mother of God 'was declared to be orthodox. But Cyril still had to reckon with the implacable hostility of the Antiochene delegation. Eventually the two sides settled on a compromise over the theological points. John of Antioch accepted that Nestorius was a heretic, and that the term 'Mother of God' was orthodox, while Cyril accepted that Christ had two natures joined together in unconfused union. Theologically Cyril managed to remain respectable. But there were many, even of his own supporters, who disliked his methods. Many thought that

[3] Full description of the proceedings in Frend, *The Early Church*, pp. 226–30.

he was bent on pursuing private animosities rather than on contending for the truth of God. His action as prosecutor, judge and jury was hardly likely to gain him a reputation for fairness. When he died in 444, a charitable man like Theodoret (bishop of Cyrrhus and a church historian) was ready to say that Cyril, his theological opponent, had gone down to hell unrepentant and plotting still greater crimes; and that while his departure from this world was a cause for relief, the dead were probably profoundly disturbed at his arrival.[4] Cyril was probably justified in protesting at the opinions of Nestorius which appeared to make Christ merely a very inspired man. The methods he used were unworthy, but sadly they were to become the standard tactics in the ensuing debate.

## The 'Robber Synod' of Ephesus (449)

Cyril was succeeded by Dioscorus, a man who had all of Cyril's ability in politics, but who lacked the wisdom Cyril had shown when he accepted a compromise with Antioch. At the time when Dioscorus took office in Alexandria, another reforming patriarch had come to Constantinople—Flavian, who was very much in the tradition of John Chrysostom and Nestorius. Flavian had become pope of Constantinople in 446, and among his clergy was a certain Eutyches, who held views very similar to those of Cyril. But Eutyches was more blatant, and insisted that during the incarnation Jesus Christ had only one nature (the divine one). Dioscorus knew that Flavian was going to investigate the views of Eutyches. He also knew that Eutyches was a favourite of the court chamberlain Chrysaphius, and that Chrysaphius had the ear of the emperor Theodosius II.

Again a synod was summoned at Ephesus.[5] It was 449. A summons for this council went to Rome, where Leo was now pope. Leo, as we have seen previously,[6] was unable to come in person, but he sent a letter outlining his doctrinal standpoint.[7] And because there was no animosity between him and Flavian, the two of them agreed

[4] The full 'obituary' by Theodoret, and also an estimate of Cyril from one of his supporters, is given in *CCC*, pp. 300–2.

[5] See *CCC*, pp. 309–13.

[6] See above, pp. 140–1.

[7] This was the famous *Tome of Leo*, given in *CCC*, pp. 315–24. A fuller examination of it in Bindley, *Oecumenical Documents of the Faith*, pp. 159–80.

**Theodosius II, emperor 402–50.** A coin in the British Museum, London.

on their doctrinal standpoint. This did not, however, save Flavian. Eutyches came to Ephesus, sure of the support of Dioscorus, who repeated Cyril's act by presiding at the council. Unfortunately, the delegation which came to the council from Syria, and which might have been expected to support Flavian, was split. Many of the monks of the Syrian desert disliked the views of Domnus of Antioch, Ibas of Edessa and Theodoret of Cyrrhus, the leaders of he Syrian delegation. Furthermore, there were only three men from Rome at the council. Thanks to the unruly Egyptian clerics who had come with Dioscorus, riot and commotion broke out almost immediately, and Dioscorus saw to it that he led the riot. The emperor wanted to see Eutyches rehabilitated. This was done. Then the packed assembly clamoured for the deposition of Flavian. In the end, the crowd condemned all those who disagreed with Dioscorus. Many who disagreed with the views of the majority were forced to sign papers supporting the acts of the council. The Roman delegation fled. Leo's reasoned doctrinal paper was left unread. And to his eternal dishonour, the emperor Theodosius II acquiesced in all this. Flavian was beaten up by the uncontrollable Egyptian delegation and died of his injuries. Small wonder that the proceedings of Ephesus in 449 were called the 'Robber Synod'.[8]

### The Council of Chalcedon

Then, in 450, the emperor Theodosius died as a result of a fall from his horse. This was generally considered a divine judgment, especially by pope Leo of Rome! Theodosius' sister, Pulcheria,

[8] The description is Leo's.

married a general called Marcian. Marcian was an orthodox Christian, and immediately he laid plans to summon another council to meet at Chalcedon.[9] This was aimed to be as representative as possible, and nearly 520 bishops attended (as compared with 130 at the Council of Ephesus in 449). Four delegates came from Rome, but otherwise the council was composed of bishops from the East. To ensure law and order, imperial officers sat in the most important places, with the various church leaders arranged around them.

Dioscorus came with his Egyptian delegation, but this time the dice were loaded against him. Meticulously the council proceeded with its agenda. First, the creed of Nicaea and the creed of the council in 381 at Constantinople were read. They were acclaimed by all. Then came other decisions of councils, culminating in the disgraceful record of what happened at Ephesus in 449 (only two years previously). At that point quite a number of those who had sided with Dioscorus at Ephesus repudiated their signatures to the decisions of that council. Whether moved by conscience or by a desire to avoid retribution, they disowned the deeds of Dioscorus and his friends. Juvenal, bishop of Jerusalem, ostentatiously led his delegation from Palestine over to the side of the orthodox. Others followed. Dioscorus and some of his leading supporters were condemned for heresy and deposed. Then the Council of Chalcedon set about drafting its own definition concerning the person of Christ.

The Chalcedonian Definition was never intended to be a complete doctrinal statement on the Person of Christ. It was a formula to exclude error. Hence, it began by reaffirming the Nicene and Constantinopolitan Creeds. By way of clarification of these basic orthodox doctrines, the definitions of Cyril of Alexandria against Nestorius were received, and also the doctrinal statement of Leo of Rome against the heresy of Eutyches. Then came the definition itself. The purport of the Chalcedonian Definition can be summed up thus, that Christ is 'truly God, truly man and truly one'. Following Leo's lead, the definition notes that Christ existed in two natures, human and divine. The human nature was completely like our nature except for the absence of sin. The divine nature was the same as that of God the Father. But these two natures were united

[9] Documents in *CCC*, pp. 332–42.

into a single Person, without being either separated or mixed together.[1] All in all, the Definition took more care to guard against the Monophysite heresy than against Nestorianism, although it would still be unacceptable to extreme Nestorians. In the view of many oriental bishops, however, the Chalcedonian Definition was a blatant canonizing of the opinions of the heretic Nestorius. Egypt and Syria were to become strong centres of resistance to Chalcedonian doctrine.[2] At the same time, the western churches would view any attempt to revise the doctrine of Chalcedon as tantamount to reviving the Monophysite heresy. Far from ending ecclesiastical strife in the East, Chalcedon was the beginning of a continuing battle.

## The Monophysite reaction after Chalcedon

In the years after Chalcedon the political power in the Eastern Empire swung in the direction of the Monophysites. This was largely for two reasons. First, the central government was weak and often unable to enforce its will. Second, the leaders of the Monophysites were often able and unscrupulous politicians, while orthodox leaders tended to be less able to enlist and whip up popular support. For example, an orthodox leader like Theodoret of Cyrrhus was bishop in a remote area of scattered villages (he had nearly 800 small congregations under his charge). He faced considerable opposition from villagers and desert monks because of his orthodox views. He also had his hands full dealing with more dangerous heretics (Gnostics and Arians), and in all this he was disadvantaged because he was a pastor rather than a church politician. In Egypt, however, the position was very different. When the emperor Marcian died in 457, the mob of Alexandria seized the orthodox patriarch Proterius and murdered him in his own church. They were led by a certain Timothy Aelurus (Timothy the Cat), who subsequently became bishop of Alexandria and who directed

[1] Perhaps it is noteworthy that Nestorius, just before he died in exile, heard of Leo's statement and the Definition of Chalcedon, and expressed himself fully satisfied. This forms the last entry in his apology, *The Book of Heracleides*, which was rediscovered in a Syriac version in 1910.
[2] The Coptic, Ethiopic and Armenian churches are still today technically Monophysite, although their members claim that they are merely supporting the theology of Cyril of Alexandria.

all his energies against those who supported the Chalcedonian Definition. Although at one time deposed and exiled, he was subsequently reinstated, and he had the almost unanimous support of the Egyptian churches against the central church of Constantinople. But a man of blood like this did no good to the spiritual state of the Egyptian church.

But while Egypt in its comparative geographical isolation could afford to indulge its internal squabbles, Constantinople was being pressed by the barbarians who had overthrown the Western Empire. After the death of Marcian, the barbarian general Aspar the Alan[3] tried to marry his way to high office by taking as wife the daughter of Marcian's successor, the weak emperor Leo. As well as Aspar, there were also two Goths, both called Theodoric, who were in a position to terrorize the Eastern Empire. But the wily officials of Constantinople succeeded in getting the two Theodorics to fight each other. The eventual victor was then sent off, ostensibly to conquer Italy for the emperor in Constantinople, and he is better known to history as Theodoric the Great.[4] As another counterweight to barbarians from the Balkans, troops from Isauria (in the mountains of central Asia Minor) were brought to the capital. Their leader, one Tarasicodissa, also married into the royal family, and eventually became emperor, assuming the Greek name Zeno!

It was during the reign of Zeno, in 482, that an attempt was made to heal the split caused by the Council of Chalcedon. It was a total failure. Zeno issued a decree, called the *Henoticon* (Edict of Unity),[5] which set aside the Chalcedonian Definition and allowed orthodoxy simply to be defined in terms of the Nicene Creed and the definitions of Cyril of Alexandria. No-one was satisfied. The Monophysites did not think that it went far enough, while the orthodox and the western Christians were scandalized at the attempt to set aside the Chalcedonian Definition. All that resulted was that the church of Rome broke off communion with the church at Constantinople, a sign of future trouble which would eventually end in the final break between East and West in the Middle Ages.

[3] The Alani were related to the Sarmatians of Eastern Europe, and took part in the barbarian invasions along with the Vandals.

[4] See above, pp. 172–5.

[5] Text in Kidd, *Documents Illustrative of the History of the Church*, vol. ii, pp. 330–2.

Zeno's hold on the throne was uncertain, and he had to contend with various would-be usurpers.[6] When he died in 491 he was succeeded by the court official Anastasius, who married the widowed empress Ariadne. Anastasius tended to favour the Monophysite faction, and this caused great offence both in Rome and in Constantinople. It was during Anastasius' reign that an attempt was made to alter the *Trisagion* hymn (a hymn to the Trinity), by inserting 'who was crucified for us' in the praise to God the Son. By this addition the Monophysites aimed to entrench their doctrine that Christ had only one nature, and that it was the divine nature which suffered on the cross. This new version was popularized in one novel way when the patriarch Peter the Fuller taught a pet parrot to recite the Monophysite version. But this attack on a hallowed formula was not allowed to pass unchallenged. The populace of Constantinople took to the streets, and Anastasius was compelled to appear at the racing stadium (the normal place for public demonstrations at Constantinople) and offer his resignation as emperor. As the crowd had no alternative emperor to suggest, Anastasius kept his title, but he wisely bowed to public pressure and the old traditional form of the *Trisagion* was restored. The incident of the *Trisagion* riot showed that even in Constantinople an emperor might be challenged. It also showed how deeply were theological divisions felt even by the ordinary people of the Byzantine Empire.

## The rise of Justinian

Anastasius died, a very old man, in 517. Under his rule the Empire had settled down to something approaching stagnation. The eternal bureaucracy ground on, maintaining the outward semblance of rule, ensuring that the taxes were collected and keeping the day-to-day affairs of the Empire going. But during Anastasius' reign two men from Macedonia had come to Constantinople, and they were to change all this. The older man was a volunteer soldier called Justin, who was rising in the imperial army, with a reputation as an efficient officer even though he could not write his own name and had to have a gold stencil with which to sign it. His nephew, called Petrus Sabbatius, had come to the big city to study. And as

[6] *E.g.* Basiliscus who took a strongly pro-Monophysite line.

the adopted son of the childless Justin, he had adopted the surname Justinian.[7]

Anastasius died without naming a successor, and there was great uncertainty as to who would be the next emperor. Finally, the court officials chose Justin. He was a man of blameless character and a firm supporter of the orthodox faith, and his election satisfied most people. Behind the elderly new emperor, in slipped his able nephew, who was soon his close, though unofficial, confidant. Although Justin was illiterate, he was a shrewd ruler. He reigned for ten years, and when he knew that he was dying he appointed Justinian as his successor, Justinian was in his forties when he ascended the throne, and it was his reign which shaped the future of the Byzantine Empire.

It is hard to discover the real Justinian behind the various façades and biased reports. He was undoubtedly a brilliant man, with schemes for the betterment of the Byzantine Empire which were quite breathtaking. He showed extraordinary diligence in matters as diverse as reforming the Roman law, building the Church of the Hagia Sophia at Constantinople, or planning the diplomatic moves to further his many conquests. His concern in matters of Christian doctrine and his attempts to solve the Monophysite controversy show a burning desire that Christian truth should prevail. His concern for the spread of the Christian faith beyond the boundaries of the Empire is praiseworthy, even if at times he did use missionary work as part of diplomatic policy. Yet, at the same time, there was a weakness in his character. He could become paralysed with fear just when action was needed. And there was a mysterious and evil aura about him, which could make the historian Procopius[8] suggest that he was the devil incarnate. He reigned as a spider at the centre of a net of power, approachable by all but never fully to be trusted. During his uncle's reign he had married an equally enigmatic woman, called Theodora. She was a former prostitute who had been converted by Monophysite monks

[7] A good survey of Justinian is given, in novel form, in R. Lamb, *The City of Constantinople*.

[8] He wrote official histories of the Persian, North African (Vandalic) and Gothic (Italian) wars; and also a *Secret History* which purports to be the damning 'truth' about Justinian, his wife Theodora, and the great general Belisarius and his wife Antonina (the confidante of Theodora). He ends the *Secret History* with the suggestion that Justinian is really a demon in a human body.

**The emperor Justinian and his wife, Theodora.** From a 6th-century mosaic in the Church of S. Vitale, Ravenna.

in Egypt. She returned to the capital city and there met Justinian, and in spite of opposition he married her. Theodora was a hard woman, with an iron will and supremely cunning. Although as empress she had no official position, she organized her own court, and could make or ruin careers as she pleased.[9] At the same time, she was greatly liked by many of the common people. She crusaded on behalf of the persecuted Monophysites, even hiding them in her own villas to escape from imperial persecutors. She also set up her reformatory for the prostitutes of Constantinople, although it is said that it had such a rigorous régime that some of the girls there flung themselves to their death from its high walls rather than endure life inside it. Such were the imperial couple who would build the Caesaro-papism of the Byzantine Empire.

Justinian took charge in 527, and his first acts were to deal with corruption in the civil service and to undertake a complete revision of Roman law. He never fully succeeded in reforming the Byzantine bureaucracy, despite his insistence that all officials should have 'clean hands'. He also imposed a terrible oath on all officials to the effect that if they failed to be scrupulously honest in their dealings, they would incur the wrath of God, the fate of Judas, the leprosy of Gehazi and the palsy of Cain. Under the eye of Tribonian, his legal adviser, the vast, unwieldly mass of Roman law was pruned down to manageable size. The end-product of this was the *Code of Justinian*, the great Latin work which stabilized Roman law. It was made up of the *Institutes* (the basic handbook for all legal students) and the *Digest* (also called the *Pandects*) which contained some simple and concise legal definitions and decisions for every subject-division of the law. The whole work was completed in 535; but supplementary laws, called *Novellae*, were issued later as required. In this mammoth undertaking Justinian showed himself a caring monarch, who merited the description 'father of his country'.

### Justinian and religious dissent

Less creditable were his dealings with the Monophysites. At first he aimed for compromise, while fiercely persecuting other heretics. Then, wearied by their obstinacy, his patience broke. Monophysites were to conform or to be harried to death. Their leader, John of

[9] *E.g.* John of Cappadocia, the rapacious head of Justinian's revenue department, whom she had forcibly confined to a monastery.

Tellas, was brutally executed by the patriarch of Antioch, and many of his followers also suffered death and torture for their opinions. But eventually the influence of Theodora and the uselessness of persecution combined to make Justinian relent. Theodora herself gave sanctuary to Jacob Baradaeus, the Syrian who became bishop of Edessa and gave his name to the still-existing Syrian Jacobite church. And even Justinian himself was ready to give encouragement to Monophysite missionaries at times, especially when their work of converting the savage Egyptian tribes might give peace on the frontier.

The outbreak of persecution was all the more regrettable, since there had been a distinct possibility that orthodox and Monophysite might have reached some measure of agreement. The great theologian Leontius of Byzantium had done much to allay Monophysite suspicion of the Chalcedonian Definition, when he described Christ as One in whom the two natures could not exist independently of each other. Leontius set himself to answer the objection that the belief in two natures in Christ meant that there were two independent personalities inside Him (the Nestorian error). His solution was to say that Christ's human nature had no independent existence apart from the divine nature, but that together the two natures formed one Christ, so avoiding any suggestion of a dichotomy in the Person of Christ. Such views were not altogether uncongenial to a moderate Monophysite like Severus of Antioch. But the extreme Monophysites were adamant. They were even going deeper into heresy by insisting that Christ's human body was incorruptible and incapable of suffering pain. With such extreme opinions there could be no compromise. Nevertheless, in 544 Justinian made another attempt to conciliate the moderate Monophysites by condemning the works of Theodore of Mopsuestia, Theodoret of Cyrrhus and Ibas of Edessa. This caused the 'Three Chapters' controversy (so called from the three documents condemned). Justinian attempted to enforce his will by summoning a general council in 553 at Constantinople, and he compelled the pope of Rome, Vigilius, to attend. After considerable pressure Vigilius bowed to Justinian's demands to condemn the 'Three Chapters'. But many churches in Italy refused to accept the compromise of Vigilius, and they broke off communion with him. Similarly, in North Africa (Byzantine since 534), Justinian could enforce his opinion only with the aid of the civil power, and disgruntled North African church leaders objected that Christ should be the head of the church, and that the emperor should only support true doctrine, not define it. But for all this, Justinian failed to reconcile the Monophysites.

## Justinian's political adventures

Justinian's most daring and damaging dream was his plan to reconquer the West. In the execution of this he was helped by the most able general of antiquity, Belisarius. Belisarius began by taking a small force to North Africa, and destroying the Vandal kingdom there in 534. Then, with an even smaller army, he crossed to Italy and contrived to seize Rome. After a year-long siege there, he finally drove off the Goths and bluffed his way north to capture Ravenna and to declare all Italy once more subject to Constantinople. But when Belisarius returned to the capital city, the Goths rose in revolt under their king Totila. Sent back with totally inadequate forces, Belisarius could not end the war. Finally he was recalled, and in 552-3 the aged eunuch Narses was sent with the

**A 6th-century fleet and fortifications.** A mosaic in the Church of S. Apollinare Nuovo, Ravenna.

first adequate army. He defeated and killed Totila at the Battle of Busta Gallorum near Rimini, and ended the war. But Italy never recovered from this, its most damaging devastation. It was in Totila's time that free distribution of bread and the horse races were for the first time discontinued in Rome, and were never reinstated. The whole of Italy was terribly devastated, and lay open to the Lombards, who invaded it on the death of Justinian.

Justinian's grand designs, just recounted, resulted in gross overspending. Even in war, he could never put two sizeable armies in the field at one time. Belisarius never commanded more than about 10,000 men, many of whom were his personal retinue. In fact, when Belisarius performed his last great military feat, in repulsing the Kutrigur Huns from the very walls of Constantinople in 559, he had a really well-armed nucleus of only a few hundred men in his motley army! Justinian, in pursuit of grandiose schemes, imposed crushing tax after crushing tax on his subjects. Great Senators who had once been immune from taxation were bled white. From the proceeds of this taxation, the eastern frontier was kept quiet by vast payments to the Persians. And huge sums were expended on beautifying Constantinople. And it was here that Justinian almost had his greatest disaster.

Public freedom of expression in the Byzantine Empire had two outlets. One was theological discussion; the other was in the rivalry of the race-course. Two factions, the Blues and the Greens, supported opposing sides in the chariot races. The old emperor Anastasius had supported the Greens. Justin and Justinian supported the Blues until their power was secure. The rivalry between Greens and Blues would make the Celtic/Rangers rivalry in Glasgow look positively anaemic. Bands of the opposing factions terrorized the streets, murdering and burning. Theology became mixed up in their rivalry, the Greens being pro-Monophysite, the Blues being pro-orthodox. Justinian viewed all this with displeasure, and decided to stop it. But when a number of leaders of both factions were tried and sentenced to death, the crowd intervened and some of the condemned men were rescued. Then the two factions united, shouting 'Victory!' (Greek, '*Nika!*'), and turned against Justinian. For several days he was besieged in the palace, while the mobs set fire to much of the city and even planned to crown a new emperor. Then, as Justinian was about to flee for his life, Theodora stepped in. She declared that she would never flee,

**The Church of Santa Sophia**, built by the emperor Justinian.

and that she considered that the imperial purple was the best shroud for her. Her resolution turned the tide. The eunuch Narses went and bribed some of the Blues to desert the Greens. At the same time Belisarius and his soldiers were let loose on the rioting crowd in the racing arena, and nearly 30,000 rioters died. Thus, in the year 534, Justinian quelled the 'Nika' riot and clamped his iron hand on the capital. Once in power, however, he took remarkably few reprisals against the rioters. And when the burnt ruins had been cleared, he set his architects to build the Church of the Holy Wisdom ('*Hagia Sophia*' in Greek) to replace the old Church of the Apostles which had been burned down. The Hagia Sophia is the acme of Byzantine architecture. Erected in spite of terrible problems, as when the piers supporting the great dome began to split, it remains today a most breathtaking edifice. In a way, too, it aptly pictures Justinian himself. Pretentious, contriving to support a vast edifice with seemingly inadequate support, it is a mixture of magnificence and terrible emptiness.

Justinian's later years were ones of impending doom and decay. After the death of Theodora (548), he gradually became more and more introverted. Never a luxurious man, he became more and more ascetic, eating little and sleeping only a few hours each night. Increasingly, he became remote from public affairs, spending time mainly in speculating on obscure points of theology, such as the nature of the resurrection body. In his reign. church and state were welded together into an almost indissoluble bond which benefited

**Inside Santa Sophia.** A mosaic decoration over the door from the vestibule into the narthex. The Virgin Mary is flanked by the figures of Constantine (right), founder of the city as the imperial capital, and Justinian (left), at whose command Santa Sophia was built.

neither. Justinian, as head of state and effective head of the church, was taking on more than a mortal man could carry. He had risen from the obscurity of a poor peasant family in Macedonia to become one of the most formidable potentates of all time, but the ascent had done him no good. Power corrupted any true Christian feeling in both him and Theodora. Of his own personal faith we can discern little, but when a close associate like Procopius can whisper that Justinian was really a body inhabited by a demon, we have some idea of how empty he had become.

## The decline after Justinian

With Justinian's death in 565, the Byzantine Empire[1] entered a period of swift decline, brought about by Justinian's grandiose foreign policy. His successor, Justin II, was forced to conclude humiliating peace treaties with both Persia and the Avars in the Balkans, and eventually died insane. He was succeeded by Tiberius, who was more capable and who tried to stabilize the terrible situation. On the death of Tiberius in 582, the throne of the Byzantine Empire was taken over by Maurice. His reign witnessed a revival in Byzantine fortunes. He profited from a civil war in Persia, by making it a condition of his support for the Persian king that Roman troops should move eastwards to the positions they had held under Justinian. Then the emperor led his army westwards in person against the Avars. Although he had incurred the wrath of Gregory the Great by insisting that soldiers and civil servants might not be ordained,[2] Maurice was successful in his campaigns. But when he ordered his troops to stay in the field over winter, so that they could follow up his victories over the Avars, there was a mutiny. Maurice was killed, and the soldiers made the leader of the mutiny, a centurion called Phocas, the new emperor. Phocas began his reign (602) with a bloody purge in the capital, but was totally unable to rule. Avars and Persians closed in on the capital, Constantinople. Then, at the moment when all seemed lost, help came from a surprising quarter.

[1] Full details in H. St B. Moss, *The Birth of the Middle Ages* (OUP, 1935), pp. 136–8.
[2] See above, p. 183.

**The column of Phocas in the forum at Rome.** It was erected on his behalf by a Byzantine governor.

## Heraclius and the church/state

The governor of North Africa, at this time a Byzantine province, was called Heraclius. He, and his son of the same name, set sail for Constantinople to seize power. They had little difficulty in disposing of the unpopular Phocas (610), and they then set about reforming Constantinople. Although Heraclius senior died in 613, his son carried on his work. But more than this, the emperor Heraclius had new and fantastic plans for rejuvenating the Byzantine Empire.

Although Heraclius, to escape the besieging Persians and Avars, had once contemplated moving the capital of the Empire to Carthage, he abandoned this plan in favour of a daring scheme to defeat Persia. And he succeeded in getting the whole population of Constantinople on his side in this endeavour. The odds against him were formidable. The Persians had swept across the Middle East, and were actually encamped across the Bosphorus at Chalcedon. On the landward side, the Avars under their khagan were right up against the walls.

Heraclius initiated the first 'crusade'. Pictures of the Virgin Mary were painted on the gates of the city as charms to ward off the invader. The patriarch Sergius handed over much church treasure to help the war effort, and actually shared the military command of the capital with the chief administrator[3] Bonus. Even the free distribution of grain in the capital was suspended for a while, and miraculously there were no riots! Everyone united to save the city. When there was an attack on Constantinople by sea, the combined Avar/Persian forces were beaten off by a new invention, 'Greek fire'.[4] Meanwhile, Heraclius left the capital city, and sailed round towards Syria, landing his army at Tarsus and defeating a Persian land army there. Then he moved north to Armenia, while the Persian king Khosroes, attempting to draw the emperor back to Constantinople, threw all his efforts into an all-out attack on the capital city. Heraclius, however, held to his plan. In 628 he swept down from Armenia into the heartland of Persia, scattering the Persian armies. Khosroes hurried back, but was killed during the confusion. The forces of the cross had won. But the victory was at the cost of making Christianity seem to be coterminous with the Byzantine Empire.

Heraclius' other claim to fame was his one last effort to try to reconcile the Monophysites. With the help of the patriarch

[3] His official title was 'patrician'.
[4] Naphtha which was poured on the water and set alight.

**Heraclius, emperor 610–41.** A coin in the British Museum, London.

Sergius, he put forward the suggestion[5] that Christ had one 'divine-human energy', thereby trying to bridge the gap between the Monophysite stress on the oneness of Jesus and the orthodox stress on the two natures in Christ. This was soon refined, with the help of the pope of Rome, Honorius, to become the doctrine of 'one will' in Christ; and hence this was called the Monothelite controversy. The fact that Christ could mention both his own will and his Father's will when praying in Gethsemane[6] might have been though sufficient to disprove this piece of theological horse-trading. But Heraclius and his successor Constans II gave it their whole-hearted support. But this new doctrine failed in its aim to reconcile the Monophysites. In any case, the Muslim conquest of Egypt and Syria soon removed the need for political *rapprochement*. Constans II, however, would not retreat; and he even arrested the pope of Rome, Martin, and exiled him to the Crimea because he would not bow to imperial pressure to support the Monothelite doctrines but held to the traditional orthodoxy. Martin died in exile, and was widely held to be a martyr, the last pope of Rome so to be honoured. At last, with the loss of the Monophysite provinces an irreversible fact, the Monothelite controversy was brought to an end at the Council of Constantinople (680–1), when Sergius, Honorius and the supporters of Monothelitism were all condemned.

[5] H. Bettenson, *Documents of the Christian Church* (OUP, 1943), pp. 128–9. See also Williston Walker, *A History of the Christian Church* (T. & T. Clark 1920), pp. 146–7.

[6] Mark 14:36.

## The advent of Islam

Even while Heraclius was celebrating his triumph over Persia, events were taking place in the Arabian peninsula which would alter the Middle East for ever. In 612 the then obscure prophet Muhammad fled with his followers from Mecca to Medina. He and his followers took to arms to defend themselves and their new-found faith, Islam. Muhammad certainly had met Jews and probably also heretical Christians, and had been influenced by them. The faith he proclaimed was a mixture of strong monotheism and very strange revelations. But it was proclaimed at a time when the tribes of the Arabian peninsula were about to burst into a tired world. Byzantium and Persia were exhausted by their long war, and could put up no real resistance. Muhammad died in 632, by which time all Arabia was under his sway. His successors, the Caliphs Omar and Othman, carried on the conquest, and the Byzantine Empire experienced its real barbarian invasion. The aged Heraclius had his army shattered at the Battle of the Yarmuk in 636. Jerusalem fell, and the patriarch mourned the onrush of Islam as the prophesied 'abomination of desolation'. In 641 Alexandria capitulated,

A 10th-century Qur'an, possibly from Baghdad, written in a neat Kufi character. The reverential care in copying is conditioned by the fact that Muslims believe the Arabic text to be the actual words of God.

with the Monophysite patriarch negotiating with the Arab forces. North Africa was overrun, as was Visigothic Spain, and for a while it seemed that the combination of Arab military strength and Islam was invincible. Two events halted the tide. In the West, Charles Martel decisively defeated the Arab forces at the Battle of Poitiers (732). In the East a new emperor, Leo the Isaurian, turned back the invaders from the walls of Constantinople (718).

## Leo the Isaurian and the revival of Byzantium

The dynasty of Heraclius had ended in civil war even while the enemy was at the gates, and Muslim forces had besieged the city in a desultory way from 672 to 678. Leo the Isaurian repeated the feat of Heraclius in revitalizing the ancient structure of the Empire. He had risen to power by way of military posts, and he directed his reforms not only to civil affairs but also to religious matters. His religious reforms were carried out by imperial dictate, and were especially directed against the veneration of the sacred pictures or 'icons'. With a puritanical background from the uplands of Asia Minor, and perhaps also influenced by the Muslim hatred of idols, he decreed that veneration of images was to cease and that they should be pulled down. The real question at issue was how far Christ's incarnation made it possible or permissible to make a picture of Him who was God. Leo was probably also attacking the great power of the monasteries, whose immunity from taxation, and many privileges, were, in his view, a drag on the war effort.

In political matters Leo was fairly successful, driving back the Muslim forces from Asia Minor (they did not reinvade for a further 300 years). On the religious front,[7] he ran straight up against all the popular piety of the Empire. The monks and the common people led bitter resistance, for they held that supernatural power was actually present in the icons. Under Leo's successor Constantine V Copronymos (Greek for 'his name is dung'), actual armed persecution was used against those who venerated images. Eventually the policy was reversed under the empress Irene, when a general council called at Nicaea in 787 decreed that icons were 'to be given due salutation and honourable reverence but not true worship'. Strange to say, although the western churches had been in favour of retaining icons, a bad translation of this decree reached the West,

[7] Bettenson, *Documents of the Christian Church*, pp. 129–30.

and so angered Charlemagne and his advisers that some forthright retorts (called the Caroline books) were issued against the veneration of images! This proved one more wedge to prise East and West apart. In the East, Leo the Isaurian, Constantine V and their supporters were execrated as heretics, and the churches celebrated the return of their icons with great joy and with imperial backing.

With Heraclius and Leo the Isaurian, the Eastern Empire assumed the form which it would continue to have until its final extinction in 1453. Church and state were so welded together that their progress was considered completely coterminous. So, when the onslaught of Islam came, the eastern churches were poorly equipped to evangelize or in parts to survive the Arab invasion. Unlike the West, where the churches formed a society within a society, the Byzantine churches were so enmeshed with the state that they could not act without being seen as agents of that state. Bishops negotiated with the Arab invaders, and became civil rulers of conquered enclaves.[8] Although some Christians did rise to great heights in the Arab civil service (for the conquering Arabs tended to take over Byzantine organization wholesale), and although Christian scholars were responsible for passing on much classical learning to Arabs (Nestorians were especially prominent in this), there was no ongoing life which could make the churches a living force. They were living off capital, and perhaps secretly hoping that some day another Constantine or Heraclius would come to re-extend the civil power against the barbarians. The Monophysite churches, already enclaves within Byzantine holdings, swiftly became enclaves within Islam, gradually fossilizing in isolation.

[8] The position of Archbishop Makarios in Cyprus until 1974 is a direct parallel.

**Leo the Isaurian, Byzantine emperor 717–741.** Note the cross, an iconclast protest against images.

And in the East, even the monasteries were lacking in the spiritual equipment which could have made them into spiritual powerhouses. The monastic ideal was seen in terms of quietistic contemplation and worship; there was no equivalent of the unruly and zealous Celtic monks who would go wandering and preaching among the barbarians.

Altogether, the rise of the Byzantine Empire shows the danger of church and state becoming too closely involved. The end product is a kingdom of this world, where the church is merely an instrument of the state, bound to rise and fall with the fortunes of that state. The foundations of this had been laid even in the time of Constantine. They had seen first real expression under Theodosius, and had been crystallized in the time of Justinian and Heraclius. If the foregoing tale makes dismal reading, it is because it is an all-too-apt commentary on the wishes of those who would see a 'Christian nation'. Such an ideal cannot exist, and it runs counter to the whole teaching of Jesus, who said that 'my kingdom is not of this world'.

# 9

# The West from Gregory the Great to Charlemagne

From some points of view, the year 600 was the point when spiritual life in the West reached its lowest ebb. Apart from the vigour of the Celtic churches in the extreme West, there was little sign of encouragement. Gregory the Great was struggling to uphold the cause of spiritual reform in Rome, but was often distracted because he had to spend time resisting Lombard attempts to overrun the church lands in middle Italy. Although there were a few spiritual men in the French churches, such as the hymn-writer Venantius Fortunatus[1] and the historian Gregory of Tours, the main picture there was of great spiritual lethargy. Indeed, such was the weakness of the Frankish churches that the impetus for the evangelization of England came from distant Rome rather than from the neighbouring churches in France.

## The evangelization of England begins

We do not know for certain how Gregory the Great first became interested in the Saxons of England.[2] The story of his seeing the fair-headed boys on sale as slaves may well have a considerable amount of truth in it. Certainly we know that he took a great

[1] Venantius himself was an Italian who had emigrated to Tours, become chaplain of a convent and subsequently bishop of Poitiers; some of his hymns occur in translation in our hymn books; e.g. 'Sing, my tongue, the glorious battle', 'The royal banners forward go.'
[2] Our main source for this period is the English historian Bede. His *History of the English Church and People* (available in the Penguin Classics series, 1970) was completed in 731. For Bede as a historian, see pp. 228ff.

interest in other remote regions (*e.g.* Visigothic Spain), and so it was quite natural that he would become concerned with the spiritual needs of England. Perhaps too, he would have received some information about England from wandering Celtic clerics, for Columbanus certainly wrote to him. And from his Frankish informants he may have heard of the marriage of the Christian princess Bertha, of the Merovingian household, to the king of Kent.

Anyway, in 596 Gregory commissioned the rather unwilling abbot of a monastery at Rome with the task of evangelizing the pagan English. This man, Augustine (not to be confused with the great theologian from North Africa), set out with a company of clergy to travel to England. Gregory smoothed his path by writing to the bishop of Arles, telling him to assist the missionaries, and eventually Augustine and his friends landed on the Isle of Thanet in East Kent (597).

Perhaps slightly to their surprise, they received a courteous welcome from king Ethelbert of Kent, and were permitted to set up a monastery in Canterbury. There they worshipped and went out to preach. The king himself invited them to preach before him, but specified that they should preach to him in the open air, because he feared that if they met him in a house they might use magic powers against him. Ethelbert was favourably impressed, and after a while he decided to ask for baptism and to join the Christian cause. His example meant that in the kingdom of Kent Christianity now possessed at least nominal supremacy.

The strategy of the churches towards the pagan barbarians differed markedly from the methods used inside the old Roman Empire. Instead of evangelizing for individual converts, there arose what has been called rather misleadingly 'mass conversions'. All efforts were directed to the rulers of a tribe, with a view to gaining their nominal adherence to Christianity and hence a secure base to deal with the rest of the tribe at leisure. In order to gain support from the king or chief, the Christian instruction given was often scanty and the degree of commitment required was small. Once the king had submitted to baptism, there was often very slow progress in evangelizing the rest of the tribe. And if the king's successor was anti-Christian, many of the nominal adherents, gained because of the royal attitude of favour to Christianity, would be lost. While the strategy of going for the leader was good, it was often an excuse for leaving evangelism in depth undone. Nobles and peasants would flock to baptism with little or no idea of what was involved, and the end result was a nation of vaguely Christianized pagans. The distinctive Christian lifestyle, which had been the glory of the early centuries, was conspicuously lacking among the mass-converted barbarians (*e.g.* the Franks). While there could be devout kings, and also outstanding saints from the rank and file, the Dark Age habit of 'mass-conversion' must bear much of the blame for formalistic Christianity in the Middle Ages.

After his success in Kent, Augustine wrote back to Gregory, asking for his advice on various points. It is somewhat astonishing that he did so, in view of the close proximity of the Frankish churches; this shows that he could expect little help from them. Augustine, used to the Roman liturgy, had been puzzled by the differing Gallican rite, and asked Gregory which should be adopted. Gregory, with remarkable wisdom, told him to select what he considered best from both rites and use that. Other queries concerned such diverse matters as how a bishop ought to be

**St Martin's Church, Canterbury,** site of Augustine's monastery and headquarters.

consecrated,[3] what were the prohibited degrees for marriage, what should be the punishment of those who robbed churches, and how the church finances ought to be organized.

Armed with Gregory's replies and with the help of more clergy sent from Rome, Augustine set about his task. There seems to have been little popular enthusiasm for Saxon paganism, and often Augustine actually reconsecrated pagan temples as Christian churches. But he failed dismally when he tried to establish relations with the Celtic bishops.

Because of their remoteness, the Celtic churches had clung to old customs much longer than the continental churches. A slight variation in the way they computed Easter meant that every so often they celebrated Easter Sunday on the Sunday before the continental churches. The monks of the Celtic church wore a different tonsure from other monks, and the organization of the church was based much more on monasteries than on town churches with a bishop. The tribal organization of the Irish and the western British had made this the most practical method. The main doctrines of orthodox Christianity, however, were shared by all the western churches. The Irish eucharistic rite[4] was similar to that of France and Spain, although it differed markedly from that of Rome. So when Augustine approached the Celtic bishops, the main point at issue was one of proper church organization rather than doctrine.

The historian Bede tells the tale of how, prior to meeting Augustine, the Celtic bishops asked a holy hermit whether Augustine was a man of God. The hermit proposed that they should see if Augustine were a humble servant of Christ (and therefore rightly their spiritual leader) by whether he rose to greet them or remained seated. The conference took place somewhere in the Bristol region in 603. Augustine, perhaps because of ill-health (he died in the following year), remained seated when the Celtic bishops arrived. They took this to be a sign of Roman arrogance, and refused to

[3] It was normal for there to be three bishops present, but it was agreed that in remote areas such as England a single bishop might officiate.

[4] Thanks to the decipherment of the palimpsest Munich Clm 14429 (dating from 675), which originates from either Northumbria or Ireland, we now know that the Irish rite was similar to the Gallican rite. Various other Irish fragments occur in the Stowe Missal and in some continental fragments collected by Bannister in *Journal of Theological Studies*, Old Series, vol. 5, pp. 49–75.

co-operate with him. The result was a sad failure to take advantage of a situation where England was wide open for the preaching of the gospel.

## The Roman mission after Augustine's death

Augustine died in 604, and was succeeded by Laurence (also a Roman cleric). Mellitus, another Roman cleric and bishop of London, went to evangelize Essex, and for a while it seemed that the mission was going well. But then there was a change of rulers. The Saxons of Essex reverted to paganism (though without martyring any missionaries), and the situation in Kent became so precarious after the death of king Ethelbert that Laurence and his friends actually prepared to abandon the whole work and flee to the continent. Only a traumatic dream, which left Laurence with weals all across his back as from a scourge, persuaded him to continue. Better days soon came; and when a Kentish princess married the king of Northumbria, another Roman cleric called Paulinus was allowed to go north with her as her chaplain. This proved to be a great opportunity. Paulinus preached before the king and his nobles, and they were impressed. Bede records how one old man at the king's court said that human life was like the flight of a sparrow in and out of the hall during winter, and that if the preachers could tell them anything of what happened before or after they should be heard. Enthusiastically, in 627, the Northumbrian king and nobles asked for baptism, and the chief priest of the pagan cult took the lead in demolishing the heathen altars which he had once consecrated.

Six years later, there was a grave setback. Penda, the pagan king of Mercia, allied with Cadwalla, the king of the Britons of Strathclyde; and they defeated the Northumbrians at the Battle of Haethfelth, near Doncaster, and killed their king. The whole of the Roman mission north of the Thames collapsed. Paulinus fled south, and was made bishop of Rochester; which office he held until his death. Perhaps the position was not quite so serious as it seemed, for we know that a certain James the Deacon contrived to stay in the North and pastor those Christian converts who stood firm. Although Penda was repulsed and Cadwalla died soon after, Northumbria was largely abandoned by the Rome-based mission.

# Map 6

## The British Isles

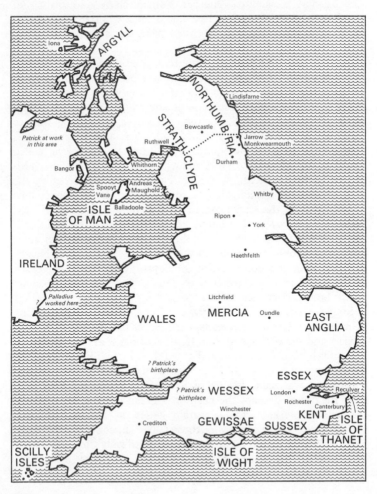

Iona

ARGYLL

NORTHUMBRIA

STRATHCLYDE

Lindisfarne

Bewcastle

*Patrick at work in this area*

Ruthwell

Jarrow
Monkwearmouth

Durham

Bangor

Whithorn

Spooyt
Vane

Andreas
Maughold

Balladoole

Whitby

ISLE
OF MAN

Ripon •

• York

IRELAND

Haethfelth •

*Palladius
worked here*
?

Litchfield

Oundle •

MERCIA

EAST
ANGLIA

WALES

*? Patrick's
birthplace*

ESSEX

*? Patrick's
birthplace*

WESSEX

London •

Reculver

Rochester •

Canterbury

Winchester

KENT

• Crediton

GEWISSAE

SUSSEX

ISLE
OF
THANET

SCILLY
ISLES

ISLE OF
WIGHT

# New moves to evangelize the Saxons

The new king of Northumbria, however, was a Christian. His name was Oswald, and he had been converted while in exile in the lowlands of Scotland. As soon as he was safely on the throne, he sent to Iona for someone to evangelize his kingdom. The first man who was sent considered the Northumbrians too barbarous to receive Christ, and returned to Iona. On his return there, he told the brethren such a grim story of them that one of his hearers asked if it would not be better to love the heathens of Northumbria rather than to condemn them. The rest suggested that he should go and try. In this way Aidan came to Northumbria. With the support first of king Oswald, and then his brother Oswy, Aidan set to work. He established his headquarters at Lindisfarne, and from there began to preach Christ in Northumbria. He was a gentle, humble, Christ-like man, whom even his opponents admired. Bede, who has little sympathy with Celtic Christians, is nevertheless unstinting in his praise of Aidan's saintliness. Aidan declined all the well-intentioned gifts of the kings, and lived and died in poverty, preaching Christ with love and determination until his death in 651.

Meanwhile, the Roman mission in Kent had turned its attention to Wessex. Although there were considerable difficulties, the work became permanent. First Birinus, an Italian cleric from Genoa, led the work. He was later joined by the Frankish bishop Angilbert,[5] but the local king disliked Angilbert's foreign accent, and appointed a Saxon bishop, Wini, who was one of the first native Englishmen to become a bishop, and who gave his name to Winchester. At the same time, the Irish and Celtic Christians were evangelizing other parts of England. An Irish abbot called Fursey settled in East Anglia, and Essex was evangelized for the second time by Cedd (another Celtic Christian). At the same time the kingdom of Mercia, which had been ruled for so long by the stubborn pagan king Penda (died 655), at last became nominally Christian through the influence of the Northumbrians.[6] These events brought the Roman and Celtic missionaries into close contact with each other in many parts of England. The differences between them could no longer be overlooked. For this reason a synod was called at Whitby by king Oswy of Northumbria, to which came delegations of Roman and Celtic clergy.

[5] The first mention of Frankish help in evangelizing England.
[6] The bishop of Mercia had his see at Lichfield.

## The Synod of Whitby

The Synod of Whitby (664) was not a clash between Protestants and Roman Catholics, as some mistakenly believe. But at the same time it was not a mere haggle over calendars and tonsures, even if these were the main points of debate. Both sides held firmly to the basic doctrines of the Christian faith (along with the various traditional accretions which had by now become attached), but they represented two distinct traditions of church life. The Celtic ideal embodied the zeal and freedom of the Spirit, with scant concern over administration. It was extremely monastic in outlook, but Celtic monks were wanderers and evangelists, not cloistered contemplatives. Because of the remoteness of Ireland and of Western Britain, the Celtic churches had preserved usages which had long since been superseded on the continent. But the Celtic clerics were far from being ignorant backwoodsmen. Their learning, acquired in their monasteries, was impressive, and they could debate with the best Roman-trained clergy on equal terms. They suffered the disadvantage of poor organization and instability, however, and it was easy for the Roman clergy to represent them as the only ones out of step. The Roman-inspired mission was a much more ordered and restrained affair. It had links back to the bishop of Rome, at that time the prime mover in spiritual reform in Western Europe. Its missionaries could claim with reasonable fairness that they were representatives of mainstream Christianity on the continent. But mainstream Christianity on the continent at that time was pretty poor stuff, and it is significant that the main spokesman for the Roman and continental party was Wilfrid, an Englishman who had received much of his early training from Celtic Christians. The Roman party, however, had the advantage of good organization and well-ordered churchmanship.

From the first, there was little idea of allowing both methods of calculating Easter to continue side by side. The synod debated which was the correct one to use, with an eye to uniformity. The Roman party made good use of the text[7] in which Christ appointed Peter as leader of the church; and king Oswy (not an acute theologian) declared that he did not want to fall foul of the man who had the keys of the kingdom. The Roman usage of Easter was declared to be the correct one, although how this could have been proved

[7] Matthew 16:17–19.

by the methods used is utterly puzzling. The Celtic bishop of Lindisfarne, Colman, who had been the Celtic spokesman, resigned his see and returned to Iona. But no sooner had the dispute been settled than a fresh disaster came over the English churches. In 665 the plague swept over Britain. Many died, including the prospective archbishop of Canterbury.[8] Of the Roman bishops only Wini remained, and although with the help of two Celtic bishops he consecrated Chad as bishop of Mercia, there was a great dearth of leadership and the prospect of an imminent breakdown of church life. A desperate letter was sent to Rome asking for help.

## Theodore and the consolidation of the English church

The pope of Rome, Vitalian (pope, 657–72), did not find it easy to find someone who would go to England. The first two men he approached both declined the offer, giving suitably devout reasons for their unworthiness but probably being horrified at the prospect of being bishop in a remote and barbarous island. And so the pope approached an elderly Greek monk, a refugee from the Muslim invasions, who had left Tarsus and had settled in a monastery at Rome. This monk, Theodore by name, agreed to go to England as archbishop. It would be hard to think of a less likely person to restore the tottering English churches and finally to put their organization on a firm footing. At sixty-six, most men of those days would be looking forward to a quiet life in retirement. Instead, Theodore the Greek began the most active part of his life at that age, and remained as archbishop of Canterbury for no less than twenty-one years!

It was Theodore's work as organizer and administrator which finally put the English churches on a sound footing, and so prepared them to undertake the great work of evangelizing North Europe and rebuilding cultural life in the eighth century. Coming from a well-ordered church situation, Theodore expected that similar customs should prevail in England. So he did hitherto unheard-of things like summoning synods of English clergy on a fairly regular basis. He travelled round inspecting the churches, and he laid the foundations for the parish system in England. Theodore did all this against a background of internecine war between the various petty

[8] The title 'archbishop' had been invented specially for the English situation by Gregory the Great.

An Anglo-Saxon cross at Ruthwell, Dumfrieshire, dating from
c. 680. It is believed that the crosses at Ruthwell and Bewcastle may have
been erected to mark preaching-points in this period before there were
church buildings.

kings, and on occasion was even called in to mediate between
disputing parties. He also had to face the problem of church
poverty. For example, the bishopric of Rochester was such a poorly
paid post that it was difficult to find anyone who would become
bishop.

Theodore had many gifted helpers in his attempts to improve
the English churches. From abroad came John, the chief church
musician from Rome. He settled with Benedict Biscop, the abbot of
Monkwearmouth, and did much to improve the church services.
At the same time, John's influence caused the spread of the Roman
rite, displacing the older Gallican/Irish service books. Celtic

bishops also fitted into Theodore's reforms, the most notable among them being Cuthbert, the hermit of Lindisfarne who was made bishop in 685. He had long been known as a keen evangelist, often travelling on foot to evangelize remote villages where paganism still persisted. Cuthbert was known by all as an eminently Christ-like man, with a gentleness similar to that of Aidan or Columba, and typical of the best in the Celtic tradition.[9] Also in the North was the redoubtable and saintly abbess Hilda, who presided over two monasteries (one for each sex) at Whitby. It was she who encouraged the cowherd turned composer, Caedmon. He was a lay brother at the monastery, who was totally unmusical until one night when he received from an angel the gift of composing songs. He composed many songs on biblical themes, using the North-umbrian vernacular.

It was in Theodore's time that the last enclaves of paganism in England were finally evangelized. There was Sussex, where a turbulent monk named Wilfrid not only taught the backward inhabitants about Christ but also helped them to avoid famine by teaching them to fish. But the final enclave of paganism was the Isle of Wight, which was evangelized after being conquered by the pro-Christian king of the Gewissae (the tribe holding Hampshire and Wiltshire). Wilfrid was also involved in this, so perhaps it is time to look at the career of this extraordinary English cleric.

## The career of Wilfrid

Wilfrid was born in about 634 in Northumbria. From early years he was attracted to Christian things, and when he was in his teens he entered the Celtic monastery at Lindisfarne. After a while, he decided that he wanted to go to Rome to study; so he wandered south to Kent, where he met Benedict Biscop.[1] The two set out together, and after some delays in France, Wilfrid and Benedict eventually reached Rome. From there Wilfrid later returned to France, and narrowly escaped execution when one of the Mero-vingian kings had his friend, bishop Dalfin of Lyons, murdered.

---

[9] After his death in 687, Cuthbert's body had several resting-places until it was finally enshrined at Durham Cathedral. His pectoral cross, silver portable altar and fragments of his vestments can still be seen there.

[1] We have already met him in his later position of abbot at Monkwear-mouth.

Wilfrid was spared on the grounds that he was a foreigner and therefore not involved in a domestic Frankish quarrel. Wilfrid returned to England, and set up a monastery near Ripon. From there he emerged to take part as the main pro-Roman spokesman at the Synod of Whitby. Perhaps as a result of this, he was sent over to France to be consecrated bishop. This was done with great splendour by Angilbert,[2] the bishop of Paris. Instead of returning to Northumbria to take up his duties, however, Wilfrid remained on the continent, and king Oswy of Northumbria got impatient. The king consecrated Chad as bishop of York in his place. Three years later, Wilfrid eventually turned up, and Chad very humbly retired to a monastery while Wilfrid took over as bishop.

Trouble soon followed, and Wilfrid was deposed by an English synod of bishops. But he was not beaten. He set off to Rome to

[2] The same Angilbert who had formerly been bishop in Wessex, as related above (p. 221).

**The Saxon crypt, Ripon Cathedral,** dating from the time of Wilfrid. The steps lead to a narrow opening, through which women were required to squeeze in order to prove their chastity. This is a good example of early medieval superstition.

appeal, no doubt basing his action on the custom that had grown up whereby the pope of Rome acted as judge of appeals against the decisions of local synods. When Wilfrid set out, however, he was blown ashore in Frisia, where he immediately set about evangelizing the natives. Eventually he reached Rome, was reinstated and returned to England, where he seems not to have returned to his see. Instead, he spent some of the next five years evangelizing the pagans of Sussex and the Isle of Wight. He did eventually return to his see, only to be expelled again by the king and some of the other bishops. Nothing daunted, he retraced his steps to Rome, appealed, was acquitted and returned yet again. By now an old and feeble man, he managed to spend his last four years in peace as bishop, and died at Oundle. The brethren of that monastery carried his body back to his old monastery at Ripon for burial.

Wilfrid is the perfect example of the combining of Roman and Celtic Christianity. From the point of organization and practice, Wilfrid was Roman to the core. But his turbulence, his wanderlust, his learning and the driving power to evangelize wherever he had opportunity, were all Celtic traits. For a while such a combination would make the English churches the spiritual powerhouse of Europe, until the zeal waned away and Roman order was succeeded by Roman torpor.

## Further English advances

While Wilfrid was still alive his example was followed in 692 by Willibrord, who set off from England and took up Wilfrid's work among the Frisians, and was eventually made bishop of Utrecht. Willibrord was helped in his missionary work by the political support of Pepin of Heristal, the mayor of the palace who effectively ruled that part of the Frankish domains. This situation marks the start of the combination of English missionaries and Frankish political power which was to be so effective during the career of Boniface. Meanwhile, the English churches were becoming completely self-supporting, and beginning to produce their own leaders and scholars. When Theodore the Greek died in 690, he was succeeded as archbishop of Canterbury by Bertwald, the abbot of the monastery at Reculver. Later in the same generation, Christian scholarship in England became world famous with the career of Bede.

**Part of Bede's History of the English Church and People**, from a manuscript probably written in southern England in the later 8th century. Bede summarized English history from the Roman invasion to Augustine (597), taken from earlier chronicles. Then he gave a more detailed history of the period 597–731.

Bede was essentially the prototype of the mediaeval Benedictine monk, seldom leaving his monastery and taking little part in the affairs of the wider world. But Bede gathered information from books and visitors as he worked in his cell at Jarrow, and he built on the foundations laid by his teachers, Benedict Biscop and Coelfrid, the abbots at Monkwearmouth and Jarrow respectively. In many ways, Bede's learning foreshadowed the characteristic attitude of the Carolingian renaissance. He gathered, systematized and preserved the wisdom of past ages. In his famous *History of the English Church and People* (the main source for the early part of this chapter), he used books like Constantius' *Life of St Germanus of Auxerre* and Gildas' *Concerning the Destruction of Britain*. For his own and for near-contemporary times he supplemented book knowledge by personal reminiscences, including some rather fantastic miracle stories. But even allowing for such limitations, Bede was a scholar who stood head and shoulders above anyone else of his day. When we remember that Bede's grandfather must have

**The Lindisfarne Gospels.** The beginning of John's Gospel in the Latin (Vulgate) manuscript of the Gospels written and illuminated at Lindisfarne c. 698.

been an illiterate pagan, the progress made is all the more surprising. Bede died at Jarrow in 735, shortly after completing a translation of John's Gospel into the Anglo-Saxon vernacular.[3] Even as Bede worked and died, events were taking place on the continent which would be highly significant for the churches there.

## The rise of the Frankish 'mayors of the palace'

Since the reign of 'good king Dagobert' in the early seventh century, there had been no strong kings[4] in the Frankish territories. Instead, power had gradually passed into the hands of the mayors of the palace in the various areas. Merovingian kings still ruled in name, but already various 'mayors of the palace' were building up their own dynasties. Foremost among these were the Arnulfings, so called because one of their famous forebears had been bishop Arnulf of Metz. In the mid-seventh century[5] the Arnulfings made an abortive attempt to seize power from the weak Merovingian kings, but the aspiring dictator Grimoald did not have popular support and was easily seized and executed. His nephew, Pepin of Heristal, became the next mayor of the palace in Austrasia (the Germanic part of the Frankish realm, as distinct from Neustria—Northern France—and Burgundy). Although only the *de facto* ruler of part of the Frankish territories, he gradually amassed sufficient power to crush his enemies decisively at the Battle of Tertry (687). Pepin of Heristal, however, did not go so far as to supplant the weak kings, even though it was his permission and support which made it possible for Willibrord to do his missionary work in Frisia. When Pepin died in 714 there followed a year or so of internal strife before his illegitimate son Charles Martel seized power as the new mayor of the palace.

Although Charles Martel was an able ruler and soldier, he had little idea of spirituality. He confiscated church lands in order to

[3] Although Bede's translation is lost, we have interlinear translations in two Anglo-Saxon manuscripts of similar age, the Lindisfarne and Rushworth Gospels, which use Northumbrian and Mercian respectively. Some scholars believe that Bede's translation is the source for the version of John in the Lindisfarne Gospels.
[4] See above, pp. 180ff.
[5] For the secular history see Moss, *The Birth of the Middle Ages*, pp. 198ff.

make them gifts to his nobles, and his general attitude to the churches in his domains was so cavalier that later churchmen considered that his actions would consign him utterly to hell. But Charles Martel did give his support to Boniface when he was beginning his missionary work in Germany, and without peace and protection Boniface admitted that he would have had an impossible task. Charles Martel was the man of the moment in one other important point. In 711, the victorious Arabs had crossed from North Africa to Spain, called in as allies in one of the internal wars of the Visigothic kingdom there. They eventually conquered the whole of the Iberian peninsula. The effect on the church there was disastrous. Not only was there great pressure to go Muslim, but the surviving church split. Some, the more conservative, were pro-Arab, and they continued to use the old Spanish rite (similar to the Gallican and Irish rites) which was henceforward dubbed 'Mo-zarabic' or Arabianizing. The anti-Arab faction, which was eventually to lead the forces of reconquest against the Arabs, allied itself with the reforming forces in Rome, and began to use the Roman rite.[6] The victorious Arabs moved north across the Pyrenes. Charles Martel, however, gathered a huge allied army and decisively defeated them at the Battle of Poitiers (732). Although the Arabs retained footholds in Provence and Septimania for some years afterwards (being finally expelled by Charlemagne), they were never again a great threat. And whatever the church leaders privately thought of Charles Martel, they enthusiastically praised God for his victory.

Charles Martel died in 741, and although his own plans had been to divide his realm between his three sons, fortunately for Frankland this idea failed. One son was easily deposed, another felt moved to enter a monastery, and this left Pepin the Short as uncontested mayor of the palace and leader of the Franks.

## Pepin the Short and Boniface

Unlike his father, Pepin had quite good relations with the churches. This, however, was not because of altruistic motives, but because he needed the support of the clergy for a momentous plan. He

[6] Eventually the Roman rite became universal in Spain, and only a modified form of the Mozarabic rite survives now, used only in a few churches in Toledo.

wanted spiritual approval for his plan to become king of the Franks. The men he turned to were Fulrad, the abbot of the monastery of St Denis at Paris, and Boniface.

Boniface was an Englishman, born at Crediton in Devon and brought up in various English monasteries.[7] In 715 he crossed over to Frisia to help Willibrord, but was so discouraged that he quickly returned to England. Soon he set out again, however, this time for Rome, where he was well received and encouraged to devote his energies to evangelizing German Thuringia. He accordingly went back to Frankish territory, and after working under Willibrord for a time he branched out on his own and started preaching Christ in Thuringia and Hesse. With the support of Charles Martel, and impelled by commendable missionary zeal, his mission went extremely well. He gathered converts by the thousands, and on a visit to Rome in 722 he was appointed bishop for the whole of Eastern Germany. His appointment was unusual in that he was directly responsible to the pope of Rome. This was perhaps natural at the time, for he would gain little help from the weak Frankish churches, where many of the top posts were filled by unspiritual, lay favourites of Charles Martel. But it was also a significant step in the growth of papal power.

Boniface was a blunt, plain-spoken preacher, but he also had a flair for the spectacular. At Geismar, in Hesse, there was a great oak sacred to the god Thor. As a demonstration of the impotence of Thor, Boniface approached the great tree with an axe and proceeded to fell it. Since no thunderbolt came to strike him down, the local people accepted this as proof of the superiority of the Christian gospel.

Boniface did not work alone. He imported many English monks and nuns to work with him in his task of pioneer evangelism. In a method reminiscent of the Irish, he set up monasteries which were to be the centres of spiritual advance. Among the famous monasteries which he founded were Fritzlar and Fulda, and such was the speed of advance that Fulda had a native abbot by 750. Boniface worked strenuously in Germany for many years. Then, in 741, the death of Charles Martel gave him an opportunity to do something about the Frankish churches. Pepin the Short turned to the aged and saintly Boniface as the man who could help him in his quest for kingship.

[7] See Walker, *The Growing Storm*, pp. 26–34.

And Boniface took advantage of this to begin reforms in the Frankish churches.

Pepin the Short had been in no hurry to rush to kingship. His father, Charles Martel, had once neglected to appoint a new king after the death of the old one for several years, and had ruled as king in all but name. Pepin's ambition was to be recognized as king, but he wanted to be sure that his move would get full support. He sent Fulrad, the abbot of St Denis, to Rome with a discreetly worded letter asking whether it was right that the feeble Merovingian puppets should continue to be called kings when the real power was so obviously elsewhere. The pope of Rome, who at that time wanted Frankish help to defend him against the ever-encroaching Lombards, readily agreed. And so the last Merovingian was deposed and sent into a monastery,[8] and Pepin was declared king. And for the first time there was a coronation, where the king was solemnly anointed. This was done at Soissons, and Boniface officiated, acting in his capacity as papal legate but also as the spiritual leader in Frankland. The sanction of the Christian church had been officially given to Pepin's seizure of power.

With the king of the Franks now a close friend of his, Boniface was able to begin the work of reforming the Frankish churches. For the first time for centuries, church synods were held in Frankish territories, and a start was made in dealing with the grosser instances of clerical immorality and disorder in the churches. Boniface's strongly moralistic sermons were needed, not only among recently converted pagans, but also for the exceedingly worldly Frankish clergy.

At heart, however, Boniface was still a missionary. In about 753 he felt the call to go out again, this time into northern Frisia. Having prudently designated his successor and packed his shroud, he set off with a group of monks. His preaching power had not waned, and soon he was gathering converts again. A year or so later, while about to baptise a group of new Christians, he and his friends were set upon and massacred by a heathen tribe. But Boniface's work had been done well. Other English and native German missionaries took up the task, and in England Boniface was soon widely regarded as a saint.

[8] This was becoming the standard way of getting rid of political rivals, and was probably preferable to splitting their heads with a battle-axe.

## Pepin and Italy

Meanwhile, Pepin the Short was being called upon for help by a churchman from another quarter. The pope who had given sanction for Pepin's kingship had died in 752, and was succeeded by Stephen II. Stephen was being harried by Aistulf, king of the Lombards in North Italy, who had finally put an end to the exarchate of Ravenna, which had ruled the fragments of Byzantine territory in North Italy. Now Aistulf was encroaching southwards into the territory which, though nominally Byzantine, was under the control of the pope of Rome. To make the pope's situation worse, south of the band of church territory which spanned the Italian peninsula were two Lombard duchies of Spoleto and Benevento. No help could be expected from Constantinople. The only possible saviour who could keep the pope of Rome from becoming a vassal bishop of the Lombards was the new king of the Franks, Pepin. So, in his distress, Stephen II came to Frankland to beg for help.

When he arrived in 754, he was required to officiate at the coronation of Pepin's two sons, Carloman and the future emperor Charlemagne. And so began the close alliance between the Frankish kingdom and the Roman papacy. A solemn assembly was held to decide what should be done on behalf of the pope. Many of the Frankish nobles were not too keen on a campaign in Italy. To complicate things further, Pepin's brother, now a monk at Monte Cassino, came at the command of his Lombard masters (Monte Cassino being in Lombard territory) to speak against the proposal. But in the end, Pepin convinced the assembly that they should undertake an expedition.

Pepin's army had little difficulty in crossing the Alps and defeating the Lombard army. Aistulf, the Lombard king, was compelled by the subsequent treaty to hand over the cities he had seized from the pope, and to make a large payment to Pepin. But no sooner had Pepin left than the Lombard king went back on his promises. He had, however, underestimated Pepin, who returned with his army and enforced the terms of the treaty (756). Having done this, Pepin returned back across the Alps once more, and took no further part in Italian politics. He devoted his attentions to pushing back the Arabs in Provence and to conquering Aquitaine, and finally died after a period of ill health in 767. In accordance with the ruinous Frankish custom, the kingdom was divided between his two sons, Charles (the future emperor Charlemagne) and Carloman.[9]

## Charlemagne

We are fortunate in possessing an almost contemporary biography of Charlmagne,[1] written by Einhard. This monk was brought from his monastery at Fulda to be architect of Charlemagne's new palace at Aachen, and remained as a quiet but observant member of Charlemagne's court circle. After retiring to be abbot of Seligenstadt on Charlemagne's death (814), he composed the king's biography in his later years, and died in 844. Using Suetonius' *Lives of the Caesars* as a model, Einhard is a usually faithful witness, preferring to remain silent when he cannot say anything good about his lord and patron. Other sources, and intelligent deduction, help to fill out the details of the story.

Charlemagne and his younger brother Carloman never got on well together, but the kingdom was spared civil war by Carloman's death three years after his accession in 771. This, however, was not the end of family trouble. The ambitious queen mother, Bertrada,

[9] It will be convenient from now on to refer to Charles, the son of Pepin the Short, as Charlemagne; even though this form of his name (meaning Charles the Great) was probably not used during his lifetime.

[1] There is also another biography, written by a monk from St Gall, sometimes called Notker Balbulus; but it is much less reliable. A good modern biography is E. M. Almedingen's *Charlemagne: a Study* (Bodley Head, 1968). See also R. Winston, *Charlemagne: from the Hammer to the Cross* (Constable, 1969).

**The emperor Charlemagne (771–814)**, the first emperor (from 800) of the 'Holy Roman Empire'. A coin in the British Museum, London. (Note the barbarous workmanship when compared with Roman coins.)

had arranged various marriage alliances between the Frankish royal family and the Lombards. The duke of Bavaria had married one daughter of Desiderius, king of the Lombards in succession to Aistulf, and Charlemagne himself had married another. When Carloman died, his wife and children fled to the Lombard king. But Charlemagne was ready for war, and he was given ample pretext when the new pope Adrian I asked for help against Lombard aggression. Charlemagne had already divorced his Lombard wife and married again, much to his mother's fury. Now, he crossed the Alps with an army, as his father Pepin had done, and soundly defeated the Lombards. But he resolved never to have such trouble again. When he finally captured the Lombard capital of Pavia, king Desiderius was sent to spend the rest of his days in a Frankish monastery, and the same fate befell Carloman's wife and children. The Lombard king's son managed to slip away to Constantinople, where he intrigued with little success for nearly twenty years. Meanwhile, Charlemagne absorbed Lombardy into his realm and took on himself the title 'king of the Lombards'.

Even while conducting the campaign in Italy, Charlemagne took the opportunity to travel to Rome. He was given a tumultuous welcome by the astute pope Adrian, who wanted to acquire the ascendent over the new lord of Italy. Promises were made about the restoration of church lands to the pope, but Charlemagne was not completely dazzled by Roman splendour. His generous donations proved to be difficult for the pope to translate into fact, for Charlemagne had no great wish to make the pope a great civil potentate, much as he admired the office of bishop of Rome. So began an ambivalent relationship between Charlemagne and the papacy. The various popes viewed Charlemagne as their earthly protector, but always tried to gain moral ascendancy over him (as Ambrose of Milan had once gained it over the emperor Theodosius). For his part, Charlemagne treated the papal domains as part of his kingdom, even sending in his officials to keep an eye on the administration. But at the same time he had a great reverence for the church of Rome as the centre of western Christendom (of which he saw himself as secular king). He was always eager to have Roman help in his reforming plans. But the primacy he accorded the various popes was a nebulous one, and he could on occasion even tell the pope what to do on matters of Christian doctrine.

## The Saxon war

The longest and bitterest war that Charlemagne fought was that against the Saxons. For thirty-three years his armies ravaged and burnt Saxony, often in reprisal against Saxon raids. But, in addition to the political motive for the war, there was a religious motive. The Saxons were pagans, and Charlemagne saw it as his duty to convert them. Unfortunately, the only method of conversion he knew was one backed up by force. We have already seen how the political support of Charles Martel and Pepin the Short had helped Boniface in the conversion of parts of Germany. Charlemagne took this support one terrible stage further. When the Saxons refused to receive normal missionaries, Charlemagne sent in his army. There followed a terrible tale of forced baptisms, Saxon revolts, savage Frankish reprisals and years of bitterness and misery. At one point, Charlemagne imposed a series of laws on Saxony which made all paganism illegal, and even made such offences as eating meat during Lent a capital offence. When the Saxons rose in revolt against this, Charlemagne replied by massacring 4,500 Saxon nobles in a single day at Verden. Eventually, Charlemagne solved the 'Saxon problem' only by mass deportations, removing almost a third of the Saxons to other parts of his kingdoms and replacing them with other inhabitants. At last, wiser and more moderate counsels prevailed. People like Alcuin (an Anglo-Saxon from England, of whom we shall hear more later) advised Charlemagne to be moderate in his laws. The savage edicts were withdrawn. When the Saxon leader Widukind eventually surrendered to Charlemagne, he suffered no punishment, and Charlemagne was his sponsor at his baptism. Instead of using the church as a means of repression, with priests having the power of death over the Saxons, Charlemagne gave to the newly established churches in Saxony the right to commute the death penalty to some lesser punishment, and the death penalty itself was limited to a few of the very worst crimes.

With the help of English missionaries, the Saxons finally began to accept the real Christ instead of the political monster preached by Charlemagne's sword. From these later attempts to evangelize the Saxons comes the curious poem called the *Heliand*. It is an attempt to put the gospel story into terms which would be congenial to the warlike Saxons. Jesus and His disciples are depicted as a great lord and his knights. Jesus' death on the cross is shown as a conquest of the devil, by which He freed those imprisoned in hell. Faith in Jesus Christ is thought of in terms of the fidelity which should be shown to a great lord by his vassal. Even if there is a bending of the gospel narrative at times, it was at least a well-intentioned attempt to make Christ seem a worth-while Lord to the pagan Saxons.

## Charlemagne's other conquests

Charlemagne extended his power in other areas with less effort. He pushed his frontier across the Pyrenees into Spain, in alliance with king Alfonso, the Christian king of Asturias. It was in one of these campaigns that there was the incident at Roncevalles, later immortalized and loaded with myth in *The Song of Roland*. He also quietened Brittany, where British emigrants from the early Saxon invasion had always been a thorn in the side of the Merovingian kings. He incorporated Bavaria into his kingdom without a war by terrifying the duke, Tassilo, into submission, and then consigning him to a monastery. Apart from wars against the Slavs and Danes, his other great military enterprise was the destruction of the Avars. They were a nomadic Asian race, who had settled in a great fortress somewhere in the region of Hungary or Rumania. From there they had raided the Eastern Roman Empire, as well as central European states. Between 789 and 796 Charlemagne's forces devastated their lands, eventually storming the allegedly impregnable 'Ring' fortress and returning with an immense booty. But although this was a war against pagans, Charlemagne did not enforce Christianity here. Some evangelistic work had already been done by Fergal[2] and Arno, successively bishops of Salzburg, and Charlemagne was content to allow evangelism in the area once dominated by the Avars to proceed normally.

In foreign policy, Charlemagne was an unashamed expansionist, and his Christianity was on occasion used as an excuse. But he could equally well turn a blind eye to religious differences, as when he struck up a friendship by letter with the Muslim Harun-al-

[2] He was a wandering Irish monk who eventually settled as bishop of Salzburg. His other claim to fame is that he believed in the existence of the Antipodes (the southern hemisphere), for which belief he was sharply censured!

Raschid of Baghdad.[3] He viewed his expansionist campaigns as part of the extension of the kingdom of God, of which Charlemagne was to be earthly king! In fact, his effect on outsiders was such that it became proverbial in Constantinople to say, 'Have a Frank for a friend, but not for a neighbour'!

## Charlemagne and his court

Charlemagne's Christianity was sincere as far as it went, but it had notable blind spots. He was not personally an ostentatious man, abhorring foreign luxury and foreign dress.[4] He was a man of vast physique (Einhard says that he was nearly 7 ft tall, and broad with it), and was a ravenous eater with an equally voracious sexual appetite. He married four times, and also had many mistresses.[5] Yet he was very severe on clerical morals, disapproved of drunkenness and was fanatically against homosexuality. Those who travelled around with his court found it a noisy and not altogether wholesome place, for Charlemagne had three daughters whose many affairs were cheerfully condoned by their father. Yet Charlemagne saw no incongruity between the goings-on at his court and regular attendance at church services—he himself being a most scrupulous attender.

Charlemagne gathered round him the finest scholars of Western Europe, and harnessed their energies to produce a revival of learning on the continent. The leader of this scholarly group was an Englishman, Alcuin. Alcuin was a Saxon from Northumbria, whom Charlemagne first met when they were both in Italy. Charlemagne persuaded Alcuin to leave his post as the head of the cathedral school at York, and to come to his court. Einhard reckoned Alcuin to be the most learned man of his day, and he was in fact the prototype of the mediaeval scholar. He never rose high in the church hierarchy, being only a deacon, although later on he was abbot of Tours in his old age. He was a dour, careful gatherer of facts and

[3] He held a position in the Muslim world analogous to that of Charlemagne. The two exchanged letters and gifts. Among the presents which Charlemagne received was an elephant, which lived for a number of years at his palace in Aachen, and was such a curiosity that chroniclers made special mention of its death after some years in captivity.

[4] Only twice in his life could he be prevailed upon to wear the Roman court dress, preferring to wear the Frankish tunic and trousers.

[5] The circumspect Einhard mentions only five!

**Alcuin's revision of the Latin Vulgate.** The 9th-century manuscript shows Wisdom 1:1–5.

an encourager of others. But Alcuin was no cloistered academic. He gave Charlemagne good and Christian advice over his treatment of the Saxons. He entered into theological debate with vigour when he had to counter the Adoptionist heresy of Felix of Urgel.[6] And Alcuin had a not uncritical eye for Charlemagne's court. In a private letter to a friend he warns him to 'beware of the crowned doves which fly all over the king's court' (a covert reference to Charlemagne's daughters), but in public he kept his own counsel.

Alcuin was not always on friendly terms with others of the court circle. He never got on very well with Angilbert, the merry adventurer who was the lover of one of Charlemagne's daughters, even though he was also a theologian and diplomat and a poet of no small merit. Alcuin also had a clash with Theodulf of Orléans, but this seems to have been an isolated incident centring round a point of church discipline.[7] Theodulf's greatest work as a member of the learned circle at court was the help he gave Charlemagne in editing and standardizing the Frankish law. Most people, however, know of him through his Palm Sunday hymn, 'All glory, laud and honour'.

A man of Alcuin's own temperament was Paul Warnefrid, usually known as Paul the Deacon. He was a Lombard monk from Monte Cassino, whom Charlemagne induced to come to court. Paul was a sombre, austere man who longed for the quiet of his cloister, and who disliked life at the Frankish court so much that he called it 'my prison'. Although a great scholar, with a command of many languages and a considerable poetical gift, he was eventually released by Charlemagne, who allowed him to return to Monte Cassino where he lived till his death in 795. Here he wrote a scholarly *History of the Lombards* and a sermon book for unlearned clergy (this latter commissioned by Charlemagne himself). The scholars from the British Isles made a great contribution to Charlemagne's renaissance. Not only was there Alcuin to lead it, but Norse raids on Ireland forced many Irish scholars to flee to the continent.[8] At least three (Clement, Dicuil and Dungal) became noted and permanent members of the court circle of Charlemagne.

[6] Felix was a bishop in the Spanish march (or borderland) who taught that Christ was Son of God only by adoption. He was forced to recant at the Synod of Frankfurt in 794.

[7] A cleric from Orléans had fled to Tours for sanctuary, and Alcuin refused to give him up.

[8] Hence also the considerable number of Irish manuscripts in continental monastic libraries.

## The Carolingian renaissance

With Charlemagne himself setting an example as an avid learner, the emphasis on learning spread down into the churches. Many monastic schools were set up; and a great effort was made to educate the clergy, many of whom were so ignorant that they hardly knew even the Lord's Prayer. Charlemagne himself issued edict upon edict, enjoining clergy to refrain from frequenting taverns, to give up immorality and to devote themselves to Christian teaching. Monks were forbidden to wander from monastery to monastery, and nuns were censured for gossip and passing on love-letters.

In his programme of reform Charlemagne looked to Rome for help. Early in his reign he was sent a Roman manual of canon law, and he tried to get this accepted as the normative form of church law in his realm. Similarly, codes of church discipline were standardized, and consequently many Irish 'penitential books', giving lists of sins and appropriately graded penances, were destroyed. Again, in the field of liturgy, he issued an 'act of uniformity' making the Roman rite the only one to be used, thereby supplanting the variegated Gallican rites.[9] But such moves took time to take effect. Mixed Gallican and Roman mass-books were produced, and Gallican liturgies were still being copied during his reign,[1] one of the latest fragments containing a pathetic prayer for deliverance 'from the Norman swords'.[2]

[9] This is the so-called *Praefatiuncula*, which occurs in a number of ninth-century manuscripts of the 'Gregorian' Missal. It stands between the Roman part of the missal, which is prescribed as obligatory, and an appendix containing various prayers of Gallican origin (which are permitted, but not required usage).

[1] The so-called *Missale Gothicum* and the *Missale Gallicanum Vetus* are examples of mass-books with both Roman and Gallican masses in one volume. The Roman rite took some while to spread, and significantly one of the oldest manuscripts of the Roman missal (*Vat. Reg. Lat.* 316) was written at the abbey of Chelles, where Charlemagne's sister Gisla was abbess.

[2] Bannister's fragment A (*Journal of Theological Studies*, Old Series, vol. 5, pp. 49–75). This fragment was written in the late eighth or early ninth century, and was torn up to be used as binding for the *Karlsruhe Bede*, which was written around 840. By 800, Hildwin, the abbot of St Denis in Paris, could report that there were no Gallican books in usable condition. The latest datable Gallican mass to be composed is the mass for St Leudegarius (died 678).

Monastic rules were revised too, and under Charlemagne's son Louis the Pious the rule of Benedict was declared to be the only legal monastic rule, thus supplanting many varied earlier rules.[3]

Finally, Charlemagne's renaissance produced an effect even on handwriting. The untidy Merovingian script gave way to a new, neat script which scholars call 'Carolingian miniscule', and which is the direct ancestor of the lower-case letters we use today.

As we can see from the foregoing actions, Charlemagne, although with no official position within the church, was its effective head. He was master of the church within his domains, but this mastery was exercised under the advice of men who had at least some devotion to Christ. But in his Romanizing policy, Charlemagne was setting the foundations for mediaeval, papal-dominated Christendom. He was a strong enough king to give orders to the various popes, but his very strength encouraged his own clerics to look to Rome as a counterbalance to the power of the king. It is from this period that the 'False Decretals' and the *Donation of Constantine* come,[4] forged documents which enhanced the claims of the Roman papacy to universal jurisdiction. They were produced by clergy who preferred to be subservient to a pope far away rather than a king close at hand. But while Charlemagne was alive, he ruled the churches. When a synod was held at Frankfurt to deal with the heresy of Felix of Urgel, Charlemagne presided. When the decrees of the eastern council against iconoclasm seemed to enjoin worship of images, Charlemagne instigated the counterblast of the 'Caroline books' which were so harsh against images that many Roman Catholic scholars at the time of the Reformation thought they were a Protestant forgery! Even on small matters, it was the king who gave judgment, rather than the bishops.

[3] This was mainly due to the advocacy of Benedict of Aniane, a Visigothic Spaniard, who was an enthusiastic supporter of the Benedictine rule and had changed his name in consequence. There were many riots (*e.g.* at Tours) when the new rule was imposed.

[4] The 'False Decretals' are decrees allegedly coming from the very early bishops of Rome (the earliest genuine 'decretal' is a letter of advice from bishop Siricius (385–399) to Himerius of Tarragona). The *Donation of Constantine* is a document purporting to be Constantine's bequest of the whole of the Western Empire to the pope of Rome in thankfulness for a cure from leprosy. Both forgeries emphasize the rights of the church of Rome in opposition to the civil power.

## Charlemagne as emperor

The junction of imperial power and papal Christianity was made official on Christmas Day 800, when Charlemagne was crowned emperor by the pope (whom he had previously helped to stay on the papal throne despite grave accusations from enemies). Charlemagne professed to be surprised and annoyed, but there is evidence that the coronation had been planned with his acquiescence. People do not usually have a crown on the altar and all the coronation trimmings available at an ordinary Christmas eucharist. Perhaps it was not the coronation which annoyed Charlemagne, but the way it was done, because it looked as if the pope was conferring something on him. It is significant that when Charlemagne's son Louis became emperor with his father in 813, there was no pope invited to perform the ceremony. Charlemagne merely gave his son a lecture on kingship and then let him take the crown from the altar himself. But whatever the details, Charlemagne was hailed as 'Roman emperor', and before the end of his reign the Byzantine emperors recognized him as such.

This act was the coping-stone on the edifice of mediaeval Christendom. The Christian church had changed from being a gathered company of believers. It was now a political entity with a visible emperor. But behind that emperor stood the spiritual and political power and prestige of the pope of Rome, soon to assert itself over even the civil power. There was the pious hope that the kingdoms of this world would now become the kingdom of Christ, but this was never likely. In his enthusiasm for building a reformed Christian state, Charlemagne had unwittingly strengthened the hand of a papacy which viewed itself as the only true head of Christendom. Control of the church by the emperor had given way to a theory of church government which would eventually become papal tyranny. The mediaeval church began definitively with Charlemagne's coronation. Although the political Empire quickly disintegrated when Charlemagne died in 814, the spiritual Empire continued. The popes of Rome did not consider relinquishing the position they had gained. The reforming spirituality faded, or else retreated into the contemplative life of the monastery. At the end of the transformation there emerged the fully developed mediaeval church.

# 10

# Epilogue

Charlemagne had intended to divide his realm between his three sons. In the event, two died before their father, and the inept Louis the Pious succeeded as sole ruler. But the cracks in the edifice of empire were widening fast. Louis the Pious reigned till his death in 840, but was so weak a ruler that at one time (in 833) he was forced to abdicate. Significantly, the church leaders were among those who forced him to do so. The feudal barons swiftly became petty kings in their own right. Linguistically also, the empire was falling apart. The debased Carolingian Latin was already existing alongside vernacular dialects[1] which would eventually become Old French and Old German.[2] Impetus for the decay was given by the Norse raids. Even during the reign of Charlemagne the Norsemen were attacking the coasts of England and Ireland. Soon after his death, nowhere within reach of the sea or a navigable river was safe. With these pagan raids came great suffering for the churches. Clergy were murdered, monasteries were burnt down, books were destroyed, and paganism saw a resurgence. But there was just sufficient life in the western churches for the savage raiders to be converted. Perhaps the best evidence of their conversion comes from the Isle of Man. At Balladoole, near Castletown, there is an early Christian cemetery within a Celtic hill fort. In the midst of this cemetery, disturbing many of the earlier graves, is a

[1] These dialects had a long pre-history themselves. Charlemagne himself spoke the old Germanic tongue of the Franks, and even edited a collection of the old heroic poems in this tongue, but this collection was destroyed by Louis the Pious because it was pagan literature.

[2] The first French document extant, *Le serment de Strasbourg*, is a treaty between the sons of Louis the Pious, dating from 842.

**A Celtic Iron Age hill fort at Chapel Hill,** Balladoole, Isle of Man. A Viking ship burial, disturbing a Christian cemetry, is marked by stones at the left end. In the centre are traces of a house, and in the top right-hand corner is a keeil and enclosure.

pagan Viking ship-burial. But the site also contains a small chapel, built by the first Christians but subsequently rebuilt in the later Viking times. The story is completed with the help of a Norse cross from Andreas, in the north of the island. On one side of the cross is the carving of Odin, the chief of the Norse gods, being devoured by the wolf of chaos at the end of the world. On the other side is a figure of a man carrying a cross and a book and trampling upon a serpent. The coming of Christian preachers is here interpreted as the end of the old gods.

On the continent, Charlemagne's renaissance faded away in the chaos of the ninth and tenth centuries; in fact, so terrible was the breakdown of government that many people thought that the year 1000 would signal the end of the world. But before the fading of the Carolingian renaissance there were two interesting church debates.[3] There was the controversy of how Christ was present in the bread of the eucharist. Paschasius Radbertus propounded (*c.* 840) an

[3] Details in Walker, *The Growing Storm*, pp. 53–5.

**Thorwald's cross, Andreas, Isle of Man.** It shows the god Odin being devoured by the Fenris wolf at the destruction of the gods.

**The reverse side of Thorwald's cross.** It shows a Christian preacher with cross and book; note also the fish.

exceedingly literalistic theory, according to which it was believed that the reconstituted flesh of Christ was actually present. Some of the best theologians of the period, such as Ratramnus and Rabanus Maurus, rejected this theory in favour of a more spiritual presence whereby the bread still was visibly bread although the faithful communicant truly received Christ at communion. But in a period of growing ignorance and superstition, the views of Paschasius eventually became those of popular piety. The other controversy concerned predestination, and centred around an unwilling monk called Gottschalk. He envisaged a theory of predestination, based on Augustine's theology, which was so extreme as to suggest that

God had immutably fixed the number and names of the elect even before the fall, and that such decrees were unaffected by any faith or works in this life. Such a view was condemned without much hesitation (870), but already the power to tackle anything but the simplest theology was fast vanishing. The eccentric John Scotus Erigena was about the last outstanding scholar of this period, even being able to understand Greek and Greek theology. But much of his theology leaned towards a kind of pantheism, and his teachings were condemned after his death. Apart from a brief afterglow of learning in king Alfred's Wessex, the light of the Carolingian renaissance went out amid the chaos of the Norse raids.

The contrast between the beginning of our period and the end is most instructive. When Constantine became emperor, the churches were loosely grouped congregations of believers. At the end of the period we have two fairly monolithic systems, the eastern one ruled by the Byzantine emperor supported by the subservient eastern patriarchs, the western system centred around the pope of Rome with secular help from the newly created 'Holy Roman Empire'. In Constantine's time, and for a century afterwards, there was a fairly wide spread of education which made theology understandable, and the Christian faith was at least partially a matter of intellectual belief and commitment. By the time of Charlemagne, general culture had become virtually nil. Only the churches and the clergy were centres of learning, and even there the Christian message had undergone serious debasement.

Under Constantine, baptism was still a rite concerned with personal commitment to Christ, although even by then it had acquired magical overtones. By the time of Charlemagne it is a magic rite to wash away sin, and to be performed on a baby as soon as reasonably possible. The free, rhetorical worship of the Constantinian churches, where a learned bishop led the congregation of his church, has been utterly lost. Under Charlemagne even local variation of prayer is officially suppressed in favour of a uniform rite which all must perform, and the state lays down what must be done. Even the preaching has withered into reading ancient sermons of the church fathers, if these happen to be available. The metamorphosis of Graeco-Roman Christianity into mediaeval religion is complete, but it has taken place without any of the participants noticing it. Roman reforming zeal has led to papal dominance. The struggle to preserve learning in the churches has forced the clergy to become an intellectual *élite*. The threat of the wrath of a saint, often used to discipline and restrain the superstitious but barbaric tyrants,[4] has led to the unrestrainable spread of superstition. Even the admiration of great Christians of the past has led to the labyrinth of the cult of the saints. But in spite of the depressing picture, all was not lost. The Bible was still there to be read. People could still hear of Jesus Christ. And whatever the darkness around, there were still the seeds of light waiting to shine out to anyone who might look for them. Although the church had become debased and mediaevalized in the period from Constantine to Charlemagne, great work for Christ had been done in that period, and the church had not departed so far from original Christianity as to be unable to be called back to it in due time.

[4] See above, pp. 172 and 179.

# Glossary

*An explanatory list of the people most prominent in the church's history from the fourth to the ninth century.*

**Adeodatus**  Illegitimate son of **Augustine of Hippo** by his mistress. Baptized with his father, but died young.

**Adrian of Rome**  Pope, 772–95 (also called Hadrian). Friend of **Charlemagne**; induced him to invade Italy and end the **Lombard** kingdom. Influenced Charlemagne considerably in liturgical and canon law reform.

**Aetius**  Master of the soldiers after the death of **Constantius** in 425. With barbarian mercenaries, he tried to preserve the holdings of the weak western emperors. In 451 led a combined army of Romans, **Goths** and other allies to defeat the **Huns** at the battle of Chalons. Assassinated by **Valentinian III** in 453.

**Alani**  A barbarian tribe, swept eastwards by the **Huns**. Some followed the **Vandals** into Spain. Others became mercenaries, and one of these, Aspar, married a daughter of the Eastern Roman emperor Leo (emperor 457–74).

**Alaric**  King of the Visigoths. At first an ally of the Romans, he turned against them when they failed to pay his soldiers, and captured Rome in 410. He died later the same year.

**Alban**  British martyr, perhaps during the persecution of Diocletian in the early fourth century. Later there was a considerable cult at his shrine.

**Alcuin**  A Saxon from Northumbria. Head of the cathedral school at York. Persuaded by **Charlemagne** to go to Aachen and lead the learned circle at his court. Charlemagne's closest confidant on religious and academic matters, and reputedly the most learned man of his age. Revised the Latin Vulgate. Retired to be abbot of Tours, and died 804.

**Aidan** Monk from Iona, who was sent at the invitation of king **Oswald** of Northumbria to evangelize northern England. Noted for his gentleness and sanctity.

**Aistulf** king of the **Lombards**. Encroaching southwards on the papal territories, he was defeated twice by **Pepin the Short**, and compelled to cede lands to the pope. Died 756.

**Alemanni** Barbarian tribe, of Germanic origin. Held territory in West Germany, Alsace and Switzerland. Defeated by **Clovis**, who incorporated them in his realm.

**Alexander of Alexandria** Bishop, 313–28. During his episcopate **Arius** began to propagate his heresy. Alexander summoned a council which condemned Arius. He also trained and encouraged the young **Athanasius**, who succeeded him.

**Ambrose of Milan** Roman governor of part of North Italy. Spontaneously acclaimed as bishop of Milan in 374. He led the fight against Arianism in North Italy, and also enforced his will against the emperor **Theodosius I** over the incidents at Callinicum and Thessalonica. Also forced the removal of the statue of Victory from the Senate house at Rome, when he clashed with **Symmachus (the elder)**. Died 397.

**Ammianus Marcellinus** Born in Antioch, he came to Rome and held various military posts, especially under **Julian the Apostate**. His history of the Roman world is the last great prose work of the classical Latin tradition, and is a very important source. Although a pagan, he had considerable admiration for the better sort of Christians.

**Anastasius** Emperor of the East, 491–518. Elderly civil servant who became emperor by marrying the widowed empress. He favoured the **Monophysites**, and tried (without success) to introduce a heretical addition to the **Trisagion** hymn.

**Antony** First famous hermit. Lived in various places in the Egyptian desert. Close friend of **Athanasius**, who wrote a biography of him.

**Apiarius** A presbyter from North Africa, condemned for misconduct but appealed to the pope of Rome. His case was a trial of strength between the growing power of the papacy and the North African churches. His appeal was not accepted in North Africa.

**Apollinaris** Bishop of Syrian Laodicaea from 361. Wrote 'Christian classics' to foil the emperor **Julian's** edict against Christian teachers. Subsequently propounded the idea that Christ was merely the Son of God concealed in a human body. His views were condemned, but were often held in modified forms by the **Monophysites**.

**Arius** Presbyter at the church of Baucalis, in the suburbs of Alexandria. Had studied under **Lucian of Antioch**. He put forward the idea that Christ was not fully God in the same sense as God the Father. Although excommunicated at the Council of Nicaea, he received considerable support in the East, but died (*c.* 342) before he could be received back into communion. The controversy he started continued unabated after his death, being finally ended within the Empire at the Council of Constantinople (381). Modified forms of his views were taken up by various barbarian tribes (*e.g.* **Goths, Vandals, Lombards**) and barbarian Arianism did not become extinct until the seventh century.

**Arnulfings** The family of **Pepin of Heristal, Charles Martel, Pepin the Short** and **Charlemagne**. So called from their ancestor Arnulf, bishop of Metz.

**Athanasius** Brought up by **Alexander of Alexandria**, he succeeded him as bishop of Alexandria in 328. The leader of the opposition to the opinions of Arius. A voluminous writer, and ardent controversialist. Gained a bad reputation early in his episcopate for harsh treatment of the Melitians. In spite of being sent into exile on five different occasions, he always managed to return to his see and continue the fight against Arianism. Wrote a biography of the hermit **Antony**, which did much to encourage the retreat to the contemplative life. Died at Alexandria in 373.

**Attila** King of the Huns, after the murder of his brother. Led the Hunnic attack on Europe in 450, but was defeated at Chalons in 451. Turned south to Italy, where he was persuaded to depart by **Leo the Great** of Rome. Died later that year.

**Augustine of Canterbury**   Roman abbot sent to evangelize the English by **Gregory the Great**. Succeeded in winning the kingdom of Kent for Christianity, but had no success in his contacts with the Celtic bishops of the West. Died 604.

**Augustine of Hippo**   Born at Thagaste, in North Africa. After study at Carthage, became a teacher of rhetoric. Became a Manichee much to the annoyance of his mother Monica. Took a mistress and had a son, **Adeodatus**. Moved to Italy, and took post as professor of rhetoric at Milan. Influenced by **Simplicianus** and **Ambrose**. Converted at Milan in 386, and baptized with several friends at Easter 387. Returned to North Africa, and became bishop of Hippo. Engaged in controversies against Manichees, Donatists, pagans, Arians and Pelagians. Very prolific writer, ánd the greatest theologian of Western Christendom. Died 430.

**Ausonius**   Professor of rhetoric and poet from Bordeaux. Tutor to the emperor **Gratian**, and corresponded with his pupil **Paulinus** (2) of Nola. Born *c.* 310. Died *c.* 395 (?).

**Avars**   Asiatic tribe, which followed the track of the Huns into Europe. Attacked Constantinople many times, and also raided Eastern Europe. Stored a vast hoard of treasure in their fortress, the 'Ring'. Eventually defeated and wiped out by **Charlemagne**.

**Avitus of Vienne**   Orthodox bishop of Vienne, 494–518. Was responsible for the Burgundians accepting orthodox Christianity and rejecting Arianism.

**Basil of Ancyra**   Pro-Arian bishop, succeeded **Marcellus of Ancyra** in 336, but subsequently became hostile to extreme Arianism, and was exiled by **Constantius** in 360.

**Basil the Great**   Came from famous church family, and studied at Athens. In 356 started a monastic community in Pontus, and produced a 'rule' which is still the basis of Eastern monasticism. In 370, became bishop of Caesarea in Cappadocia, and was by then well involved in the Trinitarian controversy. Was influential in the eventual triumph of orthodoxy, and also spent much effort in trying to heal the schism at Antioch. Died before the final triumph of orthodoxy, in 379.

**Bede**   English scholar and historian, who spent most of his life in a monastery at Jarrow. His *History of the English Church and People* is the primary source for early English Christianity. He also translated John's Gospel into Northumbrian. Died 735.

**Belisarius**   General of **Justinian**, and one of the greatest military leaders of antiquity. After campaigning on the Eastern front, he led the Byzantine forces which conquered North Africa and Italy. Gross lack of manpower prevented him from completing his victory, but he was called out of retirement in 559 to repulse the Kutrigur **Huns** outside Constantinople. Died 565.

**Benedict of Aniane**   A Visigoth from Spain, originally called Witiza, who campaigned successfully for the Benedictine rule to be the only permitted Western monastic rule, in the reign of Louis the Pious (814–40).

**Benedict Biscop**   Friend of **Wilfrid**, and a pro-Roman reformer in the English church. Subsequently became abbot of Monkwearmouth.

**Benedict of Nursia**   Founder of the Benedictine rule, which was first practised in his monastery at Monte Cassino. His rule became famous and influential after his death (*c.* 547) thanks to the support of **Gregory the Great** and later **Benedict of Aniane**.

**Boethius**   From a Roman noble family, he held high office under **Theodoric the Great**. Suspected, probably unjustly, of plotting against Theodoric, he was executed in 524. During his imprisonment before execution, he wrote the classic *On the Consolation of Philosophy*.

**Boniface**   Born at Crediton, and brought up in various English monasteries. Went to the continent, where he undertook missionary work in Germany. As legate for the pope, he anointed **Pepin the Short** as king, and conducted councils to reform the Frankish churches. Late in life he commenced missionary work again, and was martyred in Frisia in 754.

**Brunhild**   Queen of the Franks, who conducted her feud with **Fredegund** over several generations during the sixth century. **Gregory the Great** tried to enlist her help to reform the Frankish churches. She was eventually brutally executed by some of her relatives in 613.

**Caecilian**   Chief deacon at Carthage and subsequently, from 312, its bishop. Disputes over his election and consecration led to the schism in North Africa known as Donatism.

**Caesarius of Arles**   Monk from Lérins, who became bishop of Arles in 503. Noted for monastic reforms, involvement in disputes over Arianism and Semi-Pelagianism (he presided at the Council of Orange in 529). An eminent pastor and preacher. Died 542.

**Cassian (John)**   See **John Cassian**.

**Cassiodorus**   Distinguished statesman under **Theodoric the Great**. In 540, retired to found a monastery on his estate in Calabria, where he introduced the copying of manuscripts as part of the work of the monks. A great scholar and systematizer of knowledge. Died *c.* 583.

**Celestine**   Pope of Rome, 422–32. Allied with **Cyril of Alexandria** to secure the condemnation of **Nestorius**. In 430 sent a certain Palladius as bishop to Ireland.

**Charlemagne**   Son of **Pepin the Short**, became king of the Franks on his father's death in 767. Greatly expanded the Frankish kingdom by conquest, and was instrumental in many far-reaching reforms of the churches. Gathered learned circle at his court, and enforced uniformity of liturgy, canon law, *etc.*, on the churches of his realm. In close touch with the popes of Rome, but not subservient to them. In 800, crowned Roman emperor at Rome, the title subsequently accepted even at Constantinople. Died 814.

**Charles Martel**   Illegitimate son of **Pepin of Heristal**. Became mayor of the palace and effectual ruler of the Franks in 714. In 732 he defeated the Arab forces at the Battle of Poitiers and stopped the Arab advance into Europe via Spain. Supported the missionary labours of **Boniface**, but dealt with church possessions in a very cavalier manner. Died 741.

**Chrysaphius**   Lord chamberlain under **Theodosius II**. His influence helped **Eutyches** to escape condemnation at the 'Robber Synod' of Ephesus in 449. He fell from power on the death of Theodosius II.

**Chrysostom (John)**   See **John Chrysostom**.

**Claudian** Latin poet, flourished in first decade of fifth century. Most of his poems are official pieces, some in honour of **Stilicho**. Although nominally Christian, his work has almost no Christian traces. Probably died *c.* 408.

**Clovis** King of the Franks from 481. Led an expansionist programme, and in 496 declared himself a supporter of orthodox Christianity and was baptized at Soissons by Remigius of Rheims. Drove the Visigoths out of France at the battle of Vouillé. Died *c.* 517.

**Columba** Irish monk and evangelist, who left Ireland after a dispute and set up a monastery at Iona, from where he evangelized the northern Picts. Died *c.* 597.

**Columbanus** Celtic monk from Bangor, Co. Down, who travelled extensively on the continent during the sixth century, preaching and denouncing sin. He founded monasteries at Luxeuil, St Gall and Bobbio, where he died in 615.

**Constans** Son of **Constantine the Great,** and emperor of the West from 337 to 350. Pro-Nicene, he interceded for **Athanasius**. Killed in the revolt of Magnentius in 350.

**Constantine the Great** Emperor from 312, when he defeated **Maxentius** at the Battle of the Milvian bridge. Proclaimed toleration for Christianity, and gave Christians active if somewhat embarrassing support. Intervened clumsily in the Donatist and Arian disputes, and convened the Council of Nicaea. Latterly gave support to the Arians, and was baptized on his death-bed by the Arian **Eusebius of Nicomedia.** He became sole emperor in 325 when he defeated **Licinius**. Died 337.

**Constantine II** Son of **Constantine the Great**. Emperor in the West with **Constans** until his death in civil war in 340.

**Constantine V** ('Copronymos') Successor to **Leo the Isaurian** and Byzantine emperor, 740–75. Strongly opposed to veneration of images, his policies were reversed on his death and he was much reviled for his persecution of the supporters of images.

**Constantius (II)** Son of **Constantine the Great,** and not to be confused with Constantine's father, Constantius Chlorus. Became emperor in the East in 337, and sole emperor from 350. Supported the Arians, and exiled those who supported the orthodox Nicene faith. Had considerable following of 'court bishops', but eventually earned the hostility of many moderates. Enforced state Arianism at the Synods of Seleucia and Rimini in 359, but died in the next year, while preparing to fight a civil war against his colleague **Julian**.

**Constantius** Master of the soldiers after the death of **Stilicho** in 408. Tried to uphold Roman rule in Western Europe during the barbarian invasions. Married **Galla Placidia**, and was father of **Valentinian III**. Became emperor (as Constantius III) in 425 but died the same year.

**Crispus** Son of **Constantine the Great** by his first wife. Helped his father defeat **Licinius**, but was executed in mysterious circumstances in 325.

**Cyril of Alexandria** Nephew of pope **Theophilus of Alexandria**, succeeded him in 412. Led strong-arm measures against pagans in Alexandria, helped by his corps of 'sick-attendants'. In 431 presided at the council of Ephesus and secured the condemnation of **Nestorius** for heresy. A wily and unscrupulous churchman. Died 444.

**Cyril of Jerusalem** Moderate Eastern bishop, held office from 348 with several breaks of exile until 386. Gradually became more pro-Nicene. Noted for his series of lectures of instruction for candidates for baptism.

**Dagobert** Last effective king of the Franks (Merovingian), ruled from 629 to 639. Founded the famous monastery of St Denis.

**Damasus** Became pope of Rome in 366 after much street fighting. Encouraged **Jerome** to revise the Old Latin version of the Bible, and adorned many of the Catacombs. Died 384.

**Diodore of Tarsus** Bishop of Tarsus from 378, and the teacher of **Theodore of Mopsuestia** and **John Chrysostom**. A leading exponent of the 'Antiochene' Christology, which stressed both the human and divine natures in Christ. Died before 394.

**Dioscorus** Succeeded **Cyril** as pope of Alexandria in 444. Took Cyril's theology to its logical and heretical conclusion, and led the rioting at the Council of Ephesus in 449, where **Eutyches** was acquitted and **Flavian**, patriarch of Constantinople, was killed. In 451 condemned as a heretic at the Council of Chalcedon, and sent into exile.

**Donatus**   From Casae Nigrae in North Africa. Took charge of the anti-**Caecilian** party in the church at Carthage after the death of the rival bishop Majorinus. Strong personality, who welded the anti-Caecilian movement into the schismatic church which bore his name. In 347, resisted the work of the imperial commissioners Paul and Macarius, and was exiled. Continued to organize his cause from exile until his death in 355.

**Einhard**   Monk and architect from Fulda, who wrote a biography of **Charlemagne**. Member of his learned circle. After Charlemagne's death, became abbot of Seligenstadt, and died in 844.

**Ephrem Syrus**   Born at Nisibis, *c.* 306, and lived and taught there and in Edessa. Leading scholar of the Syriac-speaking churches, and even admired by Greek scholars. Died 373.

**Erigena (John Scotus)**   See **John Scotus Erigena**.

**Ethelbert**   King of Kent, who welcomed **Augustine** in 597. Gave great support to the Christian cause in Kent until his death in 616.

**Etheria**   (also called Egeria, Aetheria or Silvia).   Noble lady from southern France or Spain, who wrote an account of an extended pilgrimage she made *c.* 394 to the Holy Land and the Middle East.

**Eudoxia**   Empress of the East (and wife of emperor Arcadius), who was rebuked many times by **John Chrysostom**. She engineered his deposition and exile in 404.

**Eugenius of Carthage**   Orthodox bishop of Carthage during the **Vandal** persecution. Became bishop 478, and engaged in public debate with the Arian clergy. Exiled by king Huneric.

**Euric**   King of the Visigoths in latter part of fourth century. He expanded his kingdom into the Auvergne, was resisted by **Sidonius Apollinaris,** but eventually gained the Auvergne by treaty with the feeble Western Roman emperors. Made a notable synthesis of Roman and Gothic law.

**Eusebius of Caesarea**  Church historian, and bishop of Caesarea. Became a close friend of the emperor **Constantine the Great**, and wrote a biography of him, as well as the first extant history of the church. Suspected of Arianism before the Council of Nicaea, he was cleared at that council but held his suspect theology till his death in 339.

**Eusebius of Nicomedia**  A wily pro-Arian cleric, and organizer of the clique of ex-scholars of **Lucian of Antioch**. Supporter of **Arius** and successively bishop of Berytus, Nicomedia and Constantinople. He worked hard for the Arian cause, and engineered **Athanasius'** first exile. Baptized **Constantine** on his death-bed, and led the pro-Arian party until his death in 341/2.

**Eusebius of Vercellae**  Bishop of Vercellae and supporter of the orthodox faith. Exiled by the emperor **Constantius** at the Synod of Milan (355). Subsequently in the East with **Athanasius**, when *rapprochement* with the moderate Easterners began in 362.

**Eustathius of Sebaste**  Leader of the traditionalists at the Council of Constantinople in 381, who denied the full deity of the Holy Spirit. Probably also a supporter of the unruly monastic movement called the Messalians.

**Eutyches**  Head of a monastery at Constantinople. His views on the Person of Christ were suspected by **Flavian** (the patriarch), but he was acquitted at the 'Robber Synod' of Ephesus in 449. His views were similar to much of later **Monophysitism**, stressing the one divine nature in Christ to the detriment of His humanity. Eutyches was condemned and exiled at the Council of Chalcedon (451), but views similar to his commanded wide support in Egypt and Syria for centuries afterwards.

**Fausta**  Second wife of **Constantine the Great**, and mother of **Constantine II**, **Constantius II** and **Constans**. Died in mysterious circumstances in 325.

**Felix of Aptungi**  One of the consecrators of **Caecilian**, bishop of Carthage, in 312. Unjustly accused of having handed over copies of the Scriptures to Roman officials during the persecution, his right to consecrate Caecilian was challenged. Eventually vindicated after lengthy hearings.

**Flavian** Patriarch of Constantinople from 446. Began investigations into the heretical opinions of **Eutyches**, but was himself condemned at the 'Robber Synod' of Ephesus, when the emperor sided with Eutyches and the Egyptian delegation. Flavian was badly beaten up at the council and died of his injuries a few days later.

**Fredegund** Wife of the Merovingian king Chilperic, after procuring the murder of his previous wife. After her husband's death she carried on a feud against her arch-rival **Brunhild** (the details occupy much of **Gregory of Tours'** *History of the Franks*). After a lifetime of crime, she died in 597.

**Gaiseric** Arian king of the **Vandals**. He led his people across to North Africa, where they set up an independent kingdom. Led many piratical raids in the Mediterranean, including the famous second sack of Rome in 455. Actively persecuted orthodox Christians. Died *c.* 477.

**Galla Placidia** Daughter of **Theodosius the Great**. After the capture of Rome in 410, she was compelled to marry **Alaric's** successor Athaulf. On his death in 415 she returned to Rome, and married the master of the soldiers, **Constantius**. Their son became emperor as **Valentinian III**, but during his minority Galla Placidia ruled the Western empire as regent. She died *c.* 450.

**George** Arian bishop intruded into Alexandria by force after the exile of **Athanasius** in 356. Killed in a riot in 361, because of his widespread unpopularity.

**Germanus of Auxerre** After a spell in Roman government, he became a monk and was made bishop of Auxerre in 418. Famous bishop and preacher. Visited Britain twice. Died while on a vist to Ravenna in 448.

**Gildas** British writer, *fl. c.* 520. Wrote of the poor state of the British churches after the repulse of the Saxons by Ambrosius Aurelianus. Associated with the monastic revival in Britain.

**Goths** Central European tribe, often divided into Ostrogoths and Visigoths. Continual problem on Danube from third century. Evangelized by **Ulfilas** in mid-fourth century, and became Arians. Many settlements in Balkans in late fourth century. Took part in barbarian invasions, and Visigoths under **Alaric** took Rome in 410. Subsequently moved to Spain, where they gained control of the whole peninsula by defeating the Suevi. Ostrogoths harrassed the Eastern Empire, until under **Theodoric the Great** they moved east to seize Italy in late fifth century. Ostrogothic kingdom ended by Byzantine troops under **Belisarius** and **Narses**. Visigoths finally defeated in Spain by Arabs in early eighth century.

**Gratian**  Roman emperor 375–83. Tutored by Ausonius. Orthodox Christian, removed altar of Victory from the Roman Senate house. Killed in revolt of **Magnus Maximus**.

**Gregory of Alexandria**  Arian bishop intruded into Alexandria after **Athanasius'** exile in 339. On his death in 345 Athanasius was able to return.

**Gregory the Great**  From Roman noble family, entered monastery, and rose to become pope of Rome in 590. Built up power of papacy. Great letter-writer, diplomat. Initiated evangelization of England. Died 604.

**Gregory of Nazianzus**  Friend of **Basil the Great**, and notable Eastern theologian and monastic pioneer. In 379 called to become orthodox bishop in Constantinople. Successfully preached the orthodox faith there, and presided at the start of the Council of Constantinople in 381. Due to personal attacks and dislike of the post, he resigned in 381, and devoted the rest of his life to study and contemplation.

**Gregory of Nyssa**  Younger brother of **Basil the Great**, and a great supporter of orthodox doctrine during the later years of the Trinitarian controversy. A great preacher and theologian.

**Gregory of Tours**  Historian and bishop of Tours 573–94. His *History of the Franks* is the primary source for the history of the Merovingian period.

**Helena**  Mother of **Constantine the Great**. Made a famous pilgrimage to the Holy Land *c.* 326 which set the fashion for pilgrimages.

**Heraclius**  Byzantine emperor, 610–41. Seized power from the incompetent **Phocas**, and proceeded to shatter the power of

Persia. In his later years, unable to stem the rising tide of Arab power. With the help of the patriarch Sergius, tried to conciliate the **Monophysites** by propounding the **Monothelite** doctrine (one 'will' in Christ).

**Hilary of Arles**  Bishop of Arles in first half of fifth century, and friend of **Germanus of Auxerre**. In 445 had his jurisdiction in southern France curtailed, when papal pressure gained an imperial edict strengthening the power of the Roman church and rejecting his claim to be metropolitan of Gaul.

**Hilary of Poitiers**  Bishop from c. 350, and greatest Western orthodox theologian during the Trinitarian controversy. Exiled to the East by **Constantius**, but subsequently allowed to return. Collaborated with **Athanasius**, and on his return ensured the collapse of Western Arianism. Died 367.

**Honorius**  Roman emperor, 395–423. Weak son of **Theodosius the Great**. Continued the pro-Christian stance of his father, but retreated to Ravenna, leaving political matters in the hands of the masters of the soldiers, **Stilicho** and **Constantius**.

**Honorius**  Bishop of Rome, 625–638. Supported the **Monothelite** ideas of **Heraclius** and Sergius. Posthumously condemned as a heretic at the Council of Constantinople of 680–1.

**Hosius of Cordoba**  Became religious adviser to **Constantine the Great**, and was prominent in the moves up to the Council of Nicaea. His influence declined after this, but he gave considerable support to **Athanasius** and the orthodox faith, and was a leading figure at the Council of Sardica. In extreme old age he was forced to sign some document which supported Arianism, but he refused to condemn Athanasius. He died soon after, perhaps as the result of harrassment by the Arians, at an advanced age in c. 358.

**Huns**  Asiatic tribe, whose expansionist moves caused the first wave of barbarian invasions. In 450 they formed the second wave, but were defeated by **Aetius** at Chalons in 451. Although the main Hunnic empire collapsed, other tribes of Huns remained in central Europe and around the Volga. The Kutrigur Huns were repulsed from Constantinople in 559 by **Belisarius**. Huns were often used as mercenaries.

**Ibas of Edessa**  An orthodox leader in the Christological disputes of the fifth century. After his death, in an attempt to conciliate the **Monophysites**, a work of his was condemned; this was one of the so-called 'Three Chapters'.

**Isidore of Seville**  Visigothic church leader, and bishop of Seville, 600–36. Produced the first encyclopaedia, and sometimes regarded as the last of the Western 'church fathers'.

**Irene**  Byzantine empress (797–802) after deposing, blinding and murdering her own son. During her reign, which many regarded as invalid, **Charlemagne** was officially crowned as Roman emperor. She was a great supporter of those who worshipped the icons.

**Jacob Baradaeus**  Bishop of Edessa c. 541–78. Organizer of the **Monophysite** church in Syria (today called the Syrian Jacobites). Protected by the empress Theodora when the Monophysites were persecuted by **Justinian**.

**Jerome**  Roman theologian and monk. Travelled widely, and was very learned. Did much to popularize the monastic ideal in Rome, but was also very unpopular. Undertook the revision of the Old Latin versions of the Bible. In 385, retired to found a monastery at Bethlehem. From here he engaged in study and controversy until his death, at a great age, in 420.

**John Cassian**  Syrian monk, who came to Rome and subsequently founded a monastery at Marseilles. Famous as a monastic pioneer in the West, and also as main spokesman of the Semi-Pelagian movement.

**John Chrysostom**  Monk from Antioch, who became patriarch of Constantinople in 397. Great preacher and reformer. In 402, accused and deposed by the intervention of **Theophilus of Alexandria**. Although reinstated, was soon afterwards unjustly deposed and exiled. Died of ill treatment in 407.

**John of Antioch**  Leader of the Syrian delegation at the Council of Ephesus in 431. In 433, concluded a formula of agreement with **Cyril of Alexandria** which temporarily ended the Christological controversy.

**John Scotus Erigena**  Flourished mid-ninth century. Philosophic theologian with pantheistic leanings. Probably the last scholar in the West to understand Greek theology. An eccentric who was posthumously condemned as a heretic.

**Jovinian**  Opponent of **Jerome**, and criticized Jerome's enthusiasm for celibacy. Was condemned after being viciously attacked in a treatise by Jerome.

**Julian the Apostate**  Roman emperor 361–3. Nephew of **Constantine the Great**. Turned against Christianity by the murder of most of his relatives. Lived in seclusion until 356, when put in charge of the army in Gaul. Brilliantly repulsed the barbarians, and was about to seize the Empire when **Constantius** died. Began a pro-pagan reaction, which was not very successful. Died fighting the Persians.

**Julius of Rome**  Bishop of Rome, 337–52. Supported **Athanasius** in his fight to be reinstated, and took a prominent part at the Council of Sardica (343).

**Justin I**  Byzantine emperor, 518–27. Pro-orthodox. Uncle of **Justinian**. His decree against Arians caused the first signs of strain in **Theodoric the Great's** kingdom.

**Justina**  Wife of **Valentinian I**, and mother of the infant **Valentinian II**. Pro-Arian, she clashed with **Ambrose of Milan** in 383 when she tried to take over one of the churches in Milan for the Arians.

**Justinian**  Byzantine emperor, 528–65. Born a peasant in Macedonia, rose to power with his uncle **Justin I**. Married Theodora. Architect of Byzantine power. Revised law code; built Hagia Sophia; ended circus rivalries after the 'Nika' riot. With help of **Belisarius**, reconquered North Africa, Italy and Southern Spain. Tried with little success to conciliate the **Monophysites** (condemned the 'Three Chapters'). His grandiose schemes resulted in vast overspending. Became very withdrawn in his later years, when he spent much time in theological speculation.

**Leander of Seville**  (*c.* 549–601) Brother of Isidore, and friend of **Gregory the Great**. Leading orthodox Spanish churchman, presided at the Council of Toledo (589) when king **Recared** formally renounced Arianism.

**Leo the Great** Pope of Rome, 440–61. Major architect of Roman ecclesiastical power in the West. Gave support to orthodox side in Christological controversies at Ephesus (449) and Chalcedon (451) with his famous *Tome*. Negotiated with **Attila the Hun** and **Gaiseric**, as effective civil ruler of Rome. Enforced Roman jurisdiction against **Hilary of Arles**.

**Leo the Isaurian** Byzantine emperor, 717–40. Led Byzantine resurgence against the Muslim invaders. Initiated moves against the worship of icons (Iconoclastic controversy). Able reformer, but hated for his iconoclastic views.

**Leontius of Byzantium** Most famous Eastern theologian of the sixth century. Details of life obscure. Probably died *c.* 543. Interpreted orthodox Christology to show that the two natures of Christ did not mean a divided personality.

**Liberius of Rome** Pope of Rome, 352–66. Exiled 355–8 for his orthodox views, but subsequently allowed to return to Rome after making some compromise with the views of the emperor **Constantius**.

**Licinius** Roman emperor, 307–42. Rose to power in the East at the same time as **Constantine the Great** in the West. In 313, allied with Constantine, and defeated Maximin to rule the East. Adopted pro-Christian stance, but later abandoned this when Constantine became threatening. Defeated in 324 by Constantine and **Crispus**, and executed in the same year.

**Lombards** Germanic barbarian tribe, partly pagan, partly Arian. Invaded Italy after the death of **Justinian** (565), and held much of North and central Italy until the eighth century, when they were overthrown by **Charlemagne**. Last of the barbarian tribes to support Arianism.

**Louis the Pious** Sole surviving son of **Charlemagne**. Became emperor 814. Ineffective ruler, deposed but reinstated 833. Died 840. On his death the Empire was finally divided.

**Lucian of Antioch** Famous Christian teacher martyred during the persecution of Diocletian. Although he was not suspected of heresy, many of the prominent Arians of the fourth century had been his pupils, and they formed a powerful clique.

**Lucifer of Cagliari**　Exiled for his orthodoxy in 355. Agitated against the Arians in East. Initiated schism at Antioch by ordaining **Paulinus** (1) as bishop. Violent writer, using vulgar Latin. Subsequently formed his own sect. Died *c.* 370.

**Magnus Maximus**　Assumed imperial power in the West in 383, after defeating and killing the emperor **Gratian**. Had been governor of Britain. Supported orthodox Christianity, and acquiesced in the execution of **Priscillian** for heresy. Defeated and killed by **Theodosius** in 388.

**Mani**　Persian religious leader. Formerly an Elchesite Gnostic, he set up his own organization, and claimed to be the incarnation of the Holy Spirit. Although put to death by Zoroastrian priests, his ideas were widely proclaimed in spite of great hostility in the Roman Empire. Manichees lasted well into the Middle Ages, and **Augustine of Hippo** was a member of the sect for more than ten years. Mani held that matter was evil, and that salvation consisted in escaping from its power. Also taught dualism of good and evil.

**Marcellus of Ancyra**　Friend of **Athanasius**, and noted for his extreme anti-Arian views which amounted to Sabellianism. Exiled in 336, for a while made a common cause with Athanasius until the Council of Sardica. Had long and bitter dispute with **Eusebius of Caesarea**. Eventually condemned for heresy. The theological bogy-man of the East.

**Marius Victorinus**　Pagan rhetorician and professor. His conversion (*c.* 355) caused a great stir. Resigned his teaching post because of **Julian's** anti-Christian edict on teachers. Later reinstated. Translator of many Neo-Platonic works into Latin. Died some time after 362.

**Martin of Rome**　Pope, 649–53. Refused to accept the **Monothelite** views of **Heraclius** and Sergius. Died in exile, and was subsequently venerated as a martyr.

**Martin of Tours**　Converted soldier, and outstanding monk and evangelist. Became bishop of Tours, and instrumental in evangelizing much of rural France. Opposed the execution of **Priscillian**. Died 397. Widely venerated as a saint.

**Maurice** Byzantine emperor, 582–602. Led successful campaign against **Avars** and Persians, but killed by mutineers led by **Phocas**.

**Maxentius** Rival emperor of the West, defeated and killed by **Constantine the Great** at the Battle of the Milvian bridge.

**Meletius of Antioch** Arian bishop of Antioch, who turned orthodox in *c*. 357. Deposed, he continued as orthodox bishop with much Eastern support, although Egypt and the West supported **Paulinus**. Many fruitless attempts were made to heal the schism, which ended only after the deaths of the two men. Meletius took a leading part at the Council of Constantinople (381).

**Melitius of Alexandria** Schismatic bishop, during the time of **Peter I of Alexandria**. He set up a schismatic church among the Coptic peasants. His supporters allied with the Arians against **Athanasius**, who persecuted them.

**Mellitus** Bishop among the East Saxons. After being expelled, he eventually succeeded Laurence as archbishop of Canterbury (619).

**Monophysites** (From Greek for 'one nature'.) Collective term to describe all those Eastern theologians who stressed the divine nature of Christ to the diminution or exclusion of his human nature. While the movement might be said to have begun with **Apollinaris**, the term is properly used only after the Council of Chalcedon (451). Nationalistic feelings helped to strengthen the movement in Egypt and Syria. Some emperors were in favour of them, and many attempts were made to conciliate them, with no success. Became less important after the Muslim conquest of Syria. Some of the lesser Eastern churches (*e.g.* Copts)are still technically Monophysite.

**Monothelite** The description of the last attempt to reach a compromise with the **Monophysites**. Initiated by the patriarch Sergius and the emperor **Heraclius**, it posited 'one will' in Christ. Finally condemned at the Council of Constantinople (680), by which time it had been seen to be a total failure.

**Muhammad** Founder of Islam. After visions in the Arabian desert, he fled with his followers from Mecca to Medina (612). Returning with an army, he had conquered all Arabia by his death.

The swiftly expanding Arab tribes took up his simple monotheistic faith, and conquered the Middle East, North Africa, the Persian Empire and Spain within a century of his death.

**Narsai**   Nestorian scholar and head of the school at Edessa from 437. Fled to Nisibis *c.* 457 where he continued his work. Died *c.* 503.

**Narses**   Eunuch at the court of **Justinian**. Helped to break the alliance of the Blues and Greens in the 'Nika' riot. Subsequently completed the occupation of Italy, when he defeated the **Goths** at the Battle of Busta Gallorum (553).

**Nestorius**   Monk from Antioch, became patriarch of Constantinople in 428. Condemned for heresy at the Council of Ephesus (431),and exiled to Egypt. Died in 451, just after the Council of Chalcedon. His heresy stressed the two natures in Christ to the extent of making Christ seem a split personality. His followers fled Eastwards, and engaged in notable missionary work as far afield as India and China.

**Optatus of Milevis**   (*fl.* 365–85) A North African bishop who wrote a history of the Donatist dispute from an anti-Donatist standpoint. He preserves a number of extremely valuable original documents in his work.

**Origen**   The first great Eastern theologian. Wrote voluminous works on dogmatic theology, Bible commentaries, and made a critical edition of the Old Testament. Some of his ideas were held to foreshadow some heresies (notably Arianism), and some were condemned in the late fourth century. Origen himself died as a result of ill treatment during the persecution of Decius (254).

**Orosius**   Spanish Chronicler, and friend of **Augustine** and **Jerome**. His work covers the period to 417.

**Oswald**   King of Northumbria, 634–42. Initiated the evangelizing of Northumbria by inviting Aidan from Iona.

**Oswy**   King of Northumbria, and brother and successor of **Oswald**. Continued his brother's work after his death. Presided over the Synod of Whitby, when the Roman dating of Easter became the official usage in England. Died 670.

**Pachomius**   Founder of community monasticism. First community at Tabenissi, in Egypt, *c.* 320. Died *c.* 346.

**Patricius**   Father of **Augustine of Hippo**. Converted only very late in life. Died while Augustine was still young.

**Patrick**   British Christian. Taken as a slave to Ireland while still a boy. Escaped, but subsequently returned to Ireland as bishop. Spent about forty years evangelizing Ireland. Near end of life, wrote autobiographical *Confession*. Died *c.* 460.

**Paul of Samosata**   Bishop of Antioch and chancellor of queen Zenobia. Deposed for heresy 272. **Marcellus of Ancyra** is often thought to have held similar opinions to him.

**Paulinus** (1)   Presbyter at Antioch. After the deposition of Eustathius (330), led a small orthodox congregation. Refused to join with **Meletius'** congregation in 360, although both groups were orthodox. Ordained bishop by **Lucifer of Cagliari**. The schism at Antioch continued until after his death.

**Paulinus** (2)   Pupil of **Ausonius**. Left Spain during barbarian invasions, and became bishop of Nola (409). Conducted protracted correspondence with Ausonius. Died 431.

**Paulinus** (3)   Bishop of Trier. Welcomed **Athanasius** during his exile in 336. Later refused to disown Athanasius, and was deposed at the Synod of Milan in 355.

**Paulinus** (4)   Roman cleric who went to evangelize Northumbria in 627. On the death of the Christian king of Northumbria, he fled south, and ended his days as bishop of Rochester.

**Pelagius**   Monk from Britain. Preached in Rome *c.* 384–410. Taught that man could with effort fulfil the law of God, and so denied the need for divine grace except as a means of instruction. Vigorously combated by **Augustine** and **Jerome**. Went East and probably died there *c.* 415.

**Pepin of Heristal**   Great-grandfather of **Charlemagne** and mayor of the palace. Supported English evangelistic efforts on the continent. In 687, achieved supreme power in Frankish domains after the Battle of Tertry. Died 714.

**Pepin the Short**   Son of **Charles Martel**; succeeded his father as mayor of the palace in 741. Friend of **Boniface**. Supported reforms in the Frankish churches. In 751, anointed as king of the Franks. Twice invaded Italy to help the pope against the **Lombards** Died 768.

**Peter I of Alexandria**   Patriarch of Alexandria 300–11. **Melitius** tried to supplant him. Peter was martyred in 311.

**Peter II of Alexandria**   Succeeded **Athanasius** as bishop in 373. Endured harassment from pro-Arian emperor **Valens**. In 381, tried to get Maximus appointed as bishop of Constantinople in place of **Gregory of Nazianzus**. Died 385.

**Phocas**   Byzantine emperor, 602–10. Became emperor by leading mutiny against **Maurice**. Totally incompetent. Overthrown by **Heraclius**.

**Procopius of Caesarea**   Friend of **Belisarius** and historian of the reign of **Justinian**. Died 565.

**Prosper of Aquitaine**   Friend of **Augustine**, opponent of Semi-Pelagianism. Worked on papal staff for **Leo the Great**, and composed a chronicle.

**Pulcheria**   Sister of **Theodosius II**. After his death she married Marcian, who became emperor (450). Supported orthodox cause at Chalcedon.

**Recared**   King of the Visigoths in Spain. Accepted the orthodox faith at the Council of Toledo in 589, thus ending a long religious civil war between orthodox and Arian.

**Rufinus**   Monk from Aquileia. Travelled to the East *c.* 375. Friendly with **Jerome**, until outbreak of Origenist controversy. Issued expurgated translation of **Origen's** work *On First Principles*. Returned to Italy in 397, and lived at Aquileia until barbarian invasions drove him south. Died at Messina in 410.

**Sabellius**   Libyan of early third century. Personal history obscure. Noted for his views on the Trinity, where he stressed the oneness of God to an extent which blurred the distinction between the Persons of the Trinity. A theological bogy-man in the East for centuries.

**Saxons** Barbarian tribe from North Germany. Remained strongly pagan. Effectively wiped out Christianity in Eastern Britain. Evangelized from Rome and Ireland in their British holdings from 597 onwards. In Saxony, still pagan in the time of **Charlemagne** (eighth century.) Long war ended only by massive deportations of Saxons. Effective evangelization of Saxony only began after this.

**Schnoudi** Coptic abbot of the White Monastery. Supported **Cyril of Alexandria** at Ephesus in 431. Terrorized rural Egypt with his army of monks. Died *c.* 450, aged about 100.

**Sergius** Patriarch of Constantinople. Helped **Heraclius** in the defence of Constantinople against the Persians and **Avars**. Initiated the **Monothelite** compromise.

**Severus of Antioch** Moderate **Monophysite** theologian. Was patriarch of Antioch till deposed for his views in 518. Held opinions similar to those of **Cyril of Alexandria**, and fought against extreme Monophysites. Died *c.* 538.

**Sidonius Apollinaris** Roman country gentleman and man of letters. After outstanding public career, became bishop of Clermont (469). Defended Clermont against Visigothic forces until 474. Exiled but returned. Died *c.* 485.

**Simplicianus** Presbyter at Milan, who instructed **Ambrose** and helped **Augustine**. Became bishop of Milan after Ambrose's death.

**Stilicho** **Vandal** general, held the political power in Rome after the death of **Theodosius I** (395). Faithfully tried to uphold Roman power, but condemned to death by emperor **Honorius** in 408.

**Syagrius** Roman 'king' of Soissons in succession to his father Aegidius. His small kingdom was the last Roman holding in France, and was annexed by **Clovis** in 496.

**Symmachus (the elder)** Distinguished Roman scholar and statesman. In 382, pleaded for the restoration of the altar of Victory in the Senate house, in opposition to **Ambrose**.

**Symmachus (the younger)** Great-grandson of **Symmachus (the elder)**. One of the last representatives of the old Roman aristocracy and of classical culture. Killed in a purge shortly before the death of **Theodoric the Great** in 526.

**Theodore of Mopsuestia**  Prominent theologian and preacher of the Antiochene school of Christology. Held by many to be the inspiration of **Nestorius**. Died in 428, but posthumously condemned as a heretic.

**Theodore the Greek**  Greek monk from Tarsus. Came to Rome, and was appointed archbishop of Canterbury in 670. Organized the English churches. Died in 690.

**Theodoret**  Bishop of Cyrrhus. Condemned at the 'Robber Synod' of Ephesus (449) but reinstated at Chalcedon. Energetic pastor and leader of the orthodox party after Chalcedon. Also church historian. Died c. 466.

**Theodoric the Great**  Ostrogoth brought up at Constantinople. In 493, sent East to invade Italy for the Byzantine emperor. Became king of Italy after disposing of Odoacer. Ruled wisely in spite of being a barbarian and an Arian. In the last few years became intensely suspicious, and carried out harsh purge of orthodox leaders in Roman Senate. Died 526.

**Theodosius I**  Emperor 378–95. Last effective emperor of the West. Ensured the triumph of orthodoxy after the Council of Constantinople in 381. Close friend of **Ambrose**, and often influenced by him. Enforced Christianity as the state religion. Died 395.

**Theodosius II**  Eastern emperor, 408–50. Weak ruler, with leanings towards the **Monophysite** faction. The *Codex Theodosianus* is a product of his reign, gathering together many imperial edicts including many on church affairs. Acquiesced at the 'Robber Synod' of Ephesus. Died after a riding accident in 450.

**Theophilus of Alexandria**  Patriarch of Alexandria, 385–412. Unscrupulous prelate, who furthered his plans by force. Led the attacks on **John Chrysostom**, and secured his deposition.

**Ulfilas**  Missionary to the **Goths**. Because of his contacts with Arians when he visited Constantinople, Gothic Christianity was tainted with Arianism. Put the Gothic language into writing, and translated most of the Bible into Gothic. Made bishop c. 340 and died c. 383.

**Ursinus**   Unsuccessful claimant for the bishopric of Rome in 366, when his supporters fought in the streets with those of **Damasus**.

**Valens**   Eastern emperor, 364–78. Pro-Arian, and persecuted orthodox Christians. Died fighting **Goths** at Adrianople in 378.

**Valens of Mursa**   Arian bishop, leader of Arian party after the death of **Eusebius of Nicomedia**. Close confidant of the emperor **Constantius**. Author of the 'Blasphemy of Sirmium' in 357. Disappears after death of Constantius.

**Valentinian I**   Western emperor, 364–75. Largely neutral in church affairs, intervening only in matters of civil order.

**Valentinian II**   Western emperor, 375–92. Son of **Valentinian I** and **Justina**. Involved in clashes with **Ambrose** at Milan. Killed in revolt of Arbogast.

**Valentinian III**   Western emperor, 425–54. Son of **Constantius** and **Galla Placidia**. Largely ineffective, and power during his reign in the hands of **Aetius**. After he had assassinated Aetius, he was killed by Aetius' soldiers in 454.

**Vandals**   Germanic barbarian tribe. Took part in great invasion of 406 across Rhine, and settled in Spain. Under king **Gaiseric**, crossed to North Africa in 429, and overran it. Engaged in piracy, and sacked Rome in 455. Pro-Arian, and persecuted orthodox Christians. Eventually became effete and were easily wiped out by **Belisarius** in 534.

**Vigilantius**   Opponent of **Jerome**, who criticized his asceticism.

**Vincent of Lérins**   Monk at Lérins and Semi-Pelagian. Died *c.* 445.

**Wilfrid**   English monk. Took pro-Roman stand at the Synod of Whitby in 664. Subsequently made bishop of Northumbria, but went to continent and Chad was ordained in his place. Returned, but was deposed. Set out for Rome, preached in Frisia. Reinstated, and returned to evangelize Sussex and Isle of Wight. After second appeal to Rome, eventually returned and died at Oundle. Buried at Ripon (709).

**Willibrord**   English cleric. Preached in Frisia and eventually made bishop of Utrecht. Supported by **Pepin of Heristal**. Died 739.

**Wini**  English cleric, became bishop of Winchester in 660. Later became bishop of London.

**Zeno**  Eastern emperor, 474–91. Had been leader of Isaurian tribe (with name Tarasicodissa). Took pro-**Monophysite** stand, although tried to be conciliatory. Interceded with **Vandals** for the orthodox in North Africa. Issued *Henoticon* (Edict of Unity) to set aside decisions of Chalcedon in attempt to conciliate Monophysites.

# Index

*Numbers in bold type refer to the Glossary.*

| | DATE DUE | | |
|---|---|---|---|
| MAR 1 4 2002 | | | |
| | | | |
| | | | |
| | | | |
| | | | |
| | | | |
| | | | |
| | | | |
| | | | |
| | | | |
| | | | |